THE VOCATION OF LUTHERAN HIGHER EDUCATION

Jason A. Mahn, editor

D0093992

Lutheran University Press
Minneapolis, Minnesota

The Vocation of Lutheran Higher Education
Jason A. Mahn, editor

ISBN: 978-1-942304-21-0

Lutheran University Press, PO Box 390759, Minneapolis, MN 55439
www.lutheranupress.org
Printed in the United States of America

TABLE OF CONTENTS

Preface...5
Michael C. Maxey

Introduction 7
Jason A. Mahn

PART ONE: HISTORY

1   The Emergence of Lutheran Education:
    Listening to Luther's Troubling Questions 19
    Samuel Torvend, Pacific Lutheran University

2   The Vocation of a Lutheran College in the
    Midst of American Higher Education..30
    L. DeAne Lagerquist, St. Olaf College

3   Lutheran Colleges: Past and Prologue 46
    Paul Dovre, Concordia College

4   The Vocation Movement in Lutheran Higher Education.............59
    Mark Wilhelm, Network of ELCA Colleges and Universities

PART TWO: MARKS

5   Learning and Teaching As an Exercise in Christian Freedom.....69
    Tom Christenson, Capital University

6   The Third Path, Religious Diversity, and Civil Discourse 82
    Darrell Jodock, Gustavus Adolphus College

7   Practicing Hope:
    The Charisms of Lutheran Higher Education 100
    Martha E. Stortz, Augsburg College

PART THREE: PERSPECTIVES

8   What It Means to Build the Bridge:
Identity and Diversity at ELCA Colleges 117
Eboo Patel, Interfaith Youth Core

9   Learning to Bloom Where You're Planted:
Adapting Vocation to the Specifics of Place................................133
Mary J. Henold, Roanoke College

10 How Can We Keep from Singing?
A Mennonite Responds to
Lutheran Understandings of Vocation 144
Shirley Hershey Showalter, Goshen College

11 Integrity and Fragmentation:
Can the Lutheran Center Hold?..158
Robert Benne, Roanoke College

PART FOUR: TRAJECTORIES

12 Why Interfaith Understanding Is Integral
to the Lutheran Tradition..175
Jason A. Mahn, Augustana College

13 *Semper Reformanda*: Lutheran Higher Education
in the Anthropocene 191
Ernest Simmons, Concordia College

14 Called Forward: Educating for Vocation
in the Twenty-first Century 201
Kathryn A. Kleinhans, Wartburg College

Epilogue: Expanding the Vision 214
Darrell Jodock and Mark Wilhelm

Resources...219

Vocations of the Contributors 228

The Vocation of *Intersections*..232

PREFACE

MICHAEL C. MAXEY
President, Roanoke College, Salem, Virginia
President, Network of ELCA Colleges and Universities

Part of the Lutheran way is an awareness that intellect is God-given and that learning is a worthy commitment. American Lutheran higher education, since its inception in 1832, is a natural expression of that awareness, but the story continues to unfold.

It unfolds in this publication, and I commend it as an excellent resource for those who prize the significance and impact of Lutheran identity in higher education.

In February 2016, the colleges and universities of the ELCA, with the full support of Bishop Eaton and the ELCA Church Council, established a network of our institutions. The aim of the network is to create and sustain conversations about our grounding in the love of the Gospel along with a desire to learn and serve today. That aim is applied in twenty-six related but unique ELCA colleges and universities across the United States. Our network will help all twenty-six institutions engage in conversations about vocation. In addition, our aim is to use those conversations about our Lutheran identity to enrich the growth and development of our current and future students.

What is the vocation of Lutheran higher education? That is a central question and conversation for everyone interested in Lutheran higher education, and it is the timely focus of this book.

As president of the Network of ELCA Colleges and Universities, I speak on behalf of our network and our pride in offering this publication's contribution to the formulation of vocation and Lutheran identity in higher education. This volume shares the state of that conversation. It will spark more conversation and reflection within our communities. The book offers a welcomed resource for discussions on campus and across the ELCA. We encourage you to use the book as a common reading among faculty, administration, and staff about Lutheran identity.

The network is especially pleased to publish a book that honors the journal, *Intersections*, upon its twentieth anniversary. *Intersections* has played a valuable role in supporting conversation about the vocation of ELCA higher education for the past two decades.

Lutheran higher education is unique in its expressions at our twenty-six ELCA colleges and universities. The expression of understanding about vocation in Lutheran higher education is a treasured topic worth preserving and enhancing for all. This book is a helpful installment to that end.

INTRODUCTION

JASON A. MAHN
Augustana College, Rock Island, Illinois

What is the vocation of a Lutheran college or university once it has ceased to be a place where (mostly) Lutherans go to be educated by (mostly) Lutherans? In the early 1990s, this question—along with the retirement of faculty members and administrators who had been among the strongest proponents of Lutheran higher education—led to a new concerted effort to retrieve and redefine the missions and identities of the colleges and universities affiliated with the Evangelical Lutheran Church in America (ELCA). Leaders within the Division for Higher Education and Schools at ELCA churchwide offices joined presidents and leaders on twenty-eight ELCA college campuses to launch a series of nationwide initiatives meant to clarify and promote the vocation of Lutheran higher education. At the center was (and still is) the annual Vocation of a Lutheran College conference, which has helped to introduce new faculty, staff, and administrators to the Lutheran tradition within higher education since 1995. A year later, Tom Christenson of Capital University conceived of *Intersections*, a journal that would publish papers delivered at the "Vocation" conference, plus other articles, essays, books reviews, reports, poems, reflections, and homilies, some of which debated how best to conceive of the vocation of Lutheran higher education, much of which asked deep and important questions about how best to educate students for lives of responsible service, purpose, and meaning.

Fast-forward to the present: The twenty-second Vocation of a Lutheran College conference was held this past summer at Augsburg College in Minneapolis under the theme, "Preparing Global Leaders for a Religiously Diverse Society." In spring 2016, Mark Wilhelm (publisher of *Intersections*) and I (the journal's third editor) invited some longstanding conversation partners to contribute to a special twentieth anniversary edition of the publication.[1] Over the last two decades, additional initiatives have supported these deliberations as well. Two were nationwide initiatives on the pattern of *Intersections* and the Vocation conferences—the Lutheran Academy of Scholars summer seminar and the Thrivent Fellows Seminar for Administrative Leadership. This period also witnessed the development of several centers for "Faith and Learning" (or the like) on ELCA college and university campuses. Non-Lutheran organizations have injected new perspectives—and invaluable financial support—into our collective work. The Lilly Endowment, Inc. gave multi-million dollar grants to eight ELCA colleges/universities as part of its massive Programs for the Theological Exploration of Vocation (PTEV) initiative, and now most of the twenty-six ELCA colleges and universities partake in the Network for Vocation in Undergraduate Education (NetVUE).[2] Organizations such as the Interfaith Youth Core also have helped our schools figure out how to be both deeply grounded in a particular theological and ecclesial tradition while also building bridges between different religious and nonreligious constituents.

Having reflected and debated for twenty-some years, have we come to a conclusion about the identity and purpose—that is, the *vocation*—of Lutheran higher education, now that it is not only or primarily education for and by Lutherans? In many ways we have. There is now some consensus around the seemingly circular claim that the vocation of Lutheran higher education *is* to educate for vocation. That is, many agree that, at best, ELCA-related colleges and universities educate not exclusively or primarily to secure employment, to develop a "life of the mind," or even to cultivate citizenship and civic virtues, as important as each of these is. Lutheran institutions principally educate students so that they can discern the material, social, psychological, and spiritual needs of other human and nonhuman creatures, and then respond with committed service and out of a sense of gratitude. In the Christian tradition, such service is patterned after the life of Jesus, whose solidarity with a broken world brought salvation and healing to it. For their part, Christians from the Lutheran tradition will underscore that the character and durability of that service depends on

---

1   *Intersections* 43 (Spring 2016). All issues of *Intersections* can be found online at http://digitalcommons.augustana.edu/intersections/. The mission statement of the journal is included at the back of this book.
2   See Chapter 13 for additional descriptions of these initiatives.

whether it is offered out of a sense of being gifted or graced, or because it is demanded or expected of the one serving. But while being called to service can be construed in these particular and religious ways, "calling" and "vocation" are not the exclusive property of Christians. Rather, out of the depths of their own theological tradition, Lutheran colleges and universities educate Lutherans, other Christians, people from other religious traditions, secular humanists, and even sophomoric "whateverists"[3] for lives of meaning, purpose, and responsible service for and with a needful world.

Thus, there is consensus building over what might be called *education for vocation* as the leading leitmotif or *sine qua non* of Lutheran higher education. Still, there are a number of ways to parse this emphasis on vocation, each with differing enframing assumptions and practical implications. There are also ongoing debates about whether an emphasis on vocation leaves other central components of our Lutheran institutional identities out, as well as careful considerations of how "vocation" language might function in helpful and/or unhelpful ways.

One worthy debate largely centers on whether and how a "Christian worldview" makes a difference for learning on our campuses. Some early contributors to *Intersections* took on what they understood as a failure of nerve by those invoking Luther's "two kingdoms doctrine" and the "promiscuous use of the concept of paradox" in the Lutheran intellectual tradition.[4] That is, they questioned whether carefully demarcating a civic realm or "kingdom of this world" apart from the kingdom of the gospel could do anything other than uncritically accept the finality of so-called secular reason or keep understandings of God securely confined to personal opinions. How much epistemological ground—frameworks by which we know what is true—could be ceded to secular departments (including religion departments) and still be called a Lutheran school?[5]

A central and related debate characterized much of the first decade of *Intersections*. Does the designation "Lutheran" depend at least in part on a sufficient number of Lutherans studying, teaching, and

---

3   Gregory Bradley, *The Unintended Reformation: How a Religious Revolution Secularized Society* (Cambridge, Massachusetts: Harvard University Press, 2012), 77-78.

4   Richard VonDohlen, "A Fifth Teat on a Cow: The Irrelevance of the Lutheran Doctrine of the Two Kingdoms for Academic Life; A Response to Hughes, LaHurd, Ratke et al.," *Intersections* 9 (Summer 2000): 2-9.

5   See Chapter 11 and Robert Benne, "Response to Bishop Olson and President Tipson," *Intersections* 16 (Winter 2003): 34-36.

administering at our colleges and universities? A minority voice insisted that Lutheran *institutional* identity does in fact depend on a critical mass of *individuals* identifying as Lutheran. According to them, the diversity understandably sought on our campuses should include something like affirmative action for Lutheran employees.[6]

While this particular argument slowly gave way to Lutheran understandings of education for vocation—as opposed to the two kingdoms, "paradox," or a certain threshold of numbers of Lutheran faculty or board members—as the central marker of Lutheran institutional identities, there still were and are matters to debate. In part, this is because educating for vocation leads one to resist and reconfigure leading assumptions about the state of college today—assumptions that college is *essentially* for credentialing and employment, that colleges are leaving students "academically adrift" and graduates "lost in transition,"[7] or that robust commitment to a college's church-relatedness competes with full-bodied openness to religious and ethnic "others."[8]

Still others have raised critical questions about what they take to be a too-easy alignment of what the Lutheran tradition means by vocation and what "the world" means by a successful career or person. Writing of a dominant American culture that forms so many of us into individualism, narcissism, consumerism, "disposability rather than conservation," and careerism, Samuel Torvend (Pacific Lutheran University) recently pondered whether standard articulations of the vocation of a Lutheran college or university reinforce rather than resist such powerful cultural norms:

> I sometimes wonder if the vocation of a Lutheran college has become the calling to serve as the unwitting accomplice is such cultural formation. That is, I have begun to think that the vocation of a Lutheran college has become the calling to serve as the unwitting accomplice in the acceptance of the status quo in which, ironically, we hope our students might discover their passion, their calling, their deep commitments.

---

6   See Chapters 3 and 11.
7   References are to Richard Arum and Josipa Roksa, *Academically Adrift: Limited Learning on College Campuses* (Chicago: University of Chicago Press, 2010); and to Christian Smith, Kari Christoffersen, Hilary Davidson, and Patricia Snell Herzog, *Lost in Transition: The Dark Side of Emerging Adulthood* (New York: Oxford University Press, 2011).
8   See especially Chapters 6, 8, and 12.

And if this is so, how easy it will be to snuff out and smother that first gift of Lutheran education—that capacity to ask deep troubling questions of what you and I, our disciplines, our expertise, or our trustees might take for granted, consider normal, even sacrosanct.[9]

Marcia Bunge (then at Valparaiso University, now Gustavus Adolphus College) raised similar cautions already in 2002:

Because our culture glorifies individualism and self-fulfillment, speaking about vocation can also sometimes be a way of simply adding a spiritual gloss to a subjective sense of self-fulfillment. Here, one's vocation is what one does, whether paid or not, to find personal meaning and happiness. In this cultural context . . . there is little room for reflection on the relation of work to one's faith, to family life, to civic and environmental responsibilities, or to God's care and redemption of the world.[10]

In other words, invoking one's vocation can threaten to become nothing more than "a convenient rubber stamp of approval on our lives or institutions."[11] To resist this temptation, Bunge suggests a number of strategies to Lutheran colleges and universities, including learning from Mennonite and other faith traditions that emphasize discipleship—the conviction that one's deepest calling is to follow Christ—as well as from the Catholic tradition, with its disciplines of meditation, spiritual direction, and other practices of "listen[ing] to the One who calls us."[12]

Without these many critical, critical comments—that is, comments that are both essential and self-searching—this decades-old conversation about the vocation of Lutheran higher education might have denigrated into mere applause for our colleges and universities. Instead, it has been concerned with understanding, interrogating, debating, and strengthening—as well as celebrating—the overlapping missions and identities of our schools.

This book collects essays that have proven crucial for understanding and advancing the vocation of Lutheran higher education. Most of

---

9   Samuel Torvend, "'Greed Is an Unbelieving Scoundrel': The Common Good as Commitment to Social Justice," *Intersections* 42 (Fall 2015): 16. See also Chapter 1.

10 Marcia Bunge, "Renewing a Sense of Vocation at Lutheran Colleges and Universities: Insights from a Project at Valparaiso University," *Intersections* 14 (Summer 2002): 12.

11 Ibid., 16.

12 Ibid. See Chapters 9 and 10 for Catholic and Mennonite perspectives.

them were previously published in *Intersections*; many were also first delivered as keynote addresses at the Vocation of a Lutheran College conference. As a whole, the book is not meant to invite uncritical acceptance of a single understanding of the vocation of Lutheran higher education, but rather reflection, deliberation, conversation, critique, and maybe even robust debate. You might read it on your own, either because you are new to a Lutheran college or university or because you have heard snippets and sides of this conversation and want the fuller perspective. We think, however, that a book that emerges *from* conversation is best used *in* conversation; we hope you will discuss the questions that end each chapter with colleagues at your institution or perhaps among multiple institutions.

How This Book Unfolds

Part One, "History," includes four essays, each of which focus on one particular segment of the 500-year-old history of Lutheran higher education. In Chapter 1, Samuel Torvend (Pacific Lutheran University[13]) returns to the start of the Lutheran reform movement in sixteenth century Germany, arguing that theological and ecclesial reforms therein ineluctably led to social and civic reforms, and that chief among these was the reform of education as a crucial public service to the common good. In Chapter 2, L. DeAne Lagerquist (St. Olaf College) offers a history of Lutheran colleges and universities within the broader history of American higher education—including old-time colleges and the rise of the modern university—thus helping us to better understand who Lutheran colleges/universities are and what they are called to be. Focusing on the latter half of the twentieth century and on five Midwestern Lutheran institutions, Paul Dovre (Concordia College) in Chapter 3 traces the historical movement from what many assume was Lutheran education at its prime in the 50s and 60s, through various challenges of the 70s and 80s, and into the reclaiming and re-appropriation of Lutheran higher education in the 90s until today. Dovre also sketches the changing relationship of Lutheran colleges/universities to the Lutheran church from dependence to independence to partnership. In Chapter 4, Mark Wilhelm (Network of ELCA Colleges and Universities) turns to the most recent history in order to narrate exactly the story that the other thirteen essays here represent. He shows how and why Lutheran educators have retrieved the Lutheran "doctrine"

---

13 Please see The Vocations of the Contributors at the back of this book for full titles and short biographies of each author.

of vocation as the defining feature of their collective endeavors—gradually over the latter half of twentieth century, and then deliberately and insistently (although not unanimously) in the past twenty years.

Whereas Part One narrates the history of coming to the vocation of Lutheran higher education, the three essays that constitute Part Two, "Marks," analyze the chief features therein. In Chapter 5, Tom Christenson (formerly of Capital University and first editor of *Intersections*), lists three essential marks, attending especially to the intricate connections between Lutheran understandings of being gifted, of living into one's freedom, and of vocation. In Chapter 6, Darrell Jodock (Gustavus Adolphus College) offers six features of Lutheran higher education, each of which helps cultivate dialogue and civic discourse among different peoples, including those who come from different religious backgrounds or none at all. In Chapter 7, Martha Stortz (Augsburg College) explores five distinctive gifts or "charisms" of Lutheran education. These gifts and their attendant practices cultivate hope in uncertain times, not only for higher education, but also for a contemporary world based largely on fear. As a whole, the essays of Part Two serve as a primer into Lutheran thought for newcomers, while deepening and expanding that vision for veterans in this field.

Part Three, "Perspectives," introduces four unique points of view from which Lutheran higher education can be situated, analyzed, and assessed. In Chapter 8, the American Muslim and interfaith advocate, Eboo Patel (Interfaith Youth Core), uses his leadership in American higher education as well as his experience working with a number of Lutheran colleges and universities to show how the largest barrier to interfaith cooperation today is not necessarily fundamentalism or intolerance, but rather blasé disinterest. Patel thus encourages Lutheran colleges and universities to own their own traditions more fully; he argues that only by standing somewhere specific can they build bridges to other religious and nonreligious communities. In Chapter 9, Mary Henold (Roanoke College) tells her own story about the difficulty, as a Catholic, of sinking roots into a "nominally Lutheran" academic community. Slowly but surely, Henold has learned to use her geographic location to rediscover her personal vocation while working at a Lutheran school. This essay will be of particular importance to the many non-Lutherans who want a way to call their Lutheran college or university home. In Chapter 10, Shirley Hershey Showalter (Goshen College) similarly uses her perspective as a Mennonite Christian to reflect on the meaning of vocation. Vocation certainly plays out among Mennonites differently—given their emphases on suffering, martyrdom, and discipleship. Still, Showalter emphasizes that which brings Mennonite and Lutheran communities together: the importance of stories, solidarity with the poor, and even a penchant for singing.

Whereas the first three authors of Part Three might be described as "sympathetic outsiders," the fourth is something of a "critical insider." In Chapter 11, Robert Benne (Roanoke College) uses his lifelong experiences studying and leading Lutheran academic communities to raise serious concerns about the direction of Lutheran higher education today. Benne is among those claiming that, for a college or university to retain or strengthen it Lutheran-ness, it must carry out "affirmative action for Christians generally and Lutherans specifically" so that Christian public intellectuals comprise at least a minority voice on campus. I predict that few readers will immediately resonate with Benne's essay; that is all the more reason to take this perspective seriously.

Finally, Part Four, "Trajectories," includes four issues that promise to become increasingly important over the next twenty years—and probably into the next millennium. In Chapter 12, I (Jason Mahn, Augustana College) deconstruct standard ways that an institution's theological grounding and its openness to religious diversity are often pitted against one another. I argue that interfaith encounter, understanding, and cooperation are integral to Lutheranism from the start, and so constitute the natural flourishing of Lutheran higher education. In Chapter 13, Ernest Simmons (Concordia College) argues that education for vocation must now include education for sustainability leadership, given the realities of climate change, ecological degradation, and other characteristics of our *Anthropocene*. The vocations of our students now must include the calling to work intelligently and responsibly on behalf of an earth in peril. In Chapter 14, Kathryn Kleinhans (Wartburg College) returns to Martin Luther's understanding of vocation in light of twenty-first-century challenges within higher education as a whole. She shows how retrieving and reconceiving of this 500-year-old tradition is exactly what we need in order to face anxieties about the rising cost of higher education, the changing nature of work, and the multiple, complex callings that bear on today's students.

Each chapter ends with discussion questions geared primarily to faculty, staff, and administrators engaged in conversation about the mission, church-relatedness, and vocation of their Lutheran college or university and their own work therein. An epilogue by Jodock and Wilhelm asks whether the articulated and accomplished vocation of Lutheran higher education should not also be offered as a gift to other denominational networks of church-related colleges. To educate for vocation may very well lead to a redefinition of church-sponsored higher education; that in turn may be exactly what is needed in the church and academy today.

To support continued conversation, please also find a list of resources related to Lutheran higher education, Martin Luther, scholarship on vocation, religion and spirituality in American higher education, and the missions and identities of the twenty-six ELCA colleges and universities at the back of this book. The books ends with short bios or vocations of the authors featured here, as well as information about *Intersections*.

Acknowledgments

Hundreds of professors, residential-life leaders, coaches, chaplains, college presidents, board members, academic deans, admissions councilors, service-learning coordinators, and student life directors have written for *Intersections* throughout the past twenty years. A thousand or so more have attended the Vocation of a Lutheran College conference, teaching and learning from one another about the Lutheran intellectual tradition and our shared mission to educate for vocation and serve a world in need. Countless others have discussed and debated Lutheran mission and identity on their own campuses or through other gatherings. That is simply too many people to thank individually; I thank them here collectively for sustaining a robust conversation, a cross-section of which the present book presents.

Thank you especially to the thirteen other authors included here for permission to publish or republish their work, for sometimes substantially revising their essays, and for their leadership in Lutheran higher education. Jacqueline Bussie (Concordia), Lynn Hunnicutt (Pacific Lutheran), Darrell Jodock (Gustavus Adolphus), Tom Morgan (Augsburg), KathiTunheim (Gustavus Adolphus), and Ernie Worman (Newberry) constitute the editorial board of *Intersections* and have helped shape this publication. They are a pleasure to work with. Thank you to Kaity Lindgren for help in preparing the manuscript and to Karen Walhof at Lutheran University Press for her vision and guidance from the start.

Steven C. Bahls, the eighth president of Augustana College, Rock Island, Illinois, has sponsored and supported *Intersections* and Lutheran higher education for well over a decade. I thank him for this leadership and for encouraging me to join in. Tom Christenson first conceived of *Intersections* and was its founding editor, serving in that capacity from 1996 to 2005. He was also a beloved professor of philosophy at Capital University, Columbus, Ohio, until his death in 2013. Bob Haak, vice president of academic affairs and dean of Hiram College, Hiram, Ohio, edited the journal from 2006 until 2011, while serving as the director of the Center for Vocational Reflection at Augustana College. I thank Tom and Bob for their work with *Intersections* and for first editing a number of the essays appearing here.

Finally, thank you to the twenty-six college presidents who constitute the Board of Directors of the new Network of ELCA Colleges and Universities, which is the first formal association of ELCA schools. Members of the executive committee, Roanoke College President Michael Maxey (president of the network), and Mark Wilhelm (its executive director), have taken leadership in articulating the vision of higher education in the Lutheran intellectual tradition. Mark Wilhelm is also publisher of *Intersections* and has offered his insights, direction, experience, and wisdom to both the journal and this book. I thank Mark, President Maxey, and all the other leaders of the Network of ELCA Colleges and Universities for sponsoring the present book, which is the inaugural publication of the network.

Part One

HISTORY

CHAPTER 1

THE EMERGENCE OF LUTHERAN EDUCATION
Listening to Luther's Troubling Questions

SAMUEL TORVEND
Pacific Lutheran University, Tacoma, Washington

Between 500 and 1000 CE, Western Europe—the birthplace of the Lutheran reform movement and Lutheran education—experienced unprecedented dislocation and social trauma.[1] Such social instability was caused by a variety of forces: invasions from the north and the east that intensified in the 400s and lasted another 500 years; the loss of a sophisticated transportation infrastructure, which was once the glory of the Roman Empire; the slow dismantling of an "universal" empire governed from Rome and then, with considerable disinterest in Western concerns, from Constantinople; commercial decline due to road loss and increased brigandage; and a steady but high mortality rate. Add to this early medieval trauma the astonishing loss of life in the wake of the Black Plague during the late medieval period (1350-1500), and it is not difficult to understand why medieval Christian spirituality was suffused with a profound desire to enter "the life of the world to come."[2]

---

1   This essay was originally published as "Critical Engagement in Public Life: Listening to Luther's Troubling Questions," *Intersections* 35 (Spring 2012): 5-9.

2   A quotation from the Nicene Creed, "We look for the resurrection of the dead, and the life of the world to come," *The Book of Common Prayer* (Church Hymnal Corporation, 1979), 359. Any brief historical overview of 500-1000 years entails the risk of oversimplification. Readers may want to consult the following for more detailed narrations of the period: Karl Baus et al, *History of the Church*, ed. Hubert Jedin and John Dolan, trans. Anselm Biggs, vol. 2 (New York: Crossroad Seabury, 1980); Peter Brown, *The Rise of Western Christendom*, 2nd ed. (Blackwell, 2003); Everett Ferguson, *Church History*, vol. 1 (Grand Rapids: Zondervan, 2005); Friedrich Kempf, et al, *History of the Church*, Hubert Jedin and John Dolan, eds., Anselm Biggs, trans., vol. 2 (New York: Crossroad Seabury Press, 1969); David Knowles and Dimitri Oblensky, *The Middle Ages*, vol. 2 in *The Christian Centuries* (Paulist Press, 1979).

The World in Which Lutheran Education Emerged

In the early medieval centuries, Christianity slowly expanded into northern and central Europe, an expansion made possible by monastic missionaries who vowed stability to one place, one monastery, and from these monastic centers (which were themselves oases of human stability in the midst of much social chaos) began to establish satellite monastic centers. Their work over many centuries reconfigured the map of Europe, creating a new cultural and religious landscape. Villages, towns, and cities sprang up around monasteries. Monastic schools were the sole centers of learning, predecessors of the medieval urban universities which began to emerge after 1050. Monastic life was rooted in the local monastery where the cultivation of a common life and all that was necessary to sustain daily living took place (e.g., the construction of buildings, producing a regular food supply, creating cloth for clothing). And yet this seemingly down-to-earth existence lived in paradoxical tension with a focus on preparing for "the life of the world to come." This was due, in part, to neo-platonic impulses which had slowly but surely influenced the early and medieval Christian imagination. While the Jewish followers of Jesus of Nazareth would have imagined the human as an integral unity of body and soul, of matter and spirit, neo-platonic thought, shaped by earth-escaping tendencies, posited a more dualistic sensibility in which the noncorporeal soul alone is the object of divine grace. The neo-platonic vision suggested that this earth and all its creatures—who faced diminishment and death and thus experienced a corruptibility alien to the divine—simply did not matter in the end. Indeed, a Manichean temptation was and is ever lurking not far away from this dualistic thought form. (The Manicheans taught that the earth was created by an evil god and thus the body, indeed all matter, is simply a terrible prison for the soul. That which was considered "spiritual"/incorporeal received high religious value; that which was viewed as "material"/earthy/bodily could be readily viewed as insignificant, as an annoying obstacle to be overcome or, at worst, as a terrible and horrifying mistake.)

By the time of Luther's birth in 1483, the categories of "spiritual" and "temporal" had become a heuristic device to describe medieval society. Within the "spiritual" realm (what Luther knew as an "estate") were those persons, women and men, who had answered the call to the religious life as vowed members of an order (e.g., the Benedictines, Dominicans, or Augustinians), and those males who had a "vocation" to the priesthood, that is, to public ministry in the church. "Service to God" in the form of priestly ministry or vowed religious life was understood to be the only "calling" or vocation. Furthermore, priests and vowed religious were frequently regarded as holier because of their distance from "worldly temptations" (e.g., sexual intercourse, pursuit of wealth, ambition for social status). Within the "temporal" realm were all other baptized Christians: rulers, barmaids, lawyers, teachers, peasants, soldiers, and mothers—to list only a few. Indeed, in this construction of late medieval society, baptized laypeople were taught to be passive recipients of the priest's active work, for it was through the sacramental ministry of the priest alone that the grace of God was encountered.

These characteristics of medieval faith and life intersected with each other. Life on earth is less significant than the afterlife; what survives death is the intangible soul, not the corporeal body; in order for the soul to enter the afterlife ("heaven" or "union with God"), one must work diligently in this life and follow the teachings and practices suggested or commanded by those in spiritual authority: the church's leaders. These marks of late medieval Christian spirituality shaped the milieu in which Lutheran education emerged—emphases which ironically were called into question by a monastic priest who yearned for union with a gracious God but found only a stern and terrifying Judge.

Asking Disruptive Questions

If anything can be said of Martin Luther's sixteenth-century revolution, commonly called a reformation, it is that he reversed the focus of late medieval spirituality and thus reshaped the imagination of the West. In the late medieval world of Luther's birth, the Christian was expected to cooperate with the divine grace received in the sacraments—a divine energy, as it were, through which one could seek God, become closer to God, gain greater favor in God's sight, perform spiritual works that would demonstrate the quality of one's faith, and thus, hopefully, secure a favorable decision on that day of fear and trembling when Christ "will come again in glory to judge the living and the dead." The young Luther drank in the need to work diligently to gain divine favor. Indeed, as monk and priest he worked so steadfastly and with such anxiety that he wondered if he could ever *do enough* to receive a favorable judgment from Christ the Judge and thus enter heaven.

It was through his study of the letters of Paul (in particular, Romans and Galatians) that Luther, the university professor who lectured on the Bible, discovered what many of his theological peers had seemingly overlooked: Paul's assertion that one can do nothing to get closer to God, to gain God's favor in the hope of heaven. Instead, it is God who comes to humans in their limitations and self-centeredness, in their misery, suffering, and dying with nothing less than mercy and grace. That is, God is always advancing toward God's creatures—with "life, health, and salvation," wrote Luther—and advancing most clearly in the person of Jesus of Nazareth, son of Mary and son of God. Indeed, this emphasis on *God's advance, in Christ, toward those who dwell in the earth* effectively overturned the long-held notion that human beings can or need to make their way to God. All that striving to make oneself pleasing to God was, in the end, rubbish in the eyes of Luther.[3]

Who Benefits?

Such a scriptural discovery caused Luther to wonder if the previous 500 years of Christian teaching and practice had led Christians into unnecessary anxiety, duped them into believing that Christ was nothing but their judge, encouraged them to believe that this world was to be scorned, fostered the sense that one must indeed work hard on earth in order to gain eternal rewards. Such a discovery led Luther to ask a string of disturbing questions: Who fostered such a teaching? Who sanctioned the many spiritual works one must do in order to gain God's favor? And, who allowed the sale of spiritual favors to further one's entry into heaven, even after one's death? Would not the sale of spiritual favors actually discriminate against those, the majority of the population, who were poor? If the spiritual leader of the Western church—the bishop of Rome, the pope—can, on behalf of Christ, offer the word and consolation of forgiveness to all Christians, why does he not abolish the practices which have made such free forgiveness into a marketable commodity?[4]

---

3   See Luther's sermon, preached in 1519, on "Two Kinds of Righteousness," in which he sets forth his understanding of justification by grace, using the dialectic of "alien righteousness" and "proper righteousness," and his theology of Christ the servant; in *Luther's Works*, 55 vols., ed. Jaroslav Pelikan and Helmut Lehmann (Philadelphia and St. Louis: Fortress Press and Concordia Publishing House, 1955-1986), 31:297-306. All references to the American Edition of Luther's works will hereafter use the abbreviation LW followed by volume number.

4   These questions began to emerge in the ninety-five theses (LW 31:25-33) that Luther proposed for discussion and debate by the theology faculty of the University of Wittenberg in 1517. They are readily accessed at http://www.iclnet.org/pub/resources/text/wittenberg/luther/web/ninetyfive.html.

Continued study of Paul's letters led Luther to ask even more disturbing and disruptive questions: Is the separation of Christians into two "estates"—spiritual and temporal—fundamentally wrong? Does not Christian baptism initiate all persons into one egalitarian state in which gender, race or ethnicity, and socio-economic status no longer hold sway? If all Christians, regardless of their place in society, enjoy all the gifts of God's Spirit, should they not be able to select and, when needed, dismiss their church leaders rather than wait for them to be appointed by someone higher up the hierarchical ladder? And, if one has been freed by God's grace from the need to work diligently to receive an eternal reward, where does the act of initiation lead one—into a private experience of the divine within *or* into a religious crusade to make one's society into the church, a "Christian" nation? In response to this final "either/or," Luther and his reforming colleagues offered a resounding No. The advance of God continues, publicly, through the advance or movement of Christians into public life, not with the intent to establish a "Christian" society ruled by biblical law, but rather to engage their society ("the kingdom of this world") with concrete suggestions or proposals that would influence and shape the economic, educational, political, and social dimensions in which all citizens dwell. Thus, the Christian and the church are called to be "salt" and "leaven" within society, *neither* religious despisers of culture sitting on the sidelines *nor* religious conquerors of culture who will be tempted to transform the gospel of freedom into a new law of conformity.

Why Engage the Social, Bodily Realm?

Although he was influenced, early in his life, by an earth-escaping and body-punishing spiritual milieu, Luther's perception of matter, the earth, and the body was eventually reshaped by the social consequences of a theology of justification by grace. Remember that he was hired to teach Bible and spent much of his life studying and commenting on what Christians call the Old Testament, the Hebrew Scriptures. Luther's initial search for eternal salvation began within the austere life of the Augustinian Hermits of the Strict Observance, itself a reform movement within German religious life. Within the monastic enclosure, he punished his body with stringent spiritual practices (e.g., strict fasting, little sleep, arduous marathons of prayer, self-flagellation). And yet he abandoned monastic life for theological reasons and married Katarina von Bora, a former Cistercian nun.[5] As a biblical

---

5   See "The Judgment of Martin Luther on Monastic Vows," completed in 1521, LW 44:251-400.

scholar, he would come to accept the Hebraic emphasis on the integral unity of body and spirit, and eventually recognize that the gifts of body and earth—sexual intercourse, children, physical pleasure, food and drink, and the creation itself—flow from the generous hand of the divine Creator.

Moreover, rather than seeing the creation of the earth and all its creatures as one act of the ancient past, he would come to see the creative activity of God as something continuing in the present and into the future. Thus, it should not surprise us that later in his life, Luther would suggest that a school or a university is the place in which each discipline is called to explore and study life on this earth, a diversity of life forms continually being brought into existence by the grace and vitality of God. A school or university is that place in which students and teachers engage, rather than escape, this world and its real problems: "In order to maintain its temporal estate outwardly, the world must have good and capable men and women . . . for it is a matter of properly educating our boys and girls to that end."[6]

Calling Whom and to What End?

In the year 1520, Luther published a series of revolutionary texts that indicated his break with much (but not all) of late medieval thought and practice, a series of texts that constituted a recovery of Christian life rooted solely in the witness of the Bible. In his address, "To the Christian Nobility of the German Nation," he asked princely rulers to promote reform, a reform which began with his powerful critique of the social stratification of the baptized into two separate spheres or realms (those in holy orders/religious vows and those living "in the world").[7] One might see his criticism as a deconstruction of the hierarchical world which most of his peers took for granted. Grounding his argument in the radical act of inclusion called Christian baptism, Luther suggested that the community of faith was one in which all the baptized enjoyed all the gifts of the Holy Spirit and thus a spiritual equality.

His emerging "democratization" of the church, however, did not only end with a community more egalitarian than the one imagined by the pope or the bishops; it also led to a redefinition of the term *vocation*. While many of his peers accepted the medieval notion that

---

6   "To the Councilmen of All Cities in Germany That They Establish and Maintain Christian Schools," LW 45:368.
7   "To the Christian Nobility of the German Nation," LW 44:127-133.

only ordained priests or vowed religious had answered a "call" from God, Luther asked yet another unsettling question: Does not the act of God in baptism call a Christian, every Christian, into relationship with God, with the church, with the neighbor, and with the world? Such a question and its implied response suggested that the home, the workplace, and the public square were the very places in which all people are called by God to use their reason, employ their skills, and bear witness to the "life, health, and salvation" God intends for all. This is to suggest that Luther's evangelical reconstruction of vocation extended the medieval understanding to virtually every Christian—priest, barmaid, or lawyer—and placed one's calling, or many callings,[8] within *this world*. Thus, he would write:

> Just as those who are now called "spiritual," that is, priests, bishops, or popes, are neither different from other Christians nor superior to them, except that they are charged with the administration of the word of God and the sacraments, which is their work and office, so it is with the temporal authorities. They bear the sword and rod in their hand to punish the wicked and protect the good. A cobbler, a smith, a peasant—each has the work and office of his trade, and yet they are all alike consecrated priests and bishops. Further, everyone must benefit and serve every other by means of his own work or office so that in this way many kinds of work may be done for the bodily and spiritual welfare of the community, just as all the members of the body serve one another [1 Corinthians 12:14–26].[9]

Luther the biblical scholar also recognized that the central figure in the Christian story—Jesus of Nazareth—had been baptized into public life: "When you open the book containing the gospels and read or hear how Christ comes here or there, or how someone is brought to him, you should therein perceive the gospel through which he is coming to you . . . after that it is necessary that you turn this into an example and deal with your neighbor in the very same way, be given also to him [or her] as a gift and as example."[10] As Jesus lived a public life in which he travelled "here or there" and persons were "brought to him," so, too, the Christian is called forth from baptism into a life of service

---

8   See Chapter 14 of the present volume for the importance of considering the multiple vocations of each person.

9   Luther, "To the Christian Nobility," LW 44:130.

10   Luther, "A Brief Instruction on What to Look for and Expect in the Gospels," LW 35:121.

in the world. She or he follows the example of Christ by caring for the well-being of the neighbor. Thus, the primal sacrament of Christian identity contained a profoundly public dimension.

And this, too: Luther the priest, pastor, and professor who preached in the university church and presided at the Lord's Supper, recognized that at the center of Christian worship is a *public Christ:*

> Learn that [the Lord's Supper] is a sacrament of love. As love and support are given you, *you in turn must render love and support to Christ in his needy ones.* You must feel with sorrow all . . . the unjust suffering of the innocent, with which the world is everywhere filled to overflowing. You must fight, work, pray, and—if you cannot do more—have heart-felt sympathy. See, this is what it means to bear in your turn the misfortune and adversity of Christ and his saints. Here the saying of Paul is fulfilled, "Bear one another's burdens, and so fulfill the law of Christ" [Galatians 6:2].[11]

Such a compelling exhortation was no invitation to a private life but rather a sacramental charge to "fight" and "work" in public among the needy and the suffering. In this respect, Luther was no innovator but rather a student of early Christian practice in which the sacramental table was extended into the distribution of food and drink among the hungry poor—*a public act.*

Calling to Public Life

While Luther's reform of the Christian understanding of the relationship between God and humanity was crystallized in the teaching on justification by grace and became the powerful symbol guiding all other reforms, his theology manifested its public character within a relatively short period of time. By the early 1520s and thereafter, Luther and his colleagues—all university professors—were called upon to deal with a variety of pressing public issues: the reform of *social welfare* among the hungry poor; the delivery of *job training* for the unemployed; the establishment of *public schools* for boys and girls; the provision of *healthcare* during war and plague; the building and supervision of *orphanages* for abandoned children; the justification of *war* and the taking of human life; the rationale for *obedience to laws of the state*; and the grounds for *civil insurrection*. In other words, they were

---

11 Luther, "The Blessed Sacrament of the Holy and True Body of Christ, and the Brotherhoods," LW 35:54.

pushed to consider the relationship between contemporary public issues/crises and their teaching and learning. Their many writings on public issues and their construction of actual responses to public need suggest that the reform of theology and the church also contained the reform of ethics and society; there was not one without the other. Indeed, one could argue that the promotion of literacy—a prerequisite for reading the Bible newly translated into the vernacular—inspired the establishment of public education and the reform of university education undertaken by early Lutheran educators. One could also claim that the suppression of monastic life, which had been the center of social charity for the previous 1000 years, prompted Lutheran city councils to reform social welfare as a civic, religious, and public project, a project which in its secularized form can be found in many countries throughout the world today.

Yet the "genetic encoding" of Lutheran public engagement was not constricted to public education and social welfare.Luther would be led to write about *the power of lobbyists* who bribe political leaders, "lining their pockets with silver and gold." He would urgently propose *government regulation of banks* which charge exorbitant interest rates on loans. Aware of the increasing power of merchant capitalism to shape a society's values and practices, he asked, even begged, for the *supervision of monopolies and multinational corporations* which hoarded goods needed by all people. He vociferously argued that princes, legislators, and city councils regulate and impose fines on those business entities that would wait until a crisis to charge astounding prices on the goods they controlled, making profit from the misery of the innocent.[12] While Luther's pleas for the regulation and supervision of the private sector thrust him and his university colleagues into the public light, he voiced dismay that those who had accepted the gospel of freedom seemed immune to its ethical and public implications.

Who Benefits from Silence?

While Lutheran colleges and universities have steadfastly promoted education for service in the world, such service has frequently been focused on remarkable charitable initiatives that respond to immediate

---

12 See my *Luther and the Hungry Poor: Gathered Fragments* (Minneapolis: Fortress Press, 2008); Carter Lindberg, *Beyond Charity: Reformation Initiatives for the Poor* (Minneapolis: Fortress Press, 1993); and Kyle Session and Phillip Bebb, eds., *Pietas et Societas: New Trends in Reformation Social History* (Kirksville, Missouri: Sixteenth Century Journal Publications, 1985).

need. A closer reading of Luther's works indicates that the reformer was well aware of the systemic injustices which actually produce the need for charity in the first place. The power of greed in human life, he wrote, is an unbelieving scoundrel, a ravenous consumption of what rightly begins to all.[13] And yet Luther's works on social reform, the many Kirchenordnungen (church orders on worship and public initiatives) which blossomed in the sixteenth and seventeenth centuries, and the history of social reform in the Lutheran tradition are infrequently studied in university courses on Luther or the Lutheran heritage. One then wonders if the questions and the writings of the early sixteenth-century reformers still await study, reflection, and cultural translation for those who are eager to see the inherent relationship between faith, learning, and public engagement today.

Lutheran colleges and universities rightly resist the temptation to escape this public world into spiritual privacy and holy apathy.

They rightly resist the temptation, so strong in some sectors of American life, to urge the transformation of a pluralistic society into an allegedly Christian one.[14]

They rightly ask how teaching and learning at Lutheran institutions, a teaching and learning marked by intellectual humility and charity, might yet prepare and inspire faculty, staff, and students for public engagement, for the promotion of a just and peaceful social order.

They rightly ask how one might resist the forces that diminish and degrade what God has created for life, health, and wholeness.

They rightly ask one last troubling question: Who in this world benefits if our graduates are silent and simply satisfied with way things have always been?

---

13 Luther, "Ordinance of a Common Chest," LW 45:170.
14 One is mindful of the typology created by H. Richard Neibuhr (and still exercising considerable influence) concerning the relationship between Christ (Christians) and culture: *Christ and Culture* (New York: Harper & Row, 1951). See also Richard T. Hughes and William B. Adrian, *Models of Christian Higher Education* (Grand Rapids, Michigan: Wm. B. Eerdmans Publishing, 1997).

Questions for Discussion

1. How central is the story of Martin Luther and the Lutheran Reformation in the story that your institution tells about itself and the vocation of Lutheran higher education? What other people or events figure predominantly in its story?

2. Which central issues in Luther's reforms (e.g., his emphasis on grace, democratization of vocation, reversal of Christian otherworldliness, attention to public service, etc.) have influenced your institution or your discipline most directly or significantly?

3. How should Lutheran colleges and universities carry out the public service that Luther understands to be a direct consequence of the Christian gospel? How does the fact that our faculties and student bodies are religiously diverse qualify, underscore, or otherwise change this calling to socio-political reform and support of the common good?

4. Torvend ends his essay by asking whether and how Lutheran higher education "might yet prepare and inspire faculty, staff, and students for public engagement, for the promotion of a just and peaceful social order." Does this—and how does this—take place on your campus?

CHAPTER 2

THE VOCATION OF A LUTHERAN COLLEGE IN THE MIDST OF AMERICAN HIGHER EDUCATION

L. DE ANE LAGERQUIST
St. Olaf College, Northfield, Minnesota

My task is to examine the vocation of Lutheran colleges within the history of American higher education, to consider both the work to which these schools are called and the manner in which that work is carried out, and to suggest how Lutheran schools compare to other American schools and to one another.[1] The historical account that follows suggests both that the twenty-eight colleges and universities[2] associated with the Evangelical Lutheran Church in America have much in common with other schools and that there are significant variations within the Lutheran set.

Behind this descriptive task there lurks, unarticulated, a dual demand for justification: first, to show that the designation *Lutheran* is significant now—not only in the past—and second, to show that it matters in ways that make the schools worth maintaining and attending in the future.

Although I was an undergraduate history major and earned two graduate degrees in historical fields, I began my teaching career knowing woefully little about the history of higher education. Unfor-

---

1   The present article is an abridged version of "The Vocation of a Lutheran College in the Midst of American Higher Education," *Intersections* 12 (Summer 2001): 11-21. It is reprinted here as a historical document and does not reflect recent issues or the author's continued thinking.

2   Editor's note: There are now twenty-six ELCA colleges and universities; economic pressures forced Waldorf College to sell to a for-profit company in January 2010 and forced Dana College to close its doors in July of that same year.

tunately, few faculty members come out of graduate school informed about these topics. Our ignorance prevents a clear view either of the whole of the enterprise or of the place our schools occupy in it. My historical "plot" here is not the decline of authentic religious life on campuses under the rubric of either secularization or disengagement, nor is it a rebuttal of such a thesis.[3] Rather, I provide a brief chronological account that draws attention to commonality and difference among Lutheran colleges and between them and other American colleges. I do this because I'm convinced that knowing how our schools and their work fit into this larger scheme will allow us to understand more about our work and to do it better.

Foundings and Foundations

The founding of American institutions of higher education is generally told in three phases. The first began, of course, in 1636 with the establishment of Harvard College, a small, religiously-affiliated school on the model of English colleges, a school whose "vocation," if you will, included that "Every one shall consider the main end of his life and studies to know God and Jesus Christ, which is eternal life, and therefore to lay Christ in the bottom as the only foundation of all sound knowledge and learning."[4] Stated more generally, the purpose of producing "both a learned clergy and an educated gentry"[5] was characteristic of all nine colleges founded prior to the American Revolution and of the scores established in the following decades. This remained the primary goal and usual model for American higher education until the mid-nineteenth century. Following the Civil War another model appeared, the model of the modern research university devoted to the production of knowledge and specialized education of advanced students. The third phase, beginning in the 1940s, is characterized by rapid expansion: more students and new and bigger schools including many with two-year, non-residential programs. It may be that we are now well into a fourth phase in which the idea that learning occurs in

---

3   Compare George M. Marsden, *The Soul of the American University* (Oxford: Oxford University Press, 1994), and James T. Burtchaell, *The Dying of the Light: The Disengagement of Colleges and Universities from Their Christian Churches* (Wm. B. Eerdmans Publishing, 1998).

4   Christopher J. Lucas, *American Higher Education: A History* (New York: St. Martin's Griffin, 1994), 105. For a more recent treatment of this history, see Roger L. Geiger, *The History of American Higher Education: Learning and Culture from the Founding to World War II* (Princeton University Press, 2014).

5   F. Michael Perko, "Religion and Collegiate Education," in *Encyclopedia of American Religious Experience*, ed. Charles H. Lippy and Peter W. Williams, vol. 3 (New York: Charles Scribner's Sons, 1968), 1611.

the company of other students and teachers who share a specific place and time is under extreme challenge. Certainly at schools such as those associated with the ELCA, we are no longer in a growth mode as is attested by frequent use of phrases such as "belt-tightening," "downsizing," "out-sourcing," "strategic planning," "assessment," and "the culture of evidence."

The Old Time College

The aims and programs of the nine colonial colleges had much in common with one another and with the English tradition of the liberal arts, which, historian Christopher Lucas suggests, included a "combination of literary training, religious piety, and courtly etiquette" that produced "an archetypal conception of the ideally-educated person as a 'Christian gentleman.'"[6] The colleges' programs consisted almost entirely of rhetoric, grammar, and theology taught by Christian gentlemen whose pedagogical method—most often lectures—was designed to transfer a defined body of knowledge to their students. Students were not taught how to learn; they were given what was then judged to be the treasures of classical and Christian culture as the foundation for development of Christian character and responsible participation in civic life—often as clergymen. Close supervision of students' life outside the classroom, or at least efforts to do so, was also intended to prepare students for civic life. The number of students was small; in a peak year (1770) the total number enrolled at Yale was 413.[7]

While these schools shared goals and methods and were alike in placing Christianity at the center of both, the particular sort of Christianity varied. At the outset Harvard's supporters were Congregationalists, but by the early eighteenth century, conservatives, suspicious that the school's orthodoxy had been undermined, established The Collegiate School in Connecticut. (The school was renamed Yale in recognition of a major gift in kind from Elihu Yale.) Similarly, Yale's second, less enthusiastic thoughts about the Great Awakening contributed to the founding of Princeton by "New Side" (pro-revivalist) Presbyterians. The "sectarian" importance of establishing a college was related to the college's task in preparing clerical leadership for the sponsoring party. Using the language of a Harvard brochure published in 1643, one may point to the sponsors' dread "to leave an illiterate Ministry to

6   Lucas, *American Higher Education*, 313.
7   Ibid., 109.

Churches."[8] Although there were Lutherans in the colonies from the 1620s, and although Henry M. Muhlenberg, the patriarch of American Lutheranism who arrived in the 1740s, was concerned about the education of potential clergy, Lutherans did not found or sponsor a college in this period.[9]

Following the revolution, what we now call the "old time college" model remained the ideal with many—individuals, groups of church folks or official religious groups, and municipal boosters—rushing to found schools as the population expanded in numbers and across the continent. In the two decades between 1782 and 1802, nineteen colleges were founded; by the outbreak of the Civil War the total number reached 250, including Indiana College in Bloomington, Emory in Georgia, Roman Catholic Notre Dame, and several Lutheran colleges.[10] The stated purposes of these schools were consistent with earlier concerns. A board member at the College of California put it this way: "to make men more manly, and humanity more humane; to augment the discourse of reason, intelligence and faith, and to kindle the beacon fires of truth on all the summits of existence."[11] Other leaders were more explicitly Christian in their aims, particularly those persons deeply affected by the Second Great Awakening, those concerned to evangelize on the western frontier, or those Protestants who feared Roman Catholic expansion. Churches with a strong tradition of an educated clergy, such as Presbyterians, Congregationalists, and Lutherans, were eager founders of new institutions; Antebellum Presbyterians had forty-nine colleges.[12] Troy Female Seminary (1821) and Mount Holyoke Seminary (1837) lead the way in providing educational opportunities

8   The Harvard Guide, www.news.harvard.edu/guide
9   Having pointed to the identification of these schools with particular religious parties, I hasten to offer three cautions. First, I have used the word parties rather than denominations quite deliberately because in this time period nothing so organized or formal as a denomination existed. Second, at this stage identification with a religious party did not render a college ineligible for public financial support. William and Mary's receipt of duties paid on skins and furs and income generated by a tobacco tax provides vivid examples of the typical blurring of public/private status. This blurring continued even after 1819 when a U.S. Supreme Court decision regarding Dartmouth College began to clarify matters. Third, despite distinctions between the religious character of the colleges—Brown was Baptist, William and Mary was Anglican, Columbia was Dutch Reformed—the student body was sure to be more heterogeneous. There were no official standards of belief for enrollment.
10   Lucas, *American Higher Education*, 117.
11   Ibid, 119. The College of California was founded in 1855 by Congregationalists but became the secular University of California in 1868 (Perko, "Religion and Collegiate Education," 1614).
12   Perko, "Religion and Collegiate Education," 1613.

for young women. Oberlin College, profoundly influenced by revivalism and committed to social reform agendas, began to admit women and people of color. By the 1850s, a small handful of colleges for blacks were in operation.[13]

Regardless of who founded these schools or who staffed them, they were alike in their programs and in their small size.[14] If a calculated average enrollment was about 250, the actual enrollment at many schools was far less.[15] Even at the so-called state schools, Protestant culture and influence pervaded leadership and community life. There, as at schools which claimed religious identity, the president often was a clergyman and usually he was personally responsible for college governance. In the late 1820s, the Yale Report asserted the foundational purposes of collegiate education: "The two great points to be gained in intellectual culture are the *discipline* and the *furniture* of the mind; expanding its powers, and storing it with knowledge."[16] However, this assertion, perhaps this *reassertion*, was not universally supported. Indeed debates about educational objectives and specific curricular reforms preceded the Yale Report. The standard classical course was being supplemented by literary and scientific tasks that took account of appeals for more practical learning and responded to the expectation that education had an economic benefit for the student as well as a civic one for the nation. By the late nineteenth century, students at schools that adopted an elective system were able to select specific classes rather than committing to a prescribed series of courses.

Lutheran Colleges

More than half of the twenty-eight colleges and universities affiliated with the ELCA were founded between 1832 and 1870. Others that no longer exist, either due to merger or to closure, were also begun. All except California Lutheran were established in some form prior to

13 Lucas, *American Higher Education*, 122.
14 Here I may seem to suggest that the purposes and program of schools for women or for blacks was no different than at schools for men. That is not the case. Intense debates were carried on about precisely that point. For example, those who asserted that if women were to be allowed advanced education then the education should be of a different sort than the sort offered to men tended to reject co-education. O. M. Norlie, a graduate of co-educational St. Olaf, took this position in the early twentieth century as part of his support of the Lutheran Ladies' Seminary. See L. DeAne Lagerquist, "'As Sister, Wife, and Mother': Education for Young Norwegian-American Lutheran Women," in *Norwegian-American Studies* 33 (1992): 130-31.
15 Lucas, *American Higher Education*, 140.
16 Ibid, 133, 135.

1900. Here we cannot look carefully at each school as Richard Solberg does in his useful volume, *Lutheran Higher Education in North America*,[17] or as is done in histories of individual schools. We focus instead on ways that these schools were like or unlike other "old time colleges," like each other, and distinct from each other. The simple assertion that every Lutheran synod founded its own college is not entirely wrong and helpfully points out that the colleges thus established were distinguished by their sponsorship, by the structure of the sponsorship, and by the sorts of religious, ethnic, and geographical factors that bound the sponsoring group together. But this observation is not helpful to the degree that it obscures the key role of the colleges in linking together those many nineteenth- and early twentieth-century church bodies. The graduates of one became faculty members at another; a faculty member from a third became the president of a fourth. The Association of Lutheran College Faculty was one of the first pan-Lutheran organizations.

Describing the various sorts of Lutherans and their institutions, Philip Schaff, a nineteenth-century church historian, divided them into three types, based upon degree of Americanization and sort of commitment to confessional specificity: the Neo-Lutherans, the moderates, and the Old Lutherans.[18] Neo-Lutherans were those whose longer residence in the United States (some came from pre-Revolutionary War families) had yielded sympathy with the generalized Protestantism (then called evangelical) and manifested in cooperative societies such as the American Bible Society. Within Lutheran circles these people were also known as Americanists or Platformists in reference to the Definite Synodical Platform which offered an "American" revision of that central Lutheran document, the Augsburg Confession. The moderates were a more complex group that included both persons from these same families, quite literally, and more recently arrived immigrants. They too adapted themselves and their churches to the American setting, but were significantly more resistant to ecumenical cooperation and more devoted to confessional adherence. The Old Lutherans, which notably included the Saxons who founded the Lutheran

---

17 Richard W. Solberg, *Lutheran Higher Education in North America* (Minneapolis: Augsburg Publishing House, 1985).
18 Schaff's 1854 remarks to an audience in Germany are quoted in E. Clifford Nelson, ed., *Lutherans in North America* (Fortress Press, 1975), 211-13. For further treatment of American Lutheranism, see L. DeAne Lagerquist, *The Lutherans* (Westport: Greenwood, 1999).

Church–Missouri Synod, were the most sectarian in their corporate life. They were committed to preservation of doctrinal purity and required agreement with the largest number of confessional documents.

Sydney E. Ahlstrom, a twentieth-century church historian who was himself Lutheran, offered a different categorization of Lutherans—one that focused specifically on higher education.[19] He identified three currents of Lutheranism: the scholastic, the pietistic, and the critical. Each current emerged from a particular historical setting, yet all three claim affinities with Luther's thought and endure beyond that original setting. In the early seventeenth century the scholastic impulse toward definition and systematization was strong. The pietistic emphasis upon inner spiritual life and participation in evangelism, acts of mercy, and the moral life followed in the late seventeenth and early eighteenth centuries. Then, in the later eighteenth and much of the nineteenth century, came the investigative spirit of the critical stream. Ahlstrom observed that all of these currents can flow together within one stream: a church body, an institution, or an individual person.

Certainly the three have marked American Lutheranism both by their presence and by their interactions. Among American Lutherans during the colonial era the pietistic emphasis was strongest with leadership from key figures including Muhlenberg. Pietism was also deeply influential for many of the nineteenth-century immigrants. The notable exception was those who formed the Lutheran Church—Missouri Synod; they were more sympathetic to scholastic concerns. The relative force of these three impulses among the founders and subsequent leaders of colleges contributed to the particular nuances of Lutheranism found on Lutheran campuses and thus account in part for the differences between the schools as well as for their similarities.

Samuel S. Schmucker was both the first Lutheran clergyman to be formally trained in the United States, at Princeton, and, in 1832, the founder of the first Lutheran college in Gettysburg, Pennsylvania. In keeping with the Lutheran commitment to an educated pastorate, Schmucker first established a seminary. Finding its students frequently ill-prepared to take up theological studies, he opened the college as a remedy. Schmucker was arguably the most influential and well-known Neo-Lutheran, inside Lutheranism and out. Thus it is only to

---

19 Sydney Ahlstrom, "What's Lutheran About Higher Education?—A Critique," in *Papers and Proceedings of the 60th Annual Convention* (Washington, D.C.: Lutheran Educational Conference of North America, 1974), 8-16.

be expected that Gettysburg College, like so many other small schools founded by Protestants in these decades, depended heavily on financial backing from local, non-Lutheran supporters and included non-Lutherans on its board and in its student body. In contrast the faculty members were usually Lutheran clergymen, some of whom also taught at the nearby seminary. From the outset Gettysburg was an American college without strong ties to either an ethnic or an immigrant community. Although the Lutherans could trace their origins to Germany, they were not immigrants or the children of immigrants and tended to regard themselves primarily as Americans. Young men enrolled at Gettysburg received an education quite like what they might have gotten at any of the host of similar colleges. Indeed the primary factor that separated Gettysburg from its peers was its association with Lutherans.

For a decade Gettysburg was the single Lutheran college. Then, in the 1840s and 1850s a half-dozen additional schools more or less replicated its model and its association with the Neo-Lutheran branches of Lutheranism. Wittenberg, in Springfield, Ohio, and Newberry in South Carolina were each located near a seminary with the intention of preparing its future students. From the outset Newberry was more closely affiliated with the South Carolina Synod than Gettysburg had been with the General Synod. As was common, these Lutheran colleges did not restrict their enrollment to those called to the Lutheran pastorate. However, all founded in these decades restricted their enrollment to male students.

With the founding of Capital University (1850) in Columbus, Ohio, the variety within the set of Lutheran associated colleges increased theologically, ethnically, and programmatically. In comparison to Wittenberg, only fifty miles away, the founders of Capital were theological moderates. This confessional position allowed some of the recent German immigrants to lend their support to Capital. Thus the school was also distinguished by its ethnic identification. Rather than the American college, the model for this school was an old style European university with faculties in arts, medicine, law, and theology. Of the projected professional programs only the seminary and law schools became operative. No other nineteenth-century Lutheran school shared this aspiration. Like Capital several were associated with groups defined by moderate or orthodox theology, more or less pietist inclinations, and national origins. Muhlenberg College (1867) was founded in direct response to Gettysburg's more minimalist confessional position and lack of attention to things German.

Other Germans and Scandinavians arriving in the mid-ninteenth century soon followed the lead of their co-religionists in setting up both seminaries and colleges. The combination of theological specificity, style of piety, and ethnic identification contributed to closer ties—whether formal, informal, or symbolic—between these schools and their church bodies than was the case for the Neo-Lutheran schools.[20] Augustana College (1860) in Rock Island, Illinois, for example, was founded by direct action of the newly organized Augustana Synod and forty-nine congregations. However, since the synod provided no direct financial support the founding was a sort of unfunded mandate.[21] Dana and Grand View were both founded by Danish Lutherans distinguished by the first group's "holy" pietism and the second's "happy" Grundtvigianism. Insofar as these colleges served to—indeed were founded precisely to—supply the seminaries with students and thus the church with pastors, the colleges enrolled only male students. This was the case at Wartburg (1852), Augustana (1860), Luther (1861), and Augsburg (1869). This purpose was consistent with the long-standing Lutheran conviction that education is a necessary qualification for the office of public ministry. A personally apprehended call from God is not enough, as it sometimes was among more revivalist influenced Protestants. While lay Lutherans were capable of leading themselves in worship, and did, because a pastor was required to administer the sacraments, the need for qualified candidates was urgent. Among these schools Augsburg was remarkable for its fierce defense of a gymnasium-like program which combined college and seminary training in a nine-year sequence quite unlike the usual pattern of a four-year college course followed by a clearly articulated seminary course.

Beyond their theological and ethnic identifications, Lutheran schools in the late nineteenth century also differed from one another in ways that mirrored the variety of non-Lutheran schools in the era. There were distinctions based in the audience and in the program determined by school's stated purpose. Some institutions admitted women, either along with men as at Thiel and St. Olaf, or only women

20 Legal ownership, significant financial support, and structures of governance are examples of formal ties; overlapping membership and social interactions are examples of informal ties, which contribute to a school's symbolic role as source of group pride and visibility.
21 Solberg, *Lutheran Higher Education*, 184.

as at Elizabeth and Marion Colleges in the south and the Lutheran Ladies' Seminary in Red Wing, Minnesota.[22] By the mid-1960s the last of the Lutheran women's colleges closed. We thus tend to forget that they existed, when, in fact, there were close to three dozen, many of them established by private initiatives.[23] Most of these schools were located in the east and the south. Their programs ranged from something resembling a high school to a more rigorous curriculum which offered students a classical course as well as alternatives, for example a practical business course. The co-educational model that is now regarded as the norm was introduced among Lutherans at Thiel College (1866), founded with leadership from William A. Passavant. Seven years later Susquehanna Female Seminary merged with the Missionary Institute, forming the basis of Susquehanna University. St. Olaf and Gustavus Adolphus, founded by Norwegians in 1874 and Swedes in 1876, were co-educational from the outset.

Although some male students at these schools may have been headed for the pastorate, their curricula were not primarily pre-seminary programs. Even more than at the men's schools, there were always a certain number of students whose contributions to the world would be as teachers, business people, and medical professionals, as well as through their membership in communities, congregations, and families. The founders of co-educational colleges (or academies) recognized what might now be called the need for an informed citizenry. That view is consistent with Martin Luther's argument urging the German nobility to support schools. There, Luther set out three purposes for education: First, it supported faith by enabling the believer to understand the gospel as well as to experience it; second, education prepared the students to employ their talents in service to their neighbors; and third, pastors required sound learning to faithfully fulfill the special responsibilities of their office.[24] This view of education reflects

---

22 See Lagerquist, "As Sister, Wife, and Mother," 111-18.

23 Solberg, *Lutheran Higher Education*, 275. Fourteen were founded prior to 1860; another twenty after. Early in the twentieth century the United Lutheran Church in America Board of Education made plans to found a women's college with Mary Markely as the president. Funds were raised and property purchased, but in 1934 the project was abandoned and the moneys designated for scholarship aid for female students.

24 Martin Luther, "To the Councilmen of all Cities in Germany that they Establish and Maintain Christian Schools," in *Martin Luther's Basic Theological Writings*, ed. Timothy Lull (Minneapolis: Fortress Press, 1989), 704-35. For an account of how such ideals were addressed in Europe, see my "Welfare of the City and Why Lutherans Care about Education," *Intersections* 38 (Fall 2013): 8-16, http://digitalcommons.augustana.edu/intersections/vol2013/iss38/4/.

Luther's insistence that God's grace precedes human action; it is a gift. As in the gift economies considered by Lewis Hyde, this gift evokes a grateful response that transforms and transfers the gift to a third party.[25] Here the second act of giving is the believer's vocation to serve the neighbor. Because such service requires adequate preparation, education should be provided. Because that education undergirds faithful response to the believer's vocation, it might be termed "vocational education," but in the robust theological sense of the word and not in its narrowly technical meaning.[26]

Given this understanding of education and vocation, it is not surprising that some Lutheran schools offered occupational training for "jobs" other than that of the pastor. While nursing schools attached to deaconess hospitals might fit this category, the principle example is normal schools, such as those operated by the Lutheran Church—Missouri Synod or the Lutheran Normal School in Madison, Minnesota. The purpose of these schools was to train teachers for parochial and public teaching. The close connection between parochial schools and the interests of the sponsoring churches may account for the official and close relationship between the Lutheran Normal School and the United Church which founded it following synodical action. This is in contrast to the looser connection of overlapping "membership" between the Lutheran Ladies' Seminary and the Norwegian Synod and to the label "College of the Church" (here the United Church), for which Augsburg and St. Olaf were in competition. Even at the colleges the number of occupational offerings during this period would likely surprise us. Of course, there were lots of other normal schools, both private and public, in these years, and many colleges offered a range of practical courses. Debates about such programs included assertions of educational principles as well as appeals to economic realities. It is impossible to determine merely from lists of courses whether Lutheran involvement was a response to economic pressures, an educational

25 Lewis Hyde, *The Gift: Imagination and the Erotic Life of Property* (New York: Vintage Books, 1983), 11-24, 40-55.

26 Mark U. Edwards, Jr. often employed this usage during his tenure as president of St. Olaf College. His thinking about the particular contributions of Lutheran theology to the educational enterprise is found in Mark U. Edwards, Jr., "Characteristically Lutheran Leanings?" *Dialog* 41.1 (Spring 2002): 50-62. For my own more recent thinking, see L.DeAne Lagerquist, "'Getting a Vocation': Variations on a Lutheran Theme," in *Claiming Our Callings: Toward a New Understanding of Vocation in the Liberal Arts*, ed. Kaethe Schwehn and L. DeAne Lagerquist (Oxford: Oxford University Press, 2014), 17-28.

principle, or a manifestation of a Lutheran commitment to the centrality of service to the neighbor.

Changing Contexts

In the decades after the Civil War and into the twentieth century, the model of the old-time college was replaced by that of the modern university that crossed the Atlantic with influential scholars trained in Germany.[27] It informed establishment of new private institutions, with Johns Hopkins University (1876) as the earliest; development of public institutions such as the University of Wisconsin, many of them supported by the Morrill Acts (1862, 1890); and the transformation of some old-style colleges, Harvard among them. The modern university differed from the old-time college on several counts, all rooted in its particular purpose. Rather than transmitting a fixed body of knowledge to undergraduates and enabling them to be good citizens, the university was to discover new information and, in the case of the "land grant" universities, to facilitate its application. Some universities which grew from colleges had once been connected to a religious party, but by the late nineteenth century, that connection was usually diluted or gone. Most universities were not associated with religious groups, athough there are notable exceptions, particularly among the Roman Catholics and Methodists.[28]

No Lutheran college made this transition; nor did Lutherans found a modern university. Nonetheless, like other colleges, Lutheran colleges are affected by this powerful ideal and tend to evaluate their programs by its standards even as they assert their differences. We are devoted to the liberal arts (in some form); they are specialized. We are focused on teaching; they are focused on research. We are small; they are huge. We attend to the student's whole person, often in a residential program; they only care about the mind. Of course, these comparisons are overdrawn, on both sides, and yet they suggest the way in which the university has become the standard by which even the most prestigious colleges describe themselves and against which they justify their continuation. The challenge was put bluntly over a century ago by a

---

27 See Julie A. Reuben, *The Making of the Modern University: Intellectual Transformation and Marginalization of Morality* (Chicago: Chicago University Press, 1996) for a helpful account that considers the consequences for curriculum and student services.

28 The degree to which these schools now retain a vital relationship to their religious bodies is a point of discussion. See Marsden, *The Soul of the American University,* for a detailed account which argues the secularization thesis. My point is only that not all such institutions have always been secular.

Columbia University professor: "I confess that I am unable to divine what is to be ultimately the position of Colleges which cannot become Universities and will not be Gymnasia. I cannot see what reason they will have to exist. It will be largely a waste of capital to maintain them, and largely a waste of time to attend them."[29]

Beginning after World War II and into recent decades, American higher education was in an expansionist mode that peaked about the time that those who are now mid-career were in college. The GI Bill provided hosts of veterans with the financial resources to attend college and initiated a series of infusions of government money into higher education. Some of that money supported growth in existing institutions; some of it was used to open new schools including hundreds of non-residential, community colleges with two-year programs; some of it continues to be used to provide members of specific groups with access to college. Here are the staggering numbers. In 1947 there were 2.3 million students enrolled at 1,800 schools; in 1986, 12.3 million students were enrolled in 3,200 schools (about a third of them had two-year programs).[30] That is ten million more students in almost twice as many schools, not quite forty years later. At the same time the sorts of programs offered also expanded, both to include the occupational tracks at community colleges and in response to innovations in scholarship such as women's studies and ethnic studies.

ELCA colleges benefited from these changes. Many renovated their facilities or constructed new buildings in mid-century using federal funds. A large percentage of students now have federal or state money in their financial aid packages. Many current faculty members began their teaching careers with federally insured loans to pay off. In the 1960s and 1970s, schools increased enrollment, perhaps by 100 percent, and added classes, majors, and programs to serve those students. Lutherans even took courage to open two new colleges: The American Lutheran Church and the Lutheran Church in America cooperated at California Lutheran (1959), and the LCMS founded Christ College—Irvine, now part of the Concordia University system. (During the same years, some schools were "lost" by merger or closing.)

Certainly these schools are different today than they were when the class of 1950 was in attendance. The faculty members are less likely to come from the college's "conventional constituency." That is to

---

29 Lucas, *American Higher Education*, 143.
30 Ibid, 228-29.

say, they may not be Lutherans and they probably are not members of the ethnic group that founded the college, if one did. Similarly, they are less likely to be alumni or graduates of any liberal arts college. At the same time, they are likely to have better academic credentials. The composition of the student body has also changed. There is a smaller proportion of Lutherans. Even as colleges are trying desperately to recruit a more diverse group with regard to race and ethnicity, they long for higher board scores. As tuition and fees go up, there are still efforts to provide access to students who are without the funds to pay the current price.

The churches to which the colleges are connected have also been changing. In the 1960s and again in 1988 mergers reduced their number and diluted the relationship between the members of a smaller church and "their" college. Locally, churchwide, and internationally, Lutherans have become more actively ecumenical. While it has never been the case that all Lutherans have gone to Lutheran schools, as potential students from Lutheran congregations have been given more options and expanded their horizons, fewer have automatically selected Lutheran schools. There are lots of reasons for that. The much discussed decline in denominational loyalty is certainly one important factor. Being Lutheran in name isn't enough, especially if the word Lutheran isn't in the college's name and when many prospective students, and their parents, and their pastors, don't even know which schools are Lutheran.

Who Are These Schools Now?

What characteristics do these schools have in common today? They are small or small-ish; they are residential, more-or-less; they offer a liberal arts program, for the most part. Mission statements suggest use of a common vocabulary, including references to the whole person, diversity, community, liberal arts, and service. The statements vary more in the way they signal Lutheran connections. Some state a current formal affiliation with the ELCA or to its regional synods; others point more vaguely to Lutheran heritage or tradition. In the midst of such comparisons to the past, it is salutary to acknowledge that the past was not the same everywhere. From the start the older colleges founded by native-born, more assimilated, Neo-Lutherans have been less distinctly Lutheran than those founded by recent immigrants who were more devoted to the Confessions or more intensely pietistic.

Common characteristics place these schools with others that continue the traditions established by the old-time colleges, and mostly in Carnegie categories: BA I or II or Comprehensive University I. Within this larger pool, Lutheran colleges as a group are less expensive, have fewer financial resources, and are less selective. Based on the credentials of our faculty and the attention we give to our students' "whole lives," we stand by the quality of our programs. Indeed some of our schools are "best buys."

Now I'm a person from a family that loves to get a good deal, but I've also learned that it is not a good deal to buy something I don't need or won't use, no matter how low the price. I think that the case that these colleges are worth continuing to operate and worth attending must be made on some basis other than their comparatively low price. Moreover I'm convinced that we have something to offer that derives, not from the search for a marginal differentiation in the market, but from the Lutheran tradition.[31]

What then are the aims of Lutheran higher education? What good ends is it meant to accomplish? Students (regardless of their beliefs) are equipped to use their gifts—talents, training, and opportunities— in ways that benefit their communities (defined variously), including their role as members of families, as citizens, and as workers. This is also a good the schools themselves offer to society as a whole. For church bodies (certainly the ELCA), Lutheran education additionally aims to cultivate in their members the skills and virtues that are necessary for faithful participation in congregational life and to provide lay and clerical leadership.

What virtues help our institutions and their students accomplish these ends? Gratitude, wisdom, boldness, and humility are four key moral virtues that Lutheran education helps cultivate.[32] In fact, one

---

31 In the original version of this essay, I explore "five practices that are common on Lutheran campuses and for which explicitly Lutheran reasons can be given." They include: (1) a shared commitment to and engagement in learning; (2) student study of the Bible and the Christian tradition; (3) participation in the arts, especially, but not limited to, music; (4) application of knowledge in the service of others; and (5) regular worship on campus. See http://digitalcommons.augustana.edu/cgi/viewcontent.cgi?article=1280&context=intersections. See also Part Two of this book for comparable "marks" of Lutheran higher education.

32 I have not developed the specifically intellectual significance of these virtues but have pointed only toward their more general and moral import. Mark Schwehn, in *Exiles from Eden: Religion and the Academic Vocation in America* (Oxford: Oxford University Press, 1993) suggests that humility, faith, self-denial, and charity each have cognitive importance with potential to shape the academic enterprise. I am in sympathy with his general assertion and find much overlap between the content of the virtues he names and those I list here.

might recognize the graduates of Lutheran colleges and universities first, by their loving *gratitude*, that is, by their disposition to recognize that all that they are and have is a gift, and by their disposition to respond with thankfulness to the divine giver and with generosity and hospitality toward others; second, by their faithful *wisdom*, that is by their ability to think about matters of faith and other arenas of life with rigor and knowledge without excluding the sensual, the natural, and social; third, by their *bold freedom*, that is by their willingness to speak the truth and act with mercy and justice without undue concern about the effect upon their penultimate situation; and fourth, by their *hopeful humility*, that is by their capacity to respond to limitation and failure with good grace, knowing that all temporal things are penultimate and that God's re-creative power is at work both now and in eternity.

If the colleges and universities affiliated with the ELCA are able to engender these virtues in their students (as well as in their staff and faculty) and to accomplish these aims for students, for society, and for churches, then they are faithful to the Lutheran tradition and well worth being maintained. If they are able to do these things, then they may also offer an alternative to consumerist views of education, something that is much needed today.

Questions for Discussion

1. How does positioning Lutheran colleges and universities within a broader history of American higher education—including old-time colleges and the modern university—help to understand who Lutheran colleges/universities are and what they are called to be?

2. Can you find strands of what Schaff called the neo-Lutherans, moderates, and/or Old Lutherans, or what Ahlstrom called scholastic, pietistic, and/or critical Lutheranism in your institution's mission or identity? Where might these strands "show up"? For whom do they matter?

3. What new developments in American higher education since 2001 (when this article was written) have affected your institution's identity and mission? How is Lutheran higher education as a whole equipped to deal with these changes?

CHAPTER 3

LUTHERAN COLLEGES
Past and Prologue

PAUL DOVRE
Concordia College, Moorhead, Minnesota

As the template for the historical assessments that follow, I draw from the classical sources of persuasion as identified by Aristotle and others.[1] According to the classics, people are persuaded or convinced by three distinctive categories of proof: ethos, logos, and pathos. *Ethos* is the power of one's personality, character, and reputation. We say we are convinced because the person making the argument is deemed to be honest, trustworthy, knowledgeable, or loyal. I think that organizations and institutions have *ethos* as well, and it is derived from their mission, their narrative, their values, their traditions, and their character. The e*thos* of a college is transmitted through the people who constitute the institution, primarily the faculty and staff.

Logos has to do with arguments and evidence, that is to say, with logic. When we say that a speech was substantive and persuasive, it means that we were convinced by its arguments and supporting evidence. I believe institutions have a *logos* in that they make a case for what they stand for or what they have to offer their constituents. If they present well-formed arguments and supporting evidence, good programs, and sound learning, they are both respected and understood.

Finally, *pathos* is a form or persuasion that appeals to our wants, desires, convictions, or values. Such persuasion may appeal to either our basic instincts or our higher inclinations. Institutions also offer *pathos* to their constituents as they appeal to ideals, values, aspirations, fears, hopes, and even dreams. To the extent that people are inspired

---

1 This essay was originally published in *Intersections* 30 (Fall 2009): 16-22.

by, or in congruence with, these elements, they will be content, moved, or even inspired.

In my view, at mid-twentieth century, midwestern Lutheran colleges and universities made their case to their constituents of faculty, staff, alumni, church members, friends, and students primarily on the basis of *pathos* and *ethos*. These colleges were generally places of unity and common focus, shaped by religious and ethnic identity and a strong sense of shared values and commitments. With the passing of the generations and the presence of a more diverse faculty and a more secular and pluralistic culture, both the *pathos* and *ethos* declined in their efficacy. Many new faculty "knew not Joseph" and so the traditions, values, and general character of these places did not have a strong impact on them. Toward the end of the century, spurred by serious self-examination, growing numbers of inquiring faculty, and the support of the church, *logos* became the focus and the basis for institutional renewal. I believe that this emerging *logos* is having a significant impact upon these institutions.

The Changing Landscape of Midwestern Lutheran Colleges

As a way of explicating these matters, let me share my perceptions about the church and midwestern Lutheran colleges during this period of change.[2] The church was a major part of the context within which these colleges carried out their mission during the past half century. There have been substantial changes in the church's experience, and those changes have had an impact in the life of the schools. For example, the church has changed from a mono-ethnic institution growing from within to a multiethnic church depending on outreach for growth. At a different pace, perhaps, the schools have experienced a similar trend toward greater diversity in the ethnic, religious, and economic backgrounds of students, faculty, and staff. In similar fashion, the church has made the transition from being insular to being energetically ecumenical. Mirroring this, the colleges have attracted students from a broad ecumenical and interfaith spectrum. The church has changed from a body fairly clear about positions on moral and ethical issues to a church that is full of divisions over such matters. While the colleges may not have experienced such divisions in the ways that

---

2   In this essay, I share my perceptions on several of the key trends that have characterized the past fifty years in the history of midwestern Lutheran colleges. In both method and content, this should be regarded as autobiographical rather than academic, for it is more about reminiscence than research.

the church has, they are clearly places with a diversity of opinion and a liberal bias in such matters. At mid-century the church was a major collecting and distribution point for benevolence dollars, and the colleges enjoyed high priority in that distribution. By century's end, benevolence dollars were scarce and the colleges, thought to be able to fend more or less on their own financially, were much lower on the priority list. Somewhat shadowing this development, a church that at mid-century paid close attention to its schools and held them accountable in a number of ways, now has both less time for, and less claim upon, such accountability.

A second template identifies four key issues around which I will discuss developments in the five decades of the second half of the twentieth century. Those key issues are survival, respectability, faithfulness, and relationship to the church. We take the first three together; the last requires its own consideration.

Survival, Respectability, and Faithfulness

In the 1950s the leaders of the midwestern colleges were Stavig at Augustana (Sioux Falls, South Dakota), Christianson at Augsburg, Carlson at Gustavus, Ylvisaker at Luther, Becker at Wartburg, Granskou at St. Olaf, and Knutson at Concordia (Morehead, Minnesota). All except Carlson had ministerial preparation and parish experience. All were active leaders in their respective church bodies; they served on key boards and committees and were frequent speakers and teachers at regional and church-wide events. It should also be noted that these men gave leadership at a time when institutional authority was more centered in the office of the president than at any time since then.

Of the key issues, survival was the one that occupied most of the attention of these colleges. These were the post-Depression, post-World War II days when campus infrastructures were rundown, facilities were totally inadequate for the expanding growth caused by returning veterans, and there were not enough qualified faculty to cover all of the classes. Lutheran colleges were not unique in these regards; their state was the common state of most of higher education. A piece of good news was that although the faculty was stretched thin, there were among them some giants who defined the quality and character of these institutions.

The second issue was respectability. Most of higher education had been given a pass on rising academic standards during the survival years of the 1930s and 1940s. But in the post-war years the accrediting bodies began to flex their muscles. There was pressure to add Ph.D.s to the faculty, to improve library holdings, and to provide adequate equipment and facilities, particularly in the sciences.

With respect to the third key issue, faithfulness, the story is rather straightforward: Each college was a monoculture of the sponsoring church body; almost all of the faculty and staff were Lutheran as well as most of the students. In most cases attendance was required at daily chapel, and the religion requirement consisted of several classes taken over four years. Campus rules and norms reflected the culture and expectations of the church. The mission identity of these colleges was not a matter discussed very often; it could simply be taken for granted. The *ethos* and *logos* of these places was not very self-conscious, but it was constitutive, and one can only wonder how these institutions could have prevailed through times of testing without this reality. As a contribution to the *logos* of these institutions, the Association of Lutheran College Faculties group undertook a decade-long study that examined the theological underpinnings of a Lutheran college and their implications for the curriculum.[3] With respect to the church relationship, there was a strong tie. The financial support of the church body was a significant variable in the financial well-being of each school. The church kept a close and loving eye on these colleges. The governance relationship between the church and the colleges was very strong; in most cases, church leaders had places on the governing boards, and every board member was a member of the sponsoring church. Governing boards paid more attention to the details of managing the colleges, a practice grown out of the necessities of the 1930s and 1940s.

The decades of the 1960s and 1970s were marked by leadership changes at many of the colleges: from Stavig to Balcer at Augustana (South Dakota), from Christianson to Anderson at Augsburg, from Ylvisaker to Farwell at Luther, from Carlson to Barth at Gustavus, from Becker to Bachman at Wartburg, from Granskou to Rand at St. Olaf, and from Knutson to Dovre at Concordia toward the end of that period. It should be noted that, in several cases, the new leaders brought stronger academic credentials—but often less theological education. This was the case at Augustana (South Dakota), Luther, Wartburg, Gustavus, and Concordia.

---

3   See Harold H. Ditmanson, ed. *Christian Faith and the Liberal Arts* (Minneapolis: Augsburg Publishing House, 1960).

During these decades the schools themselves also grew in academic respectability. Faculty numbers grew and the percentages of faculty with Ph.D.s increased as well, all of which was very important to accreditation agencies. New programs were initiated on every campus, and library and laboratory facilities were upgraded. Faithfulness to mission and tradition became more challenging during this period of time for a number of reasons. With pressure for academic respectability and shortages of personnel, faculty appointments were likely to place more emphasis on academic qualifications than other factors. Most of the new academics came from research centers, shaped by a modernism that placed priority on scientific methods of establishing truth claims. This trend, in turn, placed pressure on the humanities and the religious values that were intrinsic to the distinctiveness of the schools. Curriculum changes tended to diminish the size of the religion requirement. Chapel attendance was by now voluntary but still substantial. The advent of the civil rights movement and the anti-war movement led to myriad changes in the society and its institutions. Some of those changes (e.g., more diverse faculty and student bodies) had a positive impact on the colleges while others (destructive lifestyles) did not. Other consequences were the increasing secularization of the schools, the demise of *in loco parentis*, and the restructuring of campus governance.

As it had in the 1950s, the Association of Lutheran College Faculties was minding the *logos* of Lutheran colleges, addressing both the rapidly changing culture of the late 1960s and the 1970s and the challenges for Lutheran colleges.[4] The American Lutheran Church initiated the "Theological Development Program for Faculty" in the 1970s, a program that helped shape a number of persons who would emerge as faculty and administrative leaders in the 1980s and 1990s. However, the attention given to institutional mission (*pathos*) by most colleges in the 1960s and 1970s was less than the attention given to institutional quality. The discussions of mission rarely gave systematic attention to the ways in which the mission might impact academic life. However, in most cases faculty leaders were persons who had come in the 1940s and 1950s and were infused with the *pathos* and *ethos* of which I wrote earlier.

---

4   The association's work led to the publication of Richard Baepler, *The Church-Related College in an Age of Pluralism: The Quest for a Viable Saga* (Valparaiso, Indiana: Association of Lutheran College Faculty, 1977).

Colleges of/and/or the Church

The fourth key issue—the college's changing relationship to the church—is most encompassing and complex. There were several emerging trends in these decades. To begin with, while church support was still a stable and growing part of the church's budget, reflecting the continuing priority of the colleges, church benevolence declined substantially as a percentage of the rapidly growing budgets of the colleges. Another marked trend in this period was the growing generosity of individual church members with respect to the financial needs of the colleges. In the case of the American Lutheran Church, a major church-wide campaign was very successful. During the 1970s, some Lutheran colleges revised their governing documents to include non-Lutheran members on their boards. This reflected the growing ecumenism of the church and the colleges as well as the desire to "spread a bigger net" in search of influence, financial support, and enrollment. In the Lutheran Church in America, colleges developed covenants with synods in their regions as a way of setting forth the mutual commitments that would guide the relationships. It is accurate to say that, with respect to midwestern Lutheran colleges, college presidents were still thought of as prominent in the leadership of the church.

The decade of the 1980s saw a myriad of leadership changes in these colleges. At Augsburg College, Oscar Anderson was succeeded by Charles Anderson; Augustana moved from Charles Balcer to Bill Nelson and then to Lloyd Svendsbye; St. Olaf from Sidney Rand to Harland Foss and Mel George; Luther from Elwin Farwell to H. George Anderson; Wartburg from William Jellema to Robert Vogel; and Gustavus from Ed Lindell to John Kendall. In all but one case, the new presidents came from academic backgrounds. While finance is always an issue for private colleges, financial survival was not a defining issue in the 1980s. Federal and state financial aid programs were very helpful in maintaining vigorous enrollment. Many of the schools launched and completed sophisticated and successful fund-raising programs. In terms of academic quality, the Lutheran colleges were respected by the public. It was during this decade that various national rankings of colleges first appeared, and midwestern Lutheran colleges earned high ratings. These ratings reflected the academic quality that had been built in the faculty and the attention that was being given to building strong academic programs.

Perhaps the most challenging issue in the 1980s was faithfulness to the tradition and mission. By the 1980s the academy was shaped by the Enlightenment focus on knowledge as opposed to learning, and the pedagogy of the scientific method held sway. These developments have been chronicled by many.[5] The consequences were to diminish confidence in religious knowledge and the role of faith in the life of the school. Augmented by the reality that secular values were shaping the culture, these trends were real sources of stress for most religious colleges, including Lutheran colleges in the Midwest.

In addition to the growing secularity of the schools, there was more religious diversity on the campuses in the faculty, staff, and student body. While most of the faculty in the 1950s and even into the 1960s had come through "the Lutheran pipeline," the majority of appointees in the 1970s and 1980s did not. That meant that the *ethos*, which had been carried in the DNA of the faculty in 1950s through the 1970s, could not be counted upon to carry the tradition in the 1980s, and matters of mission could no longer be taken for granted. While in the past academic criteria and institutional/missional fit were held in balance in the faculty selection process, by the 1980s academic criteria held sway. A related shift in the profile of incoming faculty in the 1970s and 1980s is that they had been shaped in ways that meant their primary allegiance was more in the direction of discipline and department, and less to the institution which they served. I do not think this was a self-conscious commitment on the part of most people, but it was nonetheless a growing reality. The consequence was a diminished religious *ethos* and *pathos.* During these decades one noted subtle changes in the rhetoric of many colleges, with a growing emphasis on academic distinctiveness and a softening in the emphasis on religious identity and mission. This was in some measure due to the fact that Lutheran schools were attracting an increasing number of students from other religious traditions whom they did not want to offend.

---

5   See especially Robert Benne, *Quality with Soul: How Six Premier Colleges and Universities Keep Faith with Their Religious Traditions* (Grand Rapids, Michigan: Wm. B. Eerdmans Publishing, 2001); James Tunstead Burtchaell, *The Dying of the Light: The Disengagement of Colleges and Universities from Their Christian Churches* (Grand Rapids, Michigan: Wm. B. Eerdmans Publishing, 1998); George M. Marsden, *The Soul of the American University: From Protestant Establishment to Established Nonbelief* (New York: Oxford University Press, 1994); Mark R. Schwehn, *Exiles from Eden: Religion and the Academic Vocation in America* (New York: Oxford University Press, 1993); and Douglas Sloan, *Faith and Knowledge: Mainline Protestantism and American Higher Education* (Louisville, Kentucky: Westminster John Knox, 1994).

The connection between the colleges and the church also changed in the 1980s. The college presidents were less likely to be church leaders. The church was stressed for resources, and hence the financial support for colleges diminished. While Lutheran colleges were included in the mission circle of the newly formed Evangelical Lutheran Church in America (ELCA), they were less central to that mission. The implication of these developments in the church meant that the colleges would assume a larger role in defining the ways and extent to which they would embrace their relationship to the Lutheran church and their mission identity. While it was clearly not the case that any of the midwestern colleges were hostile to their Lutheran identity or trying to distance themselves from their mission, the close of the 1980s became a kind of watershed for these colleges: The relationship to the church had changed, the self-understanding of these schools as institutions of the church had eroded, and the faculties were not always "at home" in the academic communities of the Lutheran church. In short, the *ethos* that had been carried by an earlier generation had largely disappeared with their retirement, the *pathos* was less clear and compelling, and the *logos* of the Lutheran academic tradition was not a significant factor.

Renewal and Renaissance

Enter the 1990s: There were myriad changes in leadership. Frame was leading Augsburg, Wagner and Halvorson led Augustana, Baker and then Torgerson came to Luther, Edwards served at St. Olaf, and Steuer led Gustavus. All of these leaders had strong academic backgrounds. Still, most of them were intrigued by the questions of relationship, identity, and mission, and they came to these conversations with a refreshing curiosity. They were leading healthy schools. While some were more robust from a financial view than others, all were viable; while some had more success in attracting students than others, all had stable numbers. Academically, these schools each continued to make one or more list of best colleges. There were centers of excellence on each campus reflecting the quality and ingenuity of the faculty. A challenge dating from the 1980s was around narrow job preparation, or "vocationalism" in this limited sense, that was sweeping the country. From grade school on students were being pressed to pick a career and pursue a professionally oriented education. This was a special concern to colleges with a strong liberal arts tradition.

Viewed through the lens of faithfulness to the Lutheran tradition, the 1990s were years of renaissance. The roots of this renaissance were both external and internal. There was a heightened awareness of a values crisis in society. At the same time, there was an emerging spirituality among the young. In the academy, the postmodern movement provided a critique of modernism, rationalism, and the scientific method. Along with a new generation of leaders came a new generation of faculty members who had, in part, been shaped by this critique—young people who were curious about religious matters and college identity and open to deep conversation about value, meaning, and faith. Providing counsel and leadership were some key faculty and administrative leaders who were schooled in the *logos* of Lutheran higher education.

Out of this crucible of change religious colleges found both incentive and support for a new self-examination of mission and identity. Many midwestern Lutheran colleges initiated formal discussions about the meaning and implications of their mission and identity as Lutheran schools. The ELCA supported these efforts with annual conferences on the vocation of Lutheran colleges. These conferences were (and are) well attended and led to the publication of *Intersections*, a journal that features essays about faith and learning. The Lilly endowment, sensing the new opening for such matters, launched a mammoth program enabling many colleges to initiate comprehensive programs centered on the Christian idea of vocation. The ELCA initiated the Lutheran Academy of Scholars, where faculty members could devote themselves to a serious intellectual engagement between faith and learning. Endowed professorships were created on a number of campuses in support of academic endeavor informed by faith commitments. A number of curriculum projects emerged, and for many the touchstone was institutional mission. The Lutheran Educational Conference of North America (LECNA) launched a major research effort designed to identify the unique impact of Lutheran colleges upon their graduates.

To return to the template of *ethos, pathos*, and *logos*, what happened in the 1990s was the beginning of the reconstruction of a *logos* on behalf of the mission of Lutheran colleges. Mirroring the leadership of their predecessors in the 1950s and 1970s, faculty members examined the Lutheran confessional, academic, and intellectual traditions and found a trove of helpful propositions upon which to build an understanding of both personal and institutional callings.[6] This *logos* is compelling enough to generate conviction—and even passion—for the cause. Thus we have the re-energizing of the *pathos* of these institutions and, over time, an emerging community *ethos* as well. This is not to suggest that questions about mission and identity are now settled. Indeed, that would defy the Lutheran tradition that is almost constantly in motion about such matters. As the society changes around these schools, the task or reinterpretation must go on.

Financial support continued to decline in 2000 as church-wide resources grew scarce and the fiscal wellbeing of most of the colleges made their need less compelling. The ELCA went through a re-organization in which higher education was joined with theological education. While church-wide direct financial support continued to decline, the ELCA continued to sponsor staff development and faculty interchanges in a variety of forums. Out of a vision of unity in mission and interconnectedness in ministry, leaders of midwestern Lutheran colleges have, in some cases, provided leadership in initiating and supporting partnerships with other institutions and agencies of the church.

One might look back on this historical survey and conclude that survival was the issue defining the 1950s, respectability was the compelling issue of the 1960s and 1970s, and faithfulness to Lutheran identity and mission emerged in the late 1980s and continues into the current decade. Over the span of the five decades, the relationship with the church evolved from dependence to independence to partnership. The profile of the presidents transitioned from churchly to academic; the cultural inclinations moved from sectarian to secular; the intellectual paradigm shifted from pre-modern, to modern, to postmodern, and the demographic profile moved from homogeneity to a growing diversity. Entering the new century, midwestern Lutheran colleges enjoyed regional and national reputations for excellence and possessed a robust attitude about their viability. Leaders of excellence mediate complex and stressful institutional agendas in a time of material uncertainty and cultural change. The case for Lutheran colleges, once resting on strong *ethos* and *pathos*, is being reconstructed around a lively and rich *logos*.

---

6   For more on how "vocation" or "calling" came to become the leading mark of Lutheran higher education, see Chapter 4 of this volume.

Conclusion: A Prologue

What then of the future of these colleges as expressions of the Lutheran tradition in higher education? Perhaps the most obvious answer is that, given the significant autonomy that characterizes Lutheran colleges, they will evolve in unique ways. Given the restructurings and downsizing of the ELCA church-wide body, it is also clear that the colleges themselves will be primary in defining their relationship to the church. Other key variables influencing the future of Lutheran colleges include the shifting demographics, increasing diversity, and complex spiritualities of the rising generations of college students. Much will depend on how we navigate the identity/diversity paradox. In recent years, we have acknowledged the value of both identity and diversity but have tended to give the greater weight to diversity. This is perhaps not surprising for institutions that were monocultural in the recent past (and defensive about it) and are well informed about, and widely influenced by, the need for diversity in higher education. The upcoming challenge will be achieving a relationship between these two powerful variables that will be consonant with the mission and identity of a Lutheran college.[7]

For many reasons, the formation of the faculty *ethos* will be of high importance. The faculties are and will be composed of a significant number of persons from non-Christian and non-Lutheran traditions. The presence of this kind of diversity presents both opportunity and challenge, the opportunity (and need) for dialogue (a Lutheran staple), and the challenge of educating those from other traditions. In reflecting on this diversity, Darrell Jodock put it this way: "In order for these colleges to retain the advantages of a tradition that challenges them to become more deeply and more profoundly what they already aspire to be, the tradition needs to be articulated more clearly and affirmed more intentionally."[8] Since persons entering the professoriate in recent years have been oriented around disciplinary identity rather than institutional identity, there will be a continuing challenge for Lutheran colleges to integrate these persons into the community and engage them in the activities that give life to it.

---

7   For more on the compatibility of Lutheran identity with interfaith practices, see Chapters 8 and 12.

8   Darrell Jodock, "The Lutheran Tradition and the Liberal Arts College: How Are They Related?" in *Called to Serve: St. Olaf and the Vocation of a Church College*, ed. Pamela Schwandt (Northfield, Minnesota: St. Olaf College, 1999), 32. Also available at http://gustavus.edu/faith/pdf/called_to_serve.pdf.

Faculty are not the only element in the human variable of course. One thinks about the important roles of presidents, other college leaders, regents, and staff. Leaders having experience and an informed commitment to the Lutheran project in education are scarce, so continuing attention to leader identification and development will be essential. The colleges will want to be self-conscious in filling leadership positions with people who share the vision and mission of Lutheran colleges. Of almost equal importance to the selection of such individuals is the provision of continuing education experiences around mission and identity. Again, if board and staff development around these issues is only left to chance, the results are likely to be drift and a growing indifference to such matters.[9]

Another variable centers on the distinctiveness of the college program, the key dimension of a school's *logos*. In recent years, and out of the impulse of the Lutheran teachings on vocation, colleges have been paying increasing attention to Lutheran narratives in the construction of curricula. While "faith and learning" is not a Lutheran invention, it has always been central to the Lutheran intellectual tradition and Lutherans have brought special resources to it. In the biblical, theological, and confessional narratives of the Lutheran tradition we find resources that apply to both the form and content of education. One thinks of Lutheran teachings on vocation, the two kingdoms, *simul justus et peccator*, original sin, and the priesthood of all believers. Or, with reference to the biblical tradition, one recognizes distinctive traditions of historical, literary, and rhetorical criticism. Concerning pedagogical matters, one thinks of the place of dialectic, the paradox, moral deliberation, and discernment in community.

The *pathos* of campus life is another significant variable in the unfolding of Lutheran identity and mission. Proclamation, prayer, and praise are staples of the Lutheran tradition and are formative of community. One calls to mind the worship centers on many campuses and the high quality programs in sacred music and art that involve large numbers of students. Given the challenge posed by individualism in religious matters and the secularism of harried lifestyles, worship will be a challenge for this group of colleges. We will need creative and winsome leaders who can both gather students in and reach out to students where they gather. Given the impulse to serve others that

---

9   This is a contested claim among participants in conversations about Lutheran higher education and the authors of the present book. See especially Chapter 4 for differing assumptions and claims.

is strongly present on our campuses, campus ministry will find ways to identify with and inform such endeavors. Under the aegis of Lilly-funded programs and church-wide initiatives, the vocation idea has taken root on many campuses and, increasingly, in the lives of many students. This trend is fortuitous for the mission and identity of these colleges.

I have often described the current decade as a time of renaissance in mission for religious colleges in America. One sees signs of this revitalization at many turns. Many midwestern Lutheran colleges have been in the vanguard of this renaissance. Hopefully, this good beginning will provide the foundation for the continuing renewal of Lutheran colleges in coming decades. Many of us believe in, and are committed to, such a future.

Questions for Discussion

1. How is your college or university Lutheran in terms of its *ethos*, *pathos*, and *logos*, as described by Dovre in this chapter?

2. Dovre here reflects on the identity and mission of five Midwestern Lutheran colleges up until the early twenty-first century. How would his findings need to change to include more recent developments, as well as Lutheran colleges and universities in eastern or western United States?

3. Some might see Dovre's historical narrative as broadly following a pattern of initial integrity, subsequent weakening of a college's Lutheran identity, and finally, a reclaiming or renewal of its mission and identity. Does this plot help make sense of the "Lutheranism" of your school? What alternative storylines or structures help narrate the Lutheran identity and mission of your institution?

CHAPTER 4

THE VOCATION MOVEMENT IN LUTHERAN HIGHER EDUCATION

MARK WILHELM
Network of ELCA Colleges and Universities, Chicago, Illinois

This article presents a brief history of the movement to urge colleges and universities related to the Evangelical Lutheran Church in America (ELCA) to view their identity and mission through the lens offered by the concept of vocation.[1] It argues that the vocation movement arose as Lutheran higher education leaders rediscovered a wisdom about higher education within the concept of vocation as expressed by the Lutheran intellectual tradition. This rediscovery enabled leaders to articulate a rationale for educating students to live meaningful, purposeful lives dedicated to the common good.

As a result of the vocation movement, reclaiming education for vocation has become the hallmark of ELCA higher education.

Changing Conditions in Lutheran Higher Education

Reclaiming vocation as the hallmark of higher education in the Lutheran tradition occurred in the context of a larger, decades-long conversation in the United States about the aims and purposes of church-related higher education. Within that larger conversation, discussions in Lutheran higher education circles about the concept of vocation developed into a *movement* intent on re-grounding Lutheran higher education in the rich intellectual tradition of the Lutheran community. The vocation movement accomplished this goal by using Martin Luther's theology of vocation to derive the aims and purposes of higher education from a Lutheran viewpoint.

---

1   This essay was previously published in *Intersections* 43 (Spring 2016): 14-18.

The movement arose to answer a very practical question: "In what sense is a college Lutheran if it no longer means being a college almost exclusively populated by Lutherans?" This question was asked with increasing frequency as the percentage of faculty, administrators, and especially students who were personally members of the Lutheran community noticeably declined. The decline grew steadily over the course of the twentieth century, and it occurred dramatically at some institutions during the last quarter of that century, where the presence of Lutherans dropped below 10 percent.

This transition accompanied the ending of Lutheran ethnic separatism, a separatism from mainstream America that had defined Lutheran colleges and all other aspects of the Lutheran community well into the early twentieth century. Ethnic separatism had also meant *defacto* that Lutheran colleges were operated by Lutherans for the service of Lutheran students. The vocation movement cannot be understood unless one realizes it was a response to the collapse of a living ethnic culture at all Lutheran colleges that had separated them from the general American public. That is, it was not just a response to a decline in the numbers of Lutherans at schools founded by the Lutheran community. The decline in Lutherans present on Lutheran campuses was the direct result of the collapse of ethnic, separatist Lutheranism.

During the eighteenth, nineteenth, and early twentieth centuries, Lutheranism in America had been an ethnic, separatist culture serving various branches of German-American and Scandinavian-American communities. These communities were separated significantly from mainstream American society by linguistic and cultural divides, in addition to religious ones. This reality of cultural, linguistic, and religious separatism was so thoroughly true that Sydney Ahlstrom, the great historian of American Christianity who taught at Yale University in the third quarter of the twentieth century and who was himself a Lutheran and an active participant in the early years of the vocation movement, labeled Lutheranism a "countervailing religion." With the label "countervailing," Ahlstrom underscored that Lutherans, Lutheranism, and its institutions—including its colleges—spent their initial existence in America set apart from and providing a counter to mainstream American society.[2] For Lutheran colleges, being ethnic, separatist institutions

---

2   Sydney E. Ahlstrom, *A Religious History of the American People,* 2nd ed. (Princeton: Princeton University Press, 2004), 515-26.

meant that they only served Lutherans, the members of their ethnic tribe, even though Lutheran colleges were formally open to the larger community and some outside of the Lutheran orbit participated in them from the beginning.

All this changed slowly during the twentieth century, and with increasing rapidity in its second half, as the Lutheran community and its institutions steadily entered mainstream American culture. This meant that its institutions, especially its institutions of higher education, were actively opened to non-Lutherans, not only for the admission of students from other backgrounds, but also to the academic subject matter and research interests of others. Lutheran scholars had always engaged the wider European-American academic community, but during the twentieth century Lutheran schools that would one day be part of the ELCA and their faculties became more deeply engaged in the mainstream of that larger academic community and in making scholarly—and hiring—decisions in concert with those who had once been outsiders to ethnic, separatist Lutheran higher education. This willingness to engage the mainstream academic community is shown in the trend among our schools during the twentieth century to join higher education accrediting bodies that expanded in the late nineteenth and early twentieth centuries in order to differentiate serious academic communities from lesser schools and programs of study, particularly the so-called Bible colleges.

The transition also meant that Lutheran students no longer felt restricted to the schools birthed by their communities. Young adult Lutherans who, in a prior generation, would have never considered attending a college outside of their community, began to accept admission to other colleges and universities, from flagship public universities to the Ivy League, in the second half of the twentieth century. The shift in practices among Lutheran students occurred within a larger breakdown of the barriers of ethnic separatism and prejudice—indeed, legalized institutional racism—that had prevailed in American culture and had prevented many persons from attending colleges outside of their community. This change was most publicly debated and made visible during the third quarter of the twentieth century by the opening of Harvard College to Jewish-Americans and by ending the segregation of African-Americans into black-only colleges.

In that larger milieu, Lutherans began to leave their own ethnic separatism behind, even as Lutheran schools increasingly opened their doors to others. As a result, the campuses of Lutheran colleges and universities were increasingly populated by persons—students, faculty, and administrators—who were not Lutherans, while Lutherans were often studying and working at non-Lutheran schools. Other economic and social factors, such as a growing professoriate trained in common programs of graduate education, also drove these changes, but addressing these factors is beyond the scope this of essay.

The increased presence of non-Lutherans among students, faculty, and administrators compelled the leaders of Lutheran institutions to ask how a college was Lutheran if it was not a college primarily operated by Lutherans for the benefit of Lutherans. The question never arose, of course, when Lutheran colleges functioned as ethnic, separatist institutions; they were simply institutions of the Lutheran community. But what made them Lutheran if they were no longer defined *de facto* by a primary—and nearly exclusive—mission to serve Lutherans?

The initial answer to this question focused on institutional markers to define a Lutheran college. Governance documents at Lutheran colleges and universities began to specify arrangements that had historically been assumed, such as specifying that the president must be a Lutheran. (In its original iteration, bylaws typically specified that the president had to be Lutheran clergy.) Constitutions mandated that certain percentages of governance board members had to be Lutherans or even Lutheran clergy. Admission practices reflected what we would today call affirmative action in favor of Lutheran students, such as the practice of reserving certain scholarships for Lutherans. Hiring practices for faculty and administrators strove to maintain a significant, albeit typically indeterminate, presence of Lutherans on campus.

The creation and policing of institutional markers such as these was the initial response to the questions arising from the opening of our schools to many non-Lutheran students, faculty, and administrators. A Lutheran college or university was Lutheran if it maintained these types of institutional markers.

No formal, collective decision by Lutheran schools or by church leadership mandated the use of such institutional factors to definitively identify a Lutheran school. In the face of declining numbers of Lutherans at Lutheran schools, the practice represented an all-too-easy capitulation to the American cultural assumption that an institution exists to serve its founding community and promote its parochial interests.

Americans, and seemingly people everywhere, believe that a religious college cannot be a genuinely a religious college—such as an authentically Lutheran college or university—unless it is parochial in its practices. They also assume that institutional markers are needed in order for a school to be properly Lutheran. These cultural assumptions about the necessarily parochial orientation of a religious college also insist that the only alternative for a school is to be secular. As Professor Darrell Jodock has taught us, most people cannot accept that a third option is available—namely, the existence of a college or university grounded in a religious tradition that does not exist to serve parochial interests.[3] Hence, Lutheran leaders assumed that they had to ensure a college or university met parochial standards if significant numbers of non-Lutherans were also involved in the school. Institutional markers demonstrated that the necessary standards for Lutheran parochial interests were being met when parochial standards were no longer culturally enforced *de facto* by a nearly exclusive population Lutherans on campus.

In the 1970s, many leaders at our schools began to question the adequacy of institutional markers as the way of defining Lutheran higher education. A search began for a more authentically Lutheran perspective on the mission of higher education that was not rooted in parochial assumptions or norms.

Reclaiming Education for Vocation

The search for a more authentic core and definition for Lutheran higher education is what I have called the vocation movement. Institutional matters, including matters of governance and administration, obviously remain important for our common work. All Lutheran colleges and universities, for example, have some type of constitutional connection to the ELCA. Service to students, scholars, and the mission of the ELCA also remain important. But the vocation movement asserts that our common identity as Lutheran schools is based in something else. The vocation movement says that a missional commitment to education for vocation is—and should be acknowledged as—the defining mark of higher education in the ELCA. The complexities of institutional issues and other aspects of the relationship between the ELCA and its colleges and universities will always be with us, but the vocation movement rightly points us to an educational ideal as the defining marker of Lutheran higher education.

---

3   Darrell Jodock, "Vocation of the Lutheran College and Religious Diversity," *Intersections* 33 (Spring 2011): 5-6. Jodock's essay is republished as Chapter 6.

Lutheran higher education leaders have been mining the Lutheran intellectual tradition for over thirty years to describe this educational ideal, its basis in the Lutheran doctrine of vocation, and a rationale for how the concept of vocation offers a wise and substantive foundation for Lutheran higher education. The annual Vocation of a Lutheran College conference, now in its twenty-first year, has been part of that process. Lutheran teaching about vocation and its implications for education form the core of a revised understanding—as promoted by the vocation movement—of what defines a Lutheran college or university.

What is the ideal of education rooted in the concept of vocation, and how is this derived from the Lutheran intellectual tradition? Here I can only offer a short summary. The doctrine of vocation is the Lutheran tradition's label for living life as God intends, namely, living lives that are purposeful, worthy, and open to considering the needs of others as well as one's own and therefore having value both in the eyes of humanity and of God. Lutheran theology teaches that people need not spend their lives trying to curry God's favor because the good news or gospel of Jesus Christ proclaims that God freely accepts persons as they are. Instead of seeking to find or impress God, to be religious is to respond to God's invitation and call to follow Jesus; that is, people are to serve rather than be served, living lives—like Jesus—that serve others and contribute to the common good or, in traditional Lutheran discourse, "serve the neighbor." The word *vocation*, of course, means calling, and Lutherans believe they are called by God to live lives of service. One way to serve the neighbor is to make opportunities for excellent higher education available to people of good will, enabling them to also pursue a meaningful life that contributes to the common good through whatever work they undertake. Persons of good will may not and need not affirm with the Lutheran tradition that God in Christ is the one who calls people to lead such lives, but from whatever religious or ethical motivation, all persons of good will can engage in education for vocation at Lutheran schools.

Gaining consensus about the educational ideal of education for vocation has not been easy, nor has it been achieved among ELCA-related schools. Education for vocation can be a "hard sell." Significant opposition remains to building the public identity of ELCA higher education around the concept of vocation. This is true even at the many institutions which have embraced vocational reflection as an important programmatic aspect of their schools' mission.

Those who object to the vocation movement and its concomitant reaffirmation of the Lutheran identity of their schools are not unreasonable. America is rife with examples of religious authority acting to interfere with a school's free exercise of its mission. Hardly a month passes without *The Chronicle of Higher Education* reporting another self-protective and detrimental move in religiously-affiliated higher education, such as the action at a small college in Indiana reported in early July 2015 to limit the teaching of evolution, bringing with that limitation a curtailment of academic freedom. Religious authority has also been a source of more sophisticated attacks against self-determination by the academy, such as the effort by the Council for Christian Colleges and Universities to seek exemption from gay rights protections. All too often it seems that the role of religion in American higher education is negative and sectarian, intruding on academic freedom, and substituting other ends for an authentic educational mission. Critics of the vocation movement ask, "Why should the Lutheran tradition and the vocation movement be any different?"[4]

Despite the challenges, I remain optimistic that the Lutheran ideal of higher education as defined by the vocation movement will find acceptance over time. Our generation has the chance to reclaim one of the great Western educational traditions by remembering the ideal of education for vocation and the Lutheran notion of a third way for non-sectarian, but authentically religious, higher education. In doing so, we will be remembering and reclaiming one of the foundational movements that produced our North Atlantic academy and the idea of the academy's unfettered freedom to explore the world and engage in teaching and learning. This essay cannot explore the links between Lutheranism and our contemporary North Atlantic academy.[5] Suffice it to say that Lutheran leaders created the influential German educational system in the sixteenth century, and their heirs were directly involved in creating the University of Berlin and the modern research university model in the nineteenth century.

This Lutheran academic tradition, although distorted through decades of ethnic, separatist existence, and now not infrequently hidden to many at our schools, continues to reside in the culture of ELCA

---

4 Still others criticize "education for vocation," especially when thought to be a *comprehensive* articulation of Lutheran church-relatedness, for overlooking or bypassing the need for confessional (or church-going) Lutherans on campus. See chapter 11 below for one clear articulation of this concern.

5 See Chapter 2 above for such links in historical perspective.

schools and inform their core commitments. Perhaps the postmodern sensibility that all persons, communities, and institutions are formed by a particular history and genealogy will make it possible for our generation to reclaim, reaffirm, and overtly practice the great Lutheran intellectual tradition in which ELCA colleges and universities stand.

In doing so, we will be affirming that Lutheran colleges and universities are not defined by their support for an ethnic culture or by their adherence to a checklist of institutional practices or markers, such as mandating minimal standards for Lutheran enrollment. Nor are they Lutheran schools because schooling provides a platform for promoting parochial Lutheran interests. They are Lutheran because they stand in a 500-year-old intellectual tradition that educates for vocation, an education of the whole person, prepared to contribute to the common good. Providing education for vocation to all persons of good will, whatever their personal religious—or non-religious—convictions is educational excellence in the Lutheran tradition. It is the vocation of Lutheran higher education.

Questions for Discussion

1. How do you or does your institution answer Wilhelm's driving question: "What makes an institution Lutheran if it is no longer defined *de facto* by a primary—and nearly exclusive—mission to serve Lutherans?"

2. Wilhelm pairs the rise of the "vocation movement" with the collapse of "ethnic, separatist Lutheranism," according to which Lutheran education was largely for and by Lutherans. When and how has that transition happened on your campus? How would you characterize the transition? As rapid, gradual, smooth, bumpy, welcomed, contested—or something else?

3. Where does "education for vocation" show up on your campus? Should it—and how might it—become more central to your work and your college's mission?

4. Why were you drawn to a Lutheran college or university? In what ways did its Lutheran or church-related identity contribute to, qualify, or otherwise bear on your desire to work/teach there?

Part Two

MARKS

CHAPTER 5

LEARNING AND TEACHING AS AN EXERCISE IN CHRISTIAN FREEDOM

TOM CHRISTENSON
Capital University, Columbus, Ohio[1]

> "More than half the work is done when we have put the question right."
>
> —Sig Royspern

What is the vocation of a Lutheran college or university? I want to both pose this question and at least begin to answer it. But before I do the latter, I want to move us away from certain natural but unhelpful ways we might have of thinking about this. The question frequently gets formulated as, "What is distinctively Lutheran about Lutheran higher education?" The phrasing of the question in this way frequently takes us in some unfruitful directions.

Asking the Wrong Question

What is distinctively Lutheran about Lutheran higher education? I want to suggest that this question is poorly framed for several reasons:

First, the question is misguided insofar as it presupposes that Lutheran education is essentially an education program *for Lutherans.* It is fine and excellent if it serves Lutherans. It isn't that we should chase Lutherans away. But we are not Lutheran institutions in proportion to the percentage of Lutherans we serve. When we do well, we serve most, if not all, of our neighbors well, not only Lutherans.

---

1   Tom Christenson was a Professor of Philosophy at Capital University, Columbus, Ohio until his death in 2013. Tom first conceived of *Intersections* and was its founding editor, serving in that capacity from 1996 to 2005. A longer version of this essay was published in *Intersections* 30 (Winter 1999): 3-11.

Second, the question is misguided insofar as it presupposes that Lutheran education is essentially an education program *by Lutherans*. It is fine and excellent that there are Lutheran faculty, administrators, and secretaries working on our campuses, and our task may be made easier by their presence (or not), but we are not Lutheran institutions in proportion to the percentage of Lutherans we employ.

Third, the question is misguided insofar as it presupposes that we are Lutheran in proportion to the ways in which we are *ethnically Lutheran*. It is fine that we celebrate a variety of ethnicities on our campuses, whether that be German or Scandinavian or Finn or (perhaps in the future) Namibian or Korean. I think it would be good to maintain those identities even if the students and staff of those institutions no longer represent those ethnicities in large numbers. These things are great, but they are not what make us essentially Lutheran institutions.

Fourth, the question is misguided insofar as "distinctiveness" connotes that we are Lutheran primarily in the ways we are *different from others*. Our differences may be obvious in some cases and not in others. The problem here is not with being different, but with taking difference as the defining essence. That's what frequently happens when marketing becomes management. If we begin with the question, "How will we be different?," we will end up in the wrong place just as often as if we begin with the question, "How can we be like everyone else?" As someone at one early Vocation of a Lutheran College conference so beautifully put it, "We should be concerned to be *essentially* Lutheran, and not worry about being *distinctively* Lutheran." I believe that if the "essential" part is taken as primary, the "distinctiveness" part will more than look after itself.

Asking the Right Question

So, if this is not the best way to pursue the question, what is a better place to start? Consider this: I'll bet that if you think of the half-dozen or so faculty who most thoroughly embody and "carry" the Lutheran-ness at your institutions (the people who are caretakers of the tradition), you will find that some of them aren't Lutheran. I know many of these faculty: the Calvinist who in his loyal criticism calls the institution to be as well-founded in its tradition as his Calvinist alma mater is in its tradition; the Catholic professor who feels genuinely blessed to be teaching at a Lutheran institution and enthusiastically shares her excitement and understanding of the place with her students; the evangelical and Baptist professors who continually challenge their students and colleagues to boldly state what they believe, who read Luther in order to engage the tradition in argument; the Jewish professor who confesses that his faith is taken more seriously at his Lutheran institution than it ever was at the state university where he previously taught; the Buddhist professor who admits a deepening of her appreciation of her own tradition through her dialogue with colleagues at a Lutheran college.

How is this possible? What is this odd thing—"Lutheran-ness"—that makes something like this possible? I assume that it has to be something communicable, something learnable—something that sensitive, perceptive, and concerned people can catch onto whether or not it is literally "their tradition." What can this be?

My answer is that what makes our institutions Lutheran is *a vision of the educational task itself* that is informed by a tradition of theological themes or principles as well as embodied in practice. Mistaken assumptions that we often make about the nature of "religious" education make us look for evidence of our Lutheran-ness in the frosting and the decorations. I believe that it's in the cake itself. We are Lutheran by means of our educational vision, a theologically informed orientation that manifests itself in what we do and our understanding of why we do it. I think that this is what Joseph Sittler intended when he said:

> Any effort properly to specify the central and perduring task of the church-related college must pierce through and below the statements of purpose that often characterize public pronouncements. . . . The church is engaged in the task of education because it is dedicated to the truth. . . . If its proposals, memories, promises, proclamations, are not related to the truth, it should get out of the expensive business of education. . . . If [our] commitment to the faith is not one with [our] commitment to the truth, no multiplication of secondary consolations . . . will suffice to sustain that commitment for [our] own integrity.[2]

Now this common theological orientation may not be so obvious to us, who are part of this tradition, as it to some of our friends and colleagues elsewhere in higher education. But there are complex issues there, too.

---

2   Joseph Sittler, "Church Colleges and the Truth," in *Faith, Learning, and the Church College: Addresses by Joe Sittler* (Northfield, Minnesota: St. Olaf, 1989), 27.

For example, many, if not most, Catholic institutions were historically founded by communities of monks and nuns. The presence of these communities has traditionally solved the problem of "the Catholic identity" of these institutions. Now, however, those religious orders are dying out. They are concerned about this. So the question they have for us is, "How do we transfer the defining essence of our institution over to the lay faculty and administrators who really make the place go? How do you Lutherans do it? Will you show us how?"

The Baptists are going through a similar crisis. The Baptist identity of colleges and universities across the nation has traditionally been guaranteed *de jure* by being owned by the Baptist conventions of their respective states. As these legal ownership ties are being severed, these institutions are asking, "How can we still be a Baptist university if we are no longer owned by the convention? How do you Lutherans do it? Will you show us how?"

What I have learned in speaking with these institutions is just how gifted Lutheran institutions are. Others have noticed our giftedness, and they are asking us to share what we may not be aware we had. So, how do we do it? What is our vision? That's the question I want to try to answer in what follows.

In order to talk about the idea I want to focus on—Christian freedom—one needs to see how this notion is situated among other concepts. I thus want to "frame" the idea of Christian freedom by also writing about two other crucial concepts: the idea of gift or giftedness, and (briefly in the conclusion) the idea of vocation. It is freedom's location between these two ideas that makes it peculiarly Christian and vital to Lutheran education.

Gift and Being Gifted

I teach gifted students, and I teach with gifted colleagues in a context of many gifts. Now I know what we usually mean when we talk about being gifted. There are special gifts: Some have the gift for music, some the gift for mathematics, some the gift for repairing things, some the gift of imagination, etc. But there are also gifts that we all share, gifts we could realize if only we would unwrap them, value them, develop them, and celebrate them.

A Christian encounters all of life and all of creation as a gift. This can make a great deal of difference. How, for example, does one teach science if one sees the cosmos and our own powers of intelligence as a gift? How does someone informed by the idea of gift teach a Bach chorale or a favorite author? There were teachers I had in college who opened the same gifts in the presence of students semester after semester. The gift may have been swamp ecology, the dialogues of Plato, the pre-Columbian history of the Americas, or the poetry of Rilke. In each case, these teachers were as excited as kids, not at finding what was in there (they had a pretty good idea already), but at *our* coming to discover what was in there. The classroom was a potlatch, a celebration of gifts, giving, opening, and receiving.

How do we approach and encounter a world given as gift? With wonder and delight (i.e., as a world with depth, not as a world reduced to the dimensions of human manipulation); with thanksgiving; as caretaker and steward; with an attitude of sharing, as part of what may be appropriately called a gift economy; and with celebration. In such a way education can become, as Nicholas Wolterstorff has said, a "eucharistic act."[3]

For Christians, of course, Christ is the paradigm of gift and giver, gift realized as God with us in person, the reign of God among us. What is it like to realize this gift? St. Paul calls it redemption, but he also calls it freedom: "For freedom Christ has set us free" (Galatians 5:1). Freedom, for a Christian, is not our natural condition, nor is it an earned achievement. It requires a death, even a crucifixion, and a resurrection to occur. Christian freedom, being a gift, needs a response (and consequently a response-ability). That is to say that freedom, being a gift, makes a call to us to which our lives are the response. The connection is explicit: gift, freedom, vocation.

Freedom

There are many mistakes the modern world has made (and continues to make), but one of the most serious and far reaching is a misunderstanding of freedom. Just consider these two contrasting ideas of freedom. Being free can mean being bound by nothing, connected to nothing. I make myself who I want to be, from nothing. Since I have no one to please but myself, my whole life is devoted to the fulfilling of my "preferences." Since there is nothing (besides myself) to give the world (or myself) value, the world frequently becomes bor-

---

3   Nicholas Wolterstorff, "Should the Work of Our Hands Have Standing in the Christian College?" in *Keeping Faith: Embracing the Tensions in Christian Higher Education* (Grand Rapids, Michigan: Wm. B. Eerdmans Publishing, 1997), 140.

ing, irrelevant, and I go from one extreme thrill to another—seeking to jolt myself into existence.

But consider an alternative view of freedom. As called by those to whom I am connected, I discover myself as I discover what I love, care about, care for, and am connected to. Hearing the call of others' needs and the call of truth, justice, love, beauty, I am encouraged and enlivened. I become who I am in the context of the call I have received. In place of a freedom that says, "What shall I buy today?" we have a freedom that can say, "Here I stand, I can do no other." Such freedom depends on vocation. As Luther might put it, "We exist by being called by God. And we exist only so long as God continues to address us."

Luther, in fact, interpreted freedom thusly in his famous treatise, *On the Freedom of the Christian:*

> A Christian is a perfectly free lord of all, subject to none. A Christian is a perfectly dutiful servant of all, subject to all. . . . Freed from the vain attempt to justify him [or her] self [the Christian] should be guided in all his [or her] works by this thought alone . . . considering nothing but the need and advantage of his [or her] neighbor. . . . This is a truly Christian life. Here faith is truly active through love, that is, it finds expression in the works of the freest service, cheerfully and lovingly done. . . .[4]

What would a college or university informed by such an understanding of freedom look like? What are we thus freed *from*? What are we thus freed *for*?

Freed from Piousness

First, Luther understood freedom as the consequence of grace, i.e., of God's gift. Thus we are freed from the necessity to work our own salvation. This also means that we are freed from the captivity of the hierarchical dualisms one usually finds in religions; we are freed to be fully human. We have no need to transcend the bodily in service of some "higher" spiritual realm; we have no need to deny the secular to serve the sacred; we have no need to depart the natural to serve the supernatural. Luther was adamant that we are called to serve where we are, in the stations in which we find ourselves, thoroughly embodied, concrete, earthen, and particular. This freedom to be fully human

---

4   Martin Luther, "The Freedom of a Christian," in *Three Treatises* (Philadelphia: Fortress Press, 1977), 277, 301-302.

also implies that we are freed to be eating, drinking, excreting, working, sweating, hoping, fearing, crying, nurturing, thinking, and sexual beings. Piety, by this view, is not a denial of part of our own reality so much as an embrace of all of it. We come before God not pure and unspotted but in our honest wholeness.

Perhaps most important for the life of our colleges and universities, we are freed to engage the problems of the world by the use of the very fallible but still useful tools to be found in our academic disciplines. We have no need to become a one dimensional "Bible college" because we are free to become engaged inquirers and learners in biology, psychology, economics, history, nursing, etc. There are no writers whose thoughts we must avoid thinking about, no books we need to consider banning, no theories we must dismiss without thorough examination. We can learn from Marx about new dimensions of human slavery and liberation; we can learn from Nietzsche a suspicion of religious and moral motivation—just as Jesus's hearers learned the meaning of neighbor from the example of the otherwise-despised Samaritan. There is no authority we may not question, no ignorance we may not admit, and no doubt that we need to silence. Why? Because our salvation is not worked by such efforts since it is not worked by us at all.

This freedom is what distinguishes education in the Lutheran sense from "religious education" that we commonly find in some other contexts. Where people see education as a means or evidence of salvation or sanctification, it frequently ends up being an indoctrination that is frightened, closed, authoritarian, and defensive. Education informed by the freedom of the Christian can be, by contrast, bold, open, multi-dimensional, dialogical, and engaging. Education, informed by freedom, is not afraid of the largeness, the darkness, the inexplicable mystery of the world.

In last December's issue of *The Christian Century*, James Schaap wrote a provocative article about the difficulty of being an avowedly Christian writer.[5] A reviewer of one of his novels told him she had liked his novel a good deal even though she had thought she wouldn't when the review was assigned to her. "Why does your novel say the word 'Christian' on the back cover?" she asked him. "Now nobody is

---

5   James Calvin Schaap, "On truth, fiction, and being a Christian writer," *Christian Century*, December 17, 1997, 1188.

going to read it."[6] God help us when the word "Christian" has come to mean "inoffensive," "sanitized," "asexual," or when Christian writers can only write about nice folks, in nice towns, doing nice things for nice reasons, in nice language. The freedom of the Christian is, among other things, a freedom from the suffocating and nauseating law of niceness. It is a freedom to see the truth and tell it. John Updike has written:

> God is the God of the living, though many of his priests and executors, to keep order and force the world into a convenient mold, will always want to make him the God of the dead, the God who chastises life and forbids and says No. . . . [As a Christian writer] I have felt free to describe life as accurately as I could, with special attention to human erosions and betrayals. What small faith I have has given me what artistic courage I have. My theory was that God already knows everything and cannot be shocked. And only truth is useful. Only truth can be built upon.[7]

Freed from Idolatry

Second, we are freed to serve the world by being skeptical of and challenging all worldly claims to ultimacy. We are called, in other words, to recognize idols when we see them. We can recognize them, in part because we know as well as anyone what it is to be tempted by them and by the power they can have over us. We call attention to them not as problems that "they" have that "we" are now going to condemn and correct, but as things by which we are all tempted, under whose influence we have fallen. But the freeing power of the gospel should also have shown us that they are false ultimacies, i.e., that they truly are idols.

Certainly materialism in all its modes is one such idol in our society. How frequently do all other concerns take a back seat to economic progress? For how many is success *defined* by income and consump-

---

6   The same novel was reviewed in the newsletter of the Christian Booksellers Association (CBA). That reviewer did not recommend it since it included references to characters who were homosexual, adulterous, and drug users. No bookstore that was a member of the CBA carried the book because it did not pass their standards for sanitized subject matter and inoffensive language. Among other writers, the CBA will not carry Flannery O'Connor (offensive language and despicable characters, too much violence), John Updike, Wendell Berry, Doris Betts, Madeleine L'Engle, and Larry Woiwode. Schaap comments that the only "offensive" book the CBA carries is the Bible.
7   John Updike, *Self Consciousness: Memoirs* (New York: Fawcett Crest, 1989), 243.

tion? David Orr states the issue very boldly in his book, *Earth in Mind*: "The plain fact is that the planet does not need more successful people. But it does desperately need more peacemakers, healers, restorers, storytellers, and lovers of every kind. It needs people who live well in their places. It needs people of moral courage. . . . And these qualities have little to do with success as our culture defines it."[8]

So many students are convinced that education serves only to get a job, and that a job serves only to earn money, and that earning money serves only the end of copious and conspicuous consumption. Why is this so widely believed? For many students it is their story because they have never heard any other story or because they have never heard anyone challenge it. May our students encounter voices like Wendell Berry: "So I have met the economy in the road, and I am expected to yield it right of way. But I will not get over. . . . I see it teaching my students to give themselves a price before they can realize in themselves a value. Its principle is to waste and destroy the living substance of the world and the birthright of posterity for monetary profit that is the most flimsy and useless of human artifacts."[9]

A Christian college or university informed by Luther's interpretation is free to challenge this and other pervasive "ultimacies." We are also called in this freedom to embody some viable alternatives, for we educate much more persuasively by what we *do* in our institutions than only by what we *say* in them. We are called to explore what Christian freedom implies for a community of inquirers, not only in regard to curriculum and campus policies, but also in regard to the economic, social, and political life of our institutions. Realizing the liberation of the gospel we become aware of the bondage we work on each other. Having been rescued from alienation we are aware of the alienation in our own midst. We are thus called not only to be honest critics but also to become communicators, peacemakers, healers, enablers of community, and bearers of hope.

Just as the freedom of the Christian articulated above frees us to something beyond "religious education," in the restricted sense, so the freedom articulated here frees us to do something that secular institutions have a hard time doing, i.e., being skeptical of the ultimacies that rule and embodying genuine alternatives to them. We serve the

---

8   David Orr, *Earth in Mind* (Washington, D.C.: Island, 1994), 12.
9   Wendell Berry, "Discovery and Hope," in *A Continuous Harmony* (New York: Harcourt Brace Jovanovich, 1972), 180.

real need of the neighbor, in this case the wider culture, neither by following the dominant voices in it nor by worshiping at all of its altars. Our colleges and universities are excellent not insofar as they teach, research, or publish more brilliantly, and not even for being more caring and friendly. They are excellent insofar as they create a space within which the liberating truth can be heard.

Our scientists ought to be free enough to recognize and critique the ends that "value free science" serves. Our artists ought to be free enough to recognize and critique the agendas of institutions that rank the arts and artists. Whom does the idea of "the high arts" or "the fine arts" serve? Whose work is demeaned by it? Our law professors ought to be free enough to recognize and critique the way in which their profession serves itself more frequently than it serves the ends of justice. Our economists ought to be free enough to recognize and critique what the international market economy has done to many working families. And so also for the rest of us, no matter what our disciplinary allegiance is.

The Liberating Arts

Third and finally, it is my belief that Christian freedom also implies something specific for the priorities of our learning and teaching. Many Christian colleges emphasize the liberal arts. I wish to make an argument here for a new agenda for the way we teach what we do. I refer to this agenda as *the liberating arts,* i.e., the arts of embodied freedom. I wish to identify four sub-groups within this general category.

The critical/deconstructive arts are the studies by which we learn critical thinking, come to recognize our own and others' presuppositions, learn to articulate our assumptions, as well as to work out the implications of our thinking. Until one realizes the assumptions with which one operates and recognizes alternatives, one cannot really be said to be choosing or acting freely. Consider Sister Alice Lubin's course at St. Elizabeth's College, The Victorian Novel, in which students not only come to identify the roles and rules that apply to women (and men) in the world of the Victorian novel, but also come to identify by contrast the roles and rules that apply to gendered life in our own society as well. The outcome is definitely a liberation, for the forces that daily pressure young women and men to specific roles and behavior here surface, are articulated, and are interrogated with a new degree of freedom.

The embodying/connecting arts are essential to university education, much of which is completely disconnected from meaningful action. Many times we have heard students say after returning from an internship or work experience, "I learned more in those weeks than I learned in the three preceding semesters." The embodying arts connect learning to doing, deciding, and to the becoming of the student. Consider the service learning semester at Goshen College, or the field-focused learning experiences of nursing students at my own university. Students not only learn their own disciplines with a sense of urgency in such situations; they come to know themselves as well. They uncover fears, prejudices, things in their preparation that need more work, and new potentialities in themselves. They learn that knowing something one can actually do is more freeing than merely knowing *about* a whole host of things. The musician who can play one instrument has more freedom than the dilettante who has heard them all but can play none.

The melioristic/creative arts avoid the optimism/pessimism binges many indulge. They ask not, "How would I like the world ideally to be?" but ask instead, "Can we make something good out of what we are given?" Such arts need to be practiced in the classroom by middle school teachers; at home by husbands, wives, parents, and children; at work by managers and employees; in public by citizens and politicians. We learn such arts in concrete problem-solving situations, where wishing for some far-off ideal or wishing we could start over are not open options. It is the art of making the best of what is left of the present semester rather than planning for the naively hopeful next one, a fantasy both students and faculty are expert at. Consider what can be learned from a year's commitment in a communal living arrangement, or from raising and caring for a pet through its whole life, or from conversations with spouses, parents, teachers, politicians. We can learn about the compromises one has to make in order to make things work. As teachers, we can design problem-solving modules where the problem must be solved with the materials at hand.

The enabling/transformative arts teach the art of making change in culture where too many find it easier to complain about how awful things are than to try to make things better. We all know the passive helplessness behind the words, "Why don't *they* do something about it?" Crime, a culture of violence, environmental problems, lowering expectations and performances in schools—these are all problems we know in a firsthand way. Yet we suppose that these are problems to be solved only by the people who make the news, not by folks like us who merely watch it. Yet only a little reflection reveals to us that this too is a learned response. How can we unlearn it? We must make our own educational institutions into arenas where learners can practice the art of change. We must make sure students meet community persons who are involved in change at all levels, including lawmakers, inventors, members of twelve-step programs, protestors, intervenors, and effective teachers. If change is not possible, education is the most tragic of all human enterprises.

These four "liberating arts" can, and in fact should, be taught in all disciplines. They would make a firm core to a goal-focused general studies requirement. They might spur a lot of creative thinking on the part of faculty and certainly would provoke a lot of argument. Luther would approve of both. I think that a place that took such an education in freedom seriously would be a fun and invigorating place to learn and to teach.

Conclusion

We should not ask, "What kind of college or university would you create if you could go to the store and buy all the right ingredients?" We should not ask, "What kind of institution would you create *ex nihilo*—out of nothing?" This is a dean's dream, I know. Instead we should open the door of our own refrigerators and ask, "Now what kind of university can we make out of this?" Our refrigerators contain our particular students, our particular faculty, our particular administrators, our physical plant, our location, and the challenges and opportunities that each of these bring. We must know ourselves, know our limits and our potentialities, know our histories and the visions for our futures. The colleges and universities I admire the most are not the most prestigious, but the ones that have found a way to serve their particular students, with their particular needs, in their particular place, and do it well.

Frederick Buechner defines vocation like this: "The kind of work God calls you to is the kind of work a) that you need most to do, and b) that the world most needs to have done. . . . The place God calls you to is the place where your own deep gladness and the world's deep hunger meet."[10] Here is some good news: We are freed to know and

---

10 Frederick Buechner, *Wishful Thinking: A Theological ABC* (New York: Harper and Row, 1973), 95.

to serve both of these needs. We are freed to be "a perfectly free lord of all, subject to none"; we are *therefore* freed to be "a perfectly dutiful servant" seeing the deep needs of the world and working in service of our actual neighbor and actual neighborhood.

So, "what is the vocation of a Lutheran college or university?" Realizing God's gifts and ourselves as gifted, we are freed to boldly engage (in our fallible way) and to tell the whole truth. We are freed to serve the deep needs of the world, and to do so to the greater glory of God.

Questions for Discussion

1. Christenson bets that "if you think of the half-dozen or so faculty who most thoroughly embody and 'carry' the Lutheran-ness at your institution . . . you will find that some of them aren't Lutheran." Who are these people on your campus? Are they Lutheran? From what other traditions or sets of convictions have they become caretakers of the "Lutheran-ness" of your institution?

2. What are the advantages and/or the disadvantages of connecting understandings of academic freedom to Lutheran understandings of freedom, as Christenson seeks to do throughout this essay?

3. How might your own or other disciplines constitute part of the liberating arts? To which particular art (critical/deconstructive, embodying/connecting, melioristic/creative, or enabling/transformative) does your discipline contribute the most?

CHAPTER 6

THE THIRD PATH, RELIGIOUS DIVERSITY, AND CIVIL DISCOURSE

DARRELL JODOCK
Gustavus Adolphus College, St. Peter, Minnesota

My job in this article is twofold—to remind us of the basics of Lutheran theology and to begin to build on those basics in responding
to religious diversity in our colleges.[1] So, if what I am saying sounds
familiar, I will not be disappointed and I hope you will not be either.
Simply regard it to be a reminder or a restatement of what you already
know and an endeavor to establish a common base for the conversation about the vocation of a Lutheran college. If what I am saying is
new and unfamiliar to you, then I hope it will serve to invite you into
the conversation and equip you for it.

The Third Path

I begin with an image of the third path. When it comes to private
colleges in this country, there are two well-known default positions.
Each has value, so I describe in order to distinguish, not to criticize. The
first I call "sectarian." The sectarian institution is deeply rooted in one
denominational and/or one religious tradition, but it is not inclusive.
It expects a good deal of homogeneity. If it is Baptist (let's say), it will
give preference to hiring faculty and staff and admitting students that
are Baptist. Sometimes the expectations are more informal, at other
times they are formulated into written statements that faculty and staff
are expected to sign when they are appointed. The sectarian college
is an enclave. It primarily serves the church and is good at nurturing
students in its own religious tradition. But a pretty clear line separates

---

1   A version of this essay was published as "Vocation of the Lutheran College and
    Religious Diversity" in *Intersections* 33 (Spring 2011): 5-12.

it from the rest of society, and this line tends to isolate it and make full participation in the surrounding world difficult. With regard to religious diversity, it has no problem, simply because religious diversity either does not exist or is not acknowledged. It is excluded from the on-campus conversation. Seventy-five or a hundred years ago, many of our ELCA colleges were more homogenous than they are now, but the homogeneity was often driven more by ethnicity or language than by religious principle. Even so, many alumni and friends of our colleges often expect them to be more sectarian than they are.

The second default model is "non-sectarian." A non-sectarian institution is religiously inclusive; it is a microcosm of the surrounding society. Unlike the sectarian institution, the line of demarcation between the college and the larger society is easily crossed. Such a college has as much religious diversity as the society around it. But it is not religiously rooted. Every religious group has equal status, and the college endeavors to have policies that are neutral. As a result, its communal religious identity is superficial—that is, its principles are borrowed from the surrounding culture rather than from a religious tradition. With regard to religious diversity, it too has no problem, but for quite different reasons. Its implicit message is that religion is not important enough to be part of the communal life of the college. Religion becomes a private matter, so there is no reason to wrestle with religious differences.

Somewhat ironically, though the intention is clearly positive, this non-sectarian approach can have quite a different result. Built as it is on the notion of tolerance, it can result in new forms of intolerance. This can happen when each religious group, lacking interaction with the others and reacting against the communal devaluing of religion, can begin to see itself as the bastion of truth. Then a new balkanization can occur as each group within the college becomes an embattled enclave. Instead of fostering cohesion, the result can be even more rigid divisions.

Often, having in mind the more positive aspects of a non-sectarian college, some voices within our colleges and some voices from without expect us to become non-sectarian. They do so in part because the model is familiar and in part because some assume it is the only alternative to being sectarian.

In our society, a college that values its Lutheran heritage does not fit either of those default models. It follows a third path. It is rooted because it takes the Lutheran tradition seriously and draws nourishment from it, and it is inclusive in at least two senses: (a) welcoming into its student body, faculty, and staff persons of diverse religious backgrounds, and (b) seeking to serve the larger community. Instead of an enclave or a microcosm, it is a well that is dug deep to nourish the whole community. One difficulty of the third path is that it is hard to explain. It does not fit either default model. Another of the difficulties is that it leaves us with an unresolved question and an unfinished task: How is a college that is rooted in the Lutheran tradition to deal with religious diversity? How can it be both rooted and inclusive?

Two Orienting Observations

I begin by observing that we are talking here about the identity and vocation of the college, about a communal identity and not a sum of individual identities. For a college to be Lutheran, not everyone in the community needs to be Lutheran or Christian. I like to think of it this way: If everyone in the college shares a vision of what the college is trying to do, this vision informs the teaching and decision-making at the school even if only some members of the community have their personal roots sunk deeply in Lutheran soil while others do not. Or, to appeal to an analogy, if a student who is not sure if he or she believes in God goes to India and comes back so moved by the plight of people there as to make helping them a priority, and another student who is a committed believer goes to India and comes back with the same priority, and both benefit from good mentoring, the two may well wind up doing the same kind of project. In either case, in some modest way the poor in India are likely to be helped. The difference is that the second student will believe that the call has come from God through the deep human need of our neighbors in India, while the first student will believe that the call has come directly from the deep human need. The first is likely to be more deeply rooted than the second; hence the two may well differ in their vocational resiliency and may also differ in other ways. But on the level of ethical action, their initial results may be the same: namely, the poor get help. Or, at the risk of overkill, allow me one more analogy. The piers that support a bridge hold up a roadway that is usually wider than the piers themselves. So, too, Lutheran roots nourish a college community that is much more inclusive than building on a denominational identity would seem to suggest.

The analogy of a bridge can be taken one step further. If we picture a college as a long bridge with a wide deck, everything that happens at the college, whether classes or athletic events or faculty meetings, happens on the deck. Decisions about what is done or is not done on the deck are influenced by the college's educational values. These are the piers/pillars of the bridge. The piers/pillars are anchored and informed by the footings—by Lutheran theological principles. Everyone at the college is invited to endorse the educational values. And everyone is invited to understand and appreciate the theological footings, but not everyone is expected to give personal subscription to the Lutheran faith out of which these principles arise. This distinction between educational values and theological principles is an important aspect of what it means to be a third-path college. A sectarian college does not make this distinction, and a non-sectarian college has severed the connection between its theological footings and the rest of the bridge.

Having made this first observation about communal identity, allow me to make a second. A community that values the deep wells of its own religious tradition is more likely to value other kinds of depth. A religiously rooted college that follows the third path is more likely to value the rootedness of a Muslim or a Buddhist or a Jew than is a non-sectarian college that dismisses the importance of religion. I do not mean that the religious differences will disappear. No, precisely the opposite, the differences will remain.[2] But what I do want to say is that a person deeply rooted in one tradition is more likely to respect the importance of religion in the life of the deeply rooted member of another religion. If they talk at some length about their religious views, their differences will not be ignored or denied, but a different kind of kinship will emerge. If all goes well, each will be enriched by the conversation, and each will appreciate new elements in his/her own faith. This is possible because each religious tradition (and specifically the Lutheran tradition) brings with it an awareness of the deep mystery of the divine. This mystery cannot be captured fully in any one set of words or any one set of symbols. A believer need not endorse the words of another tradition in order to understand that one's own words are insufficient and one still has more to learn.

Interreligious Dialogue and Civil Discourse

After this longish introduction, I'd like to try to identify some features of the Lutheran tradition that influence how a Lutheran college begins to think about interreligious relations and civil discourse—both

---

2   See also Chapters 8 and 12 in this book.

of which are badly needed today. Before doing that, however, I need to clarify what I mean by interreligious dialogue and by civil discourse, so let me provide some descriptors:

A person engaged in good *interreligious dialogue* (a) compares the "best" of one religion to the "best" of another, not the best to the worst, (b) interprets the other religion "in such a way that an informed adherent of that religion would agree with the description," (c) enters the dialogue "ready to learn something new" and "see the world differently," and (d) stays clear of merely fitting an idea from the other religion into the framework of one's own, as if the other religion were but a pale reflection of one's own, when in fact the pieces there are put together quite differently.[3]

A person engaged in *civil discourse* seeks "common ground"—that is, areas where values overlap—and does so regarding any issue of importance, including the more contentious ones such as immigration, global warming, war, abortion, same-sex relations, etc. Indeed, the conversation needs also to tackle disagreements about the relative importance of these and other issues. Some guidelines for such civil discourse include the following: Those (a) "who claim the right to dissent should assume the responsibility to debate," (b) "who claim the right to criticize should assume the responsibility to comprehend," (c) "who claim the right to influence should accept the responsibility not to inflame," and (d) "who claim the right to participate should accept the responsibility to persuade."[4]

The Lutheran Tradition

Now, what features of the Lutheran tradition influence how a college thinks about interreligious dialogue and civil discourse? I'd like to consider six; as we will see, they are interlocking.

Feature #1: Giftedness

According to the Lutheran tradition, being right with God and having dignity as a human are free gifts, for which there are no prerequisites. It is as if we were orphans and totally out of the blue came

---

3   Darrell Jodock, "Christians and Jews in the Context of World Religions," in *Covenantal Conversations: Christians in Dialogue with Jews and Judaism*, ed. Darrell Jodock (Minneapolis: Fortress Press, 2008), 131-32.

4   James Hunter, *Before the Shooting Begins: Searching for Democracy in America's Culture War* (New York: The Free Press, 1994), 239. For Hunter "common ground" is not the same as "middle ground." The latter is achieved by compromise rather than by "rational and moral suasion regarding the basic values and issues of society" (13).

adoptive parents who say, "From this point on, as far as we are concerned, you are our child, no matter what." We would have no idea
why we were selected or why the adopted parents are taking this step.
All of the initiative and all of the energy for the relationship would be
coming from the parents. And we would see that this was happening
not only to us but to others as well. For our purposes, being adopted
means being adopted into a family with siblings. The Lutheran approach says that being right with God and having dignity are both
founded on God's evaluation, not ours.

What results from being gifted is a trustworthy relationship, which
militates against fear and anxiety. I am convinced that fear and a pervasive anxiety are contributing to the polarization and the harsh rhetoric
in our society. This anxiety has more than one cause, but among them
is the deep, inarticulate worry that our way of life is not economically,
environmentally, or politically sustainable. Anxiety gets in the way of
civil discourse. According to Peter Steinke, the consequences of anxiety include the following: It (a) "decreases our capacity to learn," (b)
"stiffens our position over against another's," (c) "prompts a desire
for a quick fix," (d)"leads to an array of defensive behaviors," and
(e) "creates imaginative gridlock (not being able to think of alternatives, options, or new perspectives)."[5] He calls for non-anxious leaders
who keep the mission of the group front and center. This is as clear
a priority for college faculty and staff as for neighborhoods and the
nation as a whole. Over 200 times we find in the Bible the reassurance:
"Fear not" or "Do not be afraid." An outlook rooted in gratitude and a
trustworthy relationship with the divine goes a long ways toward per-
mitting civil discourse because it enhances our capacity to listen and
to imagine less polarized possibilities. And an outlook rooted in gratitude and a trustworthy relationship goes a long way toward freeing
us up for interreligious dialogue. Why? (a) Because we cannot know
the limits of God's free gift. If there are no prerequisites, I cannot establish any boundaries. (b) Because the identity of a gifted person is
not threatened by persons whose outlooks differ. And (c) because, as
Luther made clear, we cannot know how anyone else is related to God.
We cannot see inside that relationship; it may not be what it appears
to be. He was thinking about people who were nominally Christians,
but the same would apply to people in other religions. To hear that a

---

5   Peter Steinke, *Congregational Leadership in Anxious Times: Being Calm and Courageous
     No Matter What* (Herndon, Virginia: Alban Institute, 2006), 8-9.

person is Jewish tells me little about that person's relationship with God any more than learning a person is Christian tells me much about that person's level of commitment or relationship with God. We all know or know of Christians whose spiritual stature is so significant that it would be acknowledged by anyone. At the same time we all know or know of Christians whose narrowness and legalism make us observe, with Sam Shoemaker, that they appear to have been starched and ironed before being washed.[6] If so, we should not be surprised to find a similar diversity within other communities of faith. Some draw sustenance from their religion for enriching lives while others use their religion to intimidate, demean, or attack others. Recognizing multiple uses of religion leads to dialogue rather than predetermined generalized judgments.

If one's standing before God is a free gift, what is the role of faith? According to the Lutheran tradition, faith is an acknowledgment of what God has done and will do in one's life. To return to the analogy used earlier, faith is acknowledging one's adoption. Faith does not come first; it tags along after God has been at work. Acknowledging that a person is part of the family into which that person has been adopted does not *effect* the adoption. That's already occurred. And it does not *affect* the parents' love. That's an ongoing gift. What faith does do is to shape the self-understanding of the child or the self-understanding of the person adopted by God.

Notice that this understanding of faith puts the Lutheran tradition at odds with much of mainline Protestantism in the United States, where the understanding is "if you have faith, then you'll be right with God." This common understanding changes the nature of faith, makes it a prerequisite, and establishes boundaries that a free gift does not. That is, if faith is a prerequisite, then I can tell who is not right with God. In fact, this view is a contemporary form of exactly what caused Luther problems.[7] It leaves God passive and expects the initiative to come from the human being. For Luther this view was completely backwards and completely unworkable.

---

6   From a speech given at Luther Seminary, St. Paul, Minnesota, somewhere between 1962 and 1966.

7   He had learned the theology of Gabriel Biel, which said that God had established a path to salvation, but the individual needed to take the initiative and take the first steps on that pathway. Then God would supply what was needed to complete the journey.

The point here is that the legacy of being freely gifted provides the kind of security and freedom that encourages civil discourse and interreligious dialogue. If I have no control over my adoption into a family or a community, if I am confident that the person adopting me will love me no matter what, and if I base my dignity as a human on this giftedness, then I have nothing to defend and nothing to fear. I can listen to those who disagree and search for common ground. I can keep my eye on the goal rather than overreacting to others. In addition to providing this kind of security and freedom, the legacy of being freely gifted also provides the basis for treating others with generosity—for becoming a channel of generosity toward others.

Feature #2: The Whole World Gifted by an Engaged God

What we have already said about free gifting can only be understood when it is seen to be part of the larger reality of God's generosity toward the entire world. Unlike other traditions that see God as "up there," orchestrating and micromanaging the world in accordance with an already worked-out plan, the Lutheran tradition finds God "down here," amid the ordinary, amid the suffering and the chaos as well as the order and beauty, deeply involved in delivering good gifts to anyone and everyone through the agency of other humans and other creatures. Many Americans, I sense, feel as if civil discourse and interreligious dialogue are concessions. Things really should be black and white. Either a religious concept is right or it is not—so why talk about it? In contrast, the Lutheran tradition's vision of a down-to-earth God views deliberation as an essential feature of God's work among us. God works through deliberation and its complexity and messiness to invite us forward into deeper insights and a new perspective. On this view, God empowers but does not control. God has a goal (the kind of wholeness and peace reflected in the word *shalom*) but not a detailed plan of how to get there. For humans, the result is a remarkable freedom and a remarkable capacity for creativity, which they can use for good or for ill. The tradition affirms that all humans are invited to use that freedom and creativity to serve the goal of *shalom*.

One of the things this means is that everyone has a vocation—everyone has a calling to serve the neighbor and the community, in and through one's parenting, occupation, and contributions as a citizen. And part of the mission of a Lutheran college is to invite and challenge everyone to develop a robust sense of vocation. One evening a group sat around a dining room table. They were all parents with children at the "best" schools in the country—Williams, Swarthmore, Carleton, Macalester. All were disappointed. This prompted a search for an explanation, the result of which was an agreement that what was missing in their children's experience at these schools was a campus-wide conversation about vocation. I like to describe vocation this way: It is (a) a sense of the self as not an isolated unit but nested in a larger community, and (b) a deep sense that one's highest ethical priority is to serve that larger community (a community with ever-widening circles—from neighborhood to nation, to all of humanity, to all the creatures in our biosphere). What is distinctive about the Lutheran view is that vocation comes from outside, from the needs of the neighbor and the community rather than from an emphasis on one's own gifts and interior priorities (though these are by no means irrelevant). Earlier this summer, during a workshop on vocation for faculty at Gustavus, one of our sessions was led by three colleagues—a Jew, a Muslim, and a Buddhist—each of whom explained how his or her own religious outlook supported a robust sense of vocation. Because of the breadth of the Lutheran concept of God's activity in the world—or, we could say, God's ongoing creation—their ability to do this is not surprising. All are gifted and all are called.

Notice what has happened here. Our focus has been on the kind and quality of relationships. Doctrines and beliefs have their place and their importance, but they are not central. From the very beginning, the Lutheran tradition has relied on paradoxes—placing side by side two seemingly contradictory statements as a way of pointing beyond the statements to some deeper reality. (The believer is free lord of all, subject to none, and at the same time is the dutiful servant of all, subject to all. The believer is simultaneously right with God and a sinner. God is both hidden and revealed. In 1912 some American Lutherans decided that both predestination and free will were right. The list could go on.) Using paradoxes says that belief statements are inadequate vehicles for the full religious truth. The deeper reality is relational. If doctrines were central and faith was primarily ascribing to a list of beliefs, the rootedness of the college would have quite different consequences and the dynamics of interreligious relations would be far different.

If the whole world is gifted by an engaged God, then interreligious dialogue has something significant to explore, and such explorations can benefit the religious perceptions of every participant.

Feature #3: Wisdom

The Lutheran tradition prizes wisdom. Let us return to the concept of freedom. What acknowledging one's giftedness does is to set a person free—*free from* the endless treadmill of trying to prove oneself through success at this or that and *free for* service to others.[8] Here as elsewhere we run into terminological difficulties, because Americans commonly mean by "freedom" what I would call "freedom of choice"—that is, the absence of coercion when deciding whether to have a hamburger or a chicken sandwich. Although the Lutheran tradition affirms freedom of choice,[9] what it typically means by freedom is something far deeper. For example, when society is caught up in a mass hysteria and a group is being feared and/or blamed for what is wrong, risking all to stand with a member of that group is an expression of this deeper "freedom for." Such an action takes courage and a strong ethical commitment to the neighbor, and it also takes a deeply rooted freedom from anxiety and fear.

Now back to wisdom. If humans are free, how are they to know how to act? Luther provides no blueprint—either for the individual or for society as a whole. There are no detailed do's and don'ts. There is no prescribed plan for how to organize a society. Decisions are to be guided, not by rules, but by wisdom. As used here, wisdom is an understanding of humans and what makes for a rich and full life and an understanding of communities and what makes for justice and peace. Wisdom is not the exclusive province of one religion, but it can be enhanced by the life-affirming instruction found in the Bible. Similarly, there are enough educated fools around for us to know that wisdom is not automatically the result of education, but it can be enhanced by good learning. When Luther wrote to the city councils in Germany, recommending that they establish schools for both young men and young women, his chief argument was that the study of human history and what has gone well and what has gone wrong throughout the ages would enhance the *wisdom* of Germany's citizens so that they could lead the community and lead their households.[10]

---

8   See Chapter 5 for development of this theme.
9   With regard to everything except initiating the God-human relationship. There God takes the first step.
10 Martin Luther, "To the Councilmen of All Cities in Germany That They Establish and Maintain Christian Schools," in *Luther's Works*, American Edition. Vol. 45 (Philadelphia: Muhlenberg Press, 1962), 368-69.

The ultimate goal of Lutheran higher education is not learning nor even critical thinking, as important as these are. It is the enhancement of wisdom. Although learning and critical thinking both contribute to this goal, they are not ends in themselves. The cultivation of wisdom is the central contribution that education can make to society.

This means that education is inherently communal. I can learn new data on my own, but wisdom requires the give and take of multiple perspectives. Wisdom comes from insight gathered in community. In order to discover wisdom, civil discourse is needed. Moreover, in order to discover wisdom, interreligious dialogue is valuable. It helps us examine the most basic of human questions about meaning and purpose, drawing upon the multiple insights of major religious traditions and thereby deepening our understanding of what it means to be human.

I should add that wisdom is never objective or neutral. It is always self-engaging. So, the pursuit of wisdom does not require us to abandon beliefs that hold up under scrutiny; the pursuit of wisdom is rather a form of deep listening that helps us refine those beliefs and figure out what our neighbors and our community need so that we can determine where to put our energies. And what is the standard? The measuring stick is very pragmatic: Whatever actions benefit the neighbor and the community are good. Whatever actions do not are bad. What matters is not one's own virtue, not one's good intentions, not some ideology about small or big governments; what matters are the consequences. Does someone get fed or housed or educated or experience the dignity of work or have access to health care? Do relationships get mended? Is justice achieved? Is *shalom* fostered? What matters are the consequences.

Because Lutheran higher education aspires to cultivate wisdom, its educational values support civil discourse and interreligious dialogue.

Feature #4: Caution Regarding Claims to Know

Luther was upset about the scholastic theologians of his day who would use isolated statements from the Bible or the theological tradition as premises upon which to build arguments that would supposedly answer questions not addressed in revelation. In other words, they would use syllogisms to "fill in the spaces" between fundamental truths. Luther saw more than one problem with this approach, but the one that concerns us for the moment is that it overstepped the capacities of human knowledge. The problem was not the endeavor to learn more. The problem was the claims made about the results of those arguments. John Haught, a fine Roman Catholic theologian, has used the term "inexhaustibility" to describe human knowing.[11] In science, for example, there is always something more to know. Scientists once claimed that atoms were the smallest particles, until they learned there were still smaller ones. They expected to find that the genes were in control of human development, but soon it became clear that other chemicals and processes turn genes on and off. No matter how much we learn about the world, there is still more to learn, and that something more does not just add to our knowledge, it often changes the whole paradigm. Similarly our knowledge of another person is inexhaustible. And so is our knowledge of God. Acknowledging this inexhaustibility is a reason for caution. From Luther's perspective, who would have expected God's clearest self-revelation to be a carpenter from a remote corner of the world who identified with suffering and was executed as a criminal? Who would have expected that discipleship involves a call to "suffer with" rather than to escape suffering, a call to acknowledge the reality of suffering rather than to deny it? There are too many surprises for our claims to have much weight. For Luther, revelation shows us God, God's attitude toward us, and God's overall purposes, but it does not answer many, many other questions. Why is there suffering in the first place? What exactly is God doing at this moment? There are questions for which we have no definitive answers. The lack of full answers leaves room for freedom and the use of wisdom.

And this reminder of limits and endorsement of caution about our claims to know has a corollary: We also need to be cautious about what we do with those claims. When a person adopts bad ideas and puts them into practice, someone gets hurt. It was, for example, a bad idea that prompted Stalin to starve out three million Ukrainians when they resisted collectivization. It was a bad idea that regarded Aryans to be superior and Jews to be a threat, and this bad idea caused untold hardship during the Holocaust. It was a bad idea to cut down ancient forests and to dump toxic gases into the air without thought of the consequences. If we cannot fully understand God, cannot fully understand humans, and cannot fully understand nature, then acting as if we did know is likely to harm someone or something else.

---

11 John Haught, *What Is God? How to Think about the Divine* (New York: Paulist Press, 1986), 11-13.

If a person listens carefully to the political rhetoric of today, one is shocked by the audacity of the claims to know what society needs or does not need. A little caution or intellectual humility would go a long way toward opening the door to civil discourse and the search for common ground.

And if a person listens to some of the religious rhetoric of today, one is similarly shocked. How can one claim to know the timetable of the future? The only way is to use the method of the Scholastics to take ideas from scattered parts of the Bible and fill in the blanks. How can one claim to know that God punished Prime Minister Sharon for his withdrawal of settlers from Gaza? The only way is to assume, not only that God is a micromanager, but also that we can know what God is thinking.

A more cautious set of religious claims—not cautious in one's confidence of being gifted, but cautious in one's claims to know—allows for significant religious dialogue, where mutual learning takes place. While prizing learning, Lutheran footings include a theology of limits; they endorse epistemological humility. If our perceptions are incomplete, then civil discourse and interreligious dialogue are important ways to learn, ways to see things from a different angle, ways to appreciate the complexity of an issue, ways to challenge the adequacy of our ideas, and ways to enhance our understanding and our wisdom.

Feature #5: A High Value on Community

I have already talked about the centrality of relationships and the quality of relationships. In this tradition, humans are understood to be shaped and formed by their relationships. When my wife and I were engaged, people who knew me well commented that I seemed different. Who I was and how I responded to things was influenced by this new relationship. Relationships either enhance our humanity or cause it to shrivel. God graces us through others. So a healthy person is always simultaneously a giver and a recipient. To see oneself as part of a community is to acknowledge this mutuality—to acknowledge that I receive from others and that others can receive from me.

Once again here we run into something that is both countercultural and at odds with much religious practice in America. Our society generally regards humans to be isolated units, fully capable of discerning for themselves what it means to live the good life. On this view, hooking up with others is merely a matter of convenience. In contrast, the Lutheran tradition sees relationships as constitutive of selfhood. Luther was influenced by the biblical view that existing without relationships is best described as "death"—the person is breathing in and breathing out but is, for all practical purposes, dead. The Lutheran tradition is at odds with American individual*ism*.

Some time ago I attended a talent show put on as part of the 125th anniversary of my hometown. In that setting I listened to half a dozen gospel tunes. Some of the musicians were excellent, and on one level I even enjoyed the songs, but the lyrics were troubling—"me," "me," "me" in one song after another—a little about God and a lot about me. As I say, the Lutheran tradition is in this regard out of step, not only with American culture, but also with American religiosity, in that it sees the individual not as isolated but nested in a community. If being "spiritual but not religious" means trying to be a Christian by oneself, then the Lutheran tradition is at odds with this contemporary trend as well. If the goal of religious life is to practice *shalom*, then participating in a community of faith is essential.

When I ask students to define the word "community," very often they describe it as a group of people with shared interests. I do not know whether that is a valid use of "community," but it is not what I am talking about here. "Community" is rather the mutual interaction of people who differ—people with different occupations, priorities, and temperaments—all working together for the common good.

The community of faith may have shared commitments, but, as Paul discovered in Corinth, it also has a good deal of diversity, held together by a common mission to mend the world. And the larger community has even greater diversity. To understand the larger community as a community is not to seek to reduce diversity but to utilize that diversity in service to the common good—that is, to help mend the world and move it toward *shalom*.

We've already mentioned some consequences of this emphasis on community:

Everyone has a calling to serve the community.

Participation in community is a crucial part of any education that aims at wisdom.

When it can be harnessed by civil discourse aimed at common ground, diversity is an asset to the educational mission of a college.

When religious diversity results in interreligious dialogue, religious diversity can also be an asset to a college that is both rooted and inclusive.

Clearly, this emphasis on community includes both the priority of the community of faith and the priority of serving the larger community.

The connection to our topic becomes clear when we remind ourselves that this larger community is multi-religious. In order to foster an understanding of how to serve a community that includes persons of other philosophical persuasions and persons of other religious traditions, a Lutheran college needs to value and to practice civil discourse and interreligious dialogue.

Feature #6: An Emphasis on Service and Community Leadership

As I hope I have already made clear, the overarching goal in Lutheran education is to equip people for service to the community. However much Luther himself emphasized the God-human relationship, he also worked to establish community chests to end begging, provide for those in need, especially children and the elderly, and provide low-interest loans to shop owners. He advocated schools for all young people. He opposed hoarding that would profit at the expense of others. He encouraged the princes and peasants to negotiate rather than go to war. He advocated changes in the rules governing marriage. He opposed a crusade against Muslims. And, if we turn to Lutherans in America, they constitute about 3 percent of the population and yet are responsible for the largest social service network in the country, operate one of the two largest refugee resettlement services, and support an international relief and development service with such a high reputation that after the tsunami in Japan major secular journals suggested it was one of the best places to send donations.

An education that equips people for service to the community also equips for leadership. Vocation is my own sense of call. Leadership is helping others discern and put into action their calling. Leadership is not just being in charge or occupying a position of authority, but rather the capacity to see what a community needs, to convince others that it is important, to decide on a course of action, and to get people working together toward that goal. Any person with some vision of the whole can lead and can do so from any position in the group. Leadership comes in diverse forms—whether discerning the need or coming up with a plan or getting people on board, whether working behind the scenes or serving as a public spokesperson. What inspires and guides a community leader is a sense of vocation and a sense of agency (that is, a sense that he/she can make a difference). At a time when many feel helpless, Lutheran higher education needs to nurture a more robust sense of agency. Because the goal is service to the community, Lutheran higher education focuses on both vocation and leadership.

If leadership is to be community leadership or transformative leadership that benefits the whole, then our college graduates need to be able to engage in civil discourse and be able to work with persons of other religions.

Religious Diversity and the Lutheran Identity of a College

Do such views relativize Christian claims? Not at all; they only reclaim the Lutheran tradition of God's ongoing creation alongside the more familiar strains of redemption. The only way we can move the world toward *shalom* is to emphasize both systemic change and personal transformation. I believe that the personal transformation that Christians have emphasized is crucial. But American society has privatized and individualized this part of Christianity to the point of distortion, and in so doing it has neglected the priority of justice and wholeness in society. Ongoing creation and this quest for *shalom* are the larger framework within which personal transformation takes on meaning. Only because God is at work mending the whole world, do I have hope. And personal transformation is one part of this hope. It enhances the "freedom for" that we need to participate in this mending.

The message of our adoption by God is foundational for those of us who are members of the faith community. Whether it makes a difference to the *world* depends on what kind of Christians we are.

Even though God's free gifting and God's goal of *shalom* make all the difference to me, I can still invite those who do not share my enthusiasm for these ideas to join me in mending the world. I can remind them that they did not choose to be born, that they did not construct the natural landscape they value, that they did not build the roads or discover the medical procedures that enhance their lives and make possible their accomplishments. In other words, I can remind them that a sober assessing of their own lives rules out a sense of entitlement and supports a life of gratitude. I can remind them of their connectedness with all that is and what this means for their exercise of freedom. I can remind them how limited is the control we seem to seek and how much in this world arouses a sense of wonder. I can remind them how important wonder is for creativity in science and music and art and every other discipline. I do not have to prove that their religious convictions are wrong and I certainly do not need to abandon my Christian faith to do this inviting. I can invite them into a sense of gratitude, vocation, wonder, and connectedness, and encourage a vision of shalom. These sensitivities have the capacity to enable religions and other groups of humans to work together and to be a unifying force instead of a dividing one. Whatever their personal religious commitments or their lack of religious commitments, these are the educational values the faculty, staff, and students at a Lutheran college are invited to endorse and to practice.

Some other may ask, if all of this is true, why should a non-Christian care about the college's rootedness? Because, by fostering a sense of vocation and by aspiring to wisdom (not just learning), this rootedness deepens the educational enterprise—and because this rootedness has itself secured a place for the non-Christian's full participation in the community. That is, the Lutheran tradition has invited not only the person but also the person with his/her religious convictions to participate fully in the community. And these religiously-based invitations are more likely to endure in the midst of countervailing forces than are culturally-based invitations. As the Hillel director at Muhlenberg College once told me, "I tell Jewish parents that this is a good place to send their children, not despite the fact that it is Lutheran, but because it is Lutheran." I admit that at times the Lutheran vocabulary and outlook in a Lutheran college may make a non-Christian feel like a visitor, but the choices are these: a sectarian college where the feeling is still more intense and full participation is limited; a non-sectarian college where, in the final analysis, no one's religious commitments are welcome; or a college that follows the third path, where the living tradition of the college supports one's presence and participation. I think the third path is the one worth taking. This path supports both civil discourse and interreligious understanding.

Questions for Discussion

1. Taking Jodock's image of Lutheran education as a "third path" distinct from sectarian and secular institutions, to which model does your own college or university gravitate?

2. Which of the six features of the Lutheran tradition seem most important in the context of Lutheran higher education? Most essential for interfaith dialogue and civil discourse? Most challenging to you or to your institution?

3. Jodock claims that "the overarching goal in Lutheran education is to equip people for service to the community." Do you agree? What does this claim emphasize? What might it leave out?

CHAPTER 7

PRACTICING HOPE
The Charisms of Lutheran Higher Education

MARTHA E. STORTZ
Augsburg College, Minneapolis, Minnesota

Several years ago, on a night flight from somewhere to somewhere else, I sat next to a man who was returning from a visit to his son in a prestigious East Coast school.[1] We fell into a conversation as deep as the hour was late. This man had gone to a Jesuit college, a network of institutions I know well. We started playing Jesuit Geography and had a lot of "hits." His son, however, hadn't wanted to go to a Jesuit college, and that made him sad. I asked what he was afraid his son had missed. Without missing a beat, he said: "Going to a Jesuit College taught me three things: (1) Be a man for others; (2) Find God in all things; and (3) Always give back." What impressed me so powerfully was how quick and how unconsidered his response was. This was more than something he did; this was who he was. His Jesuit education shaped his identity in indelible ways.[2]

What would someone answer who had attended a Lutheran institution? How would that shape her? Would the answer be as ready? Perhaps someone who had been the product of Lutheran higher education could say many similar things to someone who had been through Jesuit high-

---

1   A version of this essay was first published in *Intersections* 32 (Spring 2010): 9-15.
2   For a thorough, non-nostalgic study of what Jesuit education is all about, see George W. Traub, ed., *A Jesuit Education Reader: Contemporary Writings on the Jesuit Mission in Education, Principles, the Issue of Catholic Identity, Practical Applications of the Ignatian Way, and More* (Chicago: Loyola Press, 2008). I am deeply appreciative of what Robert Benne has done in his thoughtful survey of higher education (*Quality with Soul: How Six Premier Colleges and Universities Keep Faith with Their Religious Traditions* [Grand Rapids, Michigan: Wm. B. Eerdmans Publishing, 2001]), as well as of James T. Burtchaell's work in his massive book, *The Dying of the Light: The Disengagement of Colleges and Universities from their Christian Churches* (Grand Rapids, Michigan: Wm. B. Eerdmans Publishing, 1998).

er education. After all, though one came from Protestant Saxony and the other from the Catholic Basque region of Spain, Luther (1483-1546) and Ignatius (1491-1556) were contemporaries of one another.

Translating Ignatian into Lutheran would be surprisingly easy. "Be a person for others" would be rendered "seeing the face of Christ in the neighbor" and "being the face of Christ to the neighbor." "Find God in all things" reflects Luther's insistence that the finite is capable of the infinite and his rapt attention to the ordinary graces. "Always give back" corresponds to Luther's signature emphasis on vocation.[3]

The translation can be done. But is this what Lutheran higher education really is? More pressing: Is this what Lutheran higher education really needs to be, to meet adequately the challenges of a culture of fear? Finally, what are its unique gifts? What do Lutherans bring to the table that is distinctive to this tradition? And if we don't bring it, no one else will.

I want to talk about the *charisms* of Lutheran higher education, so at the outset I need to tell you what I mean by *charism*. Quite simply, *charism* is theological language for gift—only this kind of "gift" is not something that you purchase, wrap, and give to someone else. *Charism* is not *commodity*; rather, it comes from who you are, not what you can buy. So when I ask about Lutheran higher education, I'm talking about identity. Who are Lutherans, and what are the distinctive gifts they bring to higher education simply by being who we are?

Let me illustrate with an ordinary analogy. Invited to a family picnic, I asked what I could bring to the table, and my sister-in-law said: "Just bring yourself. That's what we need most." Actually, considering the Byzantine emotional politics of my late husband's family, she was right than she knew. I brought a lot simply by not having been raised in that set of complex family dynamics. My background was equally complicated, but different. By virtue of an identity I did nothing to create but had been shaped in for decades, I brought leaven to the gathering just by virtue of being who I was. The analogy is ordinary—but apt.

Back to the question: What do Lutherans bring to higher education that no one else can? If Lutherans don't bring it, it won't be there—or it won't be there in quite the same way.

---

3   For a more sustained comparison of Luther and Ignatius Loyola, see Martha E. Stortz, "Beyond Service: What Justice Requires," *Currents in Theology and Mission* 37.3 (June 2010): 230-37.

I want to explore five charisms:

1. In a setting where stability is prized, Lutherans present *flexible, responsive institutions* by virtue of a commitment to be "always in the process of reforming"(*semper reformanda*).

2. In an academy of competing ideologies, Lutheran colleges and universities embody a spirit of *critical inquiry*, thanks to the spirit of Christian freedom.

3. In a world of strangers, even enemies, Lutherans regard the other as *neighbor*.

4. In populations searching for meaning and purpose, Lutheran institutions promote *vocational discernment*, a process that lasts a lifetime and embraces the life spheres.

5. Finally, Lutherans enter a world of poverty as a *priesthood of all believers*.

I want to survey the landscape of each of these charisms attending to *why* it's important, *what* it means institutionally, and *where* it challenges a culture of fear.[4]

Semper Reformanda: Flexible, Responsive Institutions

The first charism is that Lutherans are part of a tradition that sees itself as always in the process of becoming, i.e., ever-reforming or *semper reformanda*. They do so because they simultaneously have one foot planted firmly in the gospel and one planted firmly in the world. Let's look more carefully at that stance.

Lutherans have one foot planted firmly in the gospel—but by gospel I don't mean "book." At their best, Lutherans inhabit the middle ground between biblical literalism and biblical irrelevance.[5] "Gospel" telegraphs the "good news" that God became human in the person of Christ Jesus. God knows life on the planet intimately—and that in-

---

4   Instead of identifying *charisms*, Jason Mahn writes of distinctive "dynamic tensions" between religious formation and interfaith, between suspicion and trust, between vocation as *theological insight* and vocation as *practice*. See Jason Mahn, "Why Interfaith Understanding is Integral to the Lutheran Tradition," *Intersections* 40 (Fall 2014): 7-16; republished as Chapter 12 of this book.

5   The author of the Gospel of John saw the danger of biblical literalism early on: "You search the scriptures because you think that in them you have eternal life; and it is they that testify on my behalf. Yet you refuse to come to me to have life" (John 5:39-40, NRSV).

timacy is not limited to the human species. The apostle Paul rightly identified the scope of divine concern. It was not just "the human condition" but "the whole creation [that] has been groaning in labor pains until now."[6]

The impact of incarnation continues, as Lutherans simultaneously have the other foot firmly planted in the world, where they look for traces of God's ongoing activity with and for the whole creation. Hauntingly, fourth-century North African theologian Augustine of Hippo called these "vestiges of the Trinity," *vestigiae trinitatis*.[7] The Latin is even more concrete: "footprints" of the Trinity.

One foot planted firmly in the gospel, one foot planted firmly in the world—this stance, this sense of being bi-locational, as George Lindbeck puts it, calls for a kind of stereoscopic vision, whereby Lutherans are prompted by the gospel to listen for God's word to God's creation *now* and simultaneously prompted to examine the world for traces of God's presence.[8] Of course, there are footprints of all kinds of things in the world. How does one recognize a "footprint" of the presence of God?

Identification calls for discernment, and that's where the gospel helps. If something comports with the Spirit of God in Christ Jesus, it is a good spirit. If it doesn't, it's bad. The apostle Paul named the "fruit" of that Spirit: "love, joy, peace, patience, kindness, generosity, faithfulness, gentleness, self-control."[9] Textual scholars confirm these habits of the heart that contour relationships with God (love, joy, peace), the neighbor (patience, kindness, generosity), and the self (faithfulness, gentleness, self-control). So if these dispositions are manifest or produced, there is a "footprint" of the presence of God. Because the Creator walked the earth with the creation, these footprints are everywhere.

The charism of being a community that is ever-reforming invites— even demands—a kind of institutional vigilance for insights outside

---

6   Romans 8:22, NRSV. That incarnation continues through a community of believers who continue to participate in the mystery, incorporating themselves into the body of Christ through baptism and incorporating the body of Christ into themselves through the Lord's Supper. It is a mutual interpenetration.

7   St. Augustine, *The Trinity (De Trinitate)*, trans. Edmund Hill (Hyde Park, New York: New City Press), 12.11.16.

8   George Lindbeck, "Martin Luther and the Rabbinic Mind," in *Understanding the Rabbinic Mind: Essays on the Hermeneutic of Max Kadushin*, ed. Peter Ochs (Atlanta: Scholars, 1990), 114-64.

9   Galatians 5:22.

of the Lutheran tribe. New Testament descriptions of the disciples advise broad consultation, because the closest were clueless. That is, those who considered themselves "closest" to Jesus, those in his inner circle, were also the most clueless about his true identity and his real purpose. Pointedly and all too often, outsiders were the ones who "got" it: a Samaritan woman in John's Gospel,[10] a centurion at the end of Mark's,[11] again, in John's, a blind man begging.[12] Moreover, the demons always know precisely who Jesus was. Disciples expected someone else. These stories constitute a caveat to the "insiders," reminding them to keep their noses outside the tent, sniffing the wind for signs of God's presence.

This gift of always being in the process of reforming means that Lutheran colleges and universities depend on a certain critical mass of non-Lutheran faculty, staff, and students who bring the world into the quad.[13] Practicing being *semper reformanda* keeps these Lutheran institutions flexible and nimble, alert to cross-currents in the culture. It counsels them to let form follow function and be bold in editing out structures that have become stagnant and no longer pulse with mission.

For example, look at the way Lutheran institutions of higher education adapt to context. Pacific Lutheran University finds itself in a region that professor Patricia Killen evocatively calls the "none" zone. More people here identify their religious affiliation as "none" than any other part of the country. It sustains a vibrant campus ministry that has developed a kind of "perfect pitch" for a student body that runs the gamut from cradle Lutherans to seekers.[14] Jewish students find a home in East Coast Lutheran colleges and universities, in part because one doesn't have to hide or apologize for belief. I think particularly of the Institute for Jewish-Christian Understanding at Muhlenberg College. L. DeAne Lagerquist relates a story about a mission statement St. Olaf College put out for its 100th anniversary. When, twenty-five years later, the college put out another statement, some people object-

---

10 John 4.
11 Mark 15:39.
12 John 9:8.
13 This is tougher in a seminary context, where Lutheran identity has a different purchase. Seminaries have to be a kind of confessional "hot-house," often doing a fair amount of remedial catechesis or confessional calisthenics, so that we train church leaders flexible enough to stand in the gospel as well as in the world.
14 Patricia Killen, *Religion and Public Life in the Pacific Northwest: The None Zone* (Lanham, Maryland: AltaMira Press, 2004).

ed: "Wasn't the centennial statement good enough?" Yes, came the response, that statement was good for *then*.[15] Whether it was good for *now* was another story. *Semper reformanda!*

Institutions change at a glacial pace—even in a time of global warming—but particularly in a culture of fear. Above all things, a culture of fear fears change. It registers change as loss, whether loss of identity or loss of spine. Yet, I think it is precisely the Lutheran commitment to being always in the process of reforming that keeps institutions flexible and structures pliant, like green wood that bends in a stiff wind.

The Freedom of a Christian: Critical Inquiry

In an academy often torn by competing ideologies, Lutheran higher education embodies a spirit of critical inquiry. This is the Lutheran spirit of both/and, or *simul . . . et . . .*, expressed most powerfully in Luther's understanding of the human person as both saint and sinner, both *justus* and *peccator*. This insight turns out to be not only an accurate description of human nature, but a good way of navigating the strong ideological currents that course through the academy and the culture as a whole. These often register as binary opposites, brooking no rapprochement, forcing students and colleagues to choose one side or another. Only one side is "right," and there are no "third sides."[16]

Lutheran institutions tend to be suspicious of ideological absolutisms. That gives us a fighting chance of breaking through some of the most controversial issues of our time. Think of the abortion debate, which divides into irreconcilable differences between "pro-life" and "pro-choice." The very positions suggest that the opposition is either "anti-life" or "anti-choice," a way of setting up debate that paralyzes discussion. I remember walking into a room where I was supposed to address the topic. The rage was palpable, but beneath it was pure fear. As we talked, the anger dissipated somewhat, and we could explore the underlying fear. We discovered that maybe the fear was the same: fear for children and fear that their potential was being snuffed out, by the practice of abortion, by poverty, by shame of illegitimacy, by the costs of medical care and child-rearing, by cultural practices that were as abortifacient as the practice of abortion itself, by practices that sub-

---

15 Conversation with L. DeAne Lagerquist, July 28, 2009.
16 The term is from William Ury, *The Third Side: Why We Fight and How We Can Stop* (New York: Penguin, 2000). See also his TED Talk, "The Walk from 'No' to 'Yes,'" https://www.ted.com/talks/william_ury?language=en

tly discriminate against children and unwed mothers. It was a much more complicated issue than being "for" or "against." The freedom of a Christian invites people to move behind anger to underlying fear.[17]

Further, this Lutheran habit of the heart holds seeming opposites in a creative and dynamic tension. It imagines both poles to have at least some purchase on the truth and to be connected with "and," not "or." Something can be both "cost-effective" and "missional." Or "traditional" and "innovating." Moreover, the freedom to shake loose from shackling binaries breaks through to the possibility of a third side, a third way, a *via media*, a path as yet unseen, which might lead all parties out of their entrenched oppositions.

Finally, this charism admits that, as the apostle Paul put it, "we see in a mirror, dimly. . . ."[18] Lutherans confess that they don't yet have a promised, eschatological "face-to-face" view. This side of heaven the best they can hope for are "partial truths," as anthropologist James Clifford calls them. He relates the story of a Cree Indian in Canada who is summoned to testify at a trial on land and water rights. When asked to the "the truth, the whole truth, and nothing but the truth," he paused, then responded: "I can only tell you what I know."[19] This charism signals humility, openness to a spectrum of options, and a refusal to cling to only one.

A culture of fear fears humility, despising it as weakness. Everything is agonistic, and only one side is right—and everything and everyone else is dangerously, fatally wrong. Practicing hope counsels critical inquiry and the search for a "third side" or middle ground.

Meeting the Other as "Neighbor"

The third charism in Lutheran higher education emphasizes a distinctive stance in regard to the "other." Coming out of a monastic context, Luther was used to more familial forms of address, particularly male ones. His fellow Augustinian monks would have been "brothers," his superiors would have been "fathers." Further, drawing on patristic language, those called to religious life understood themselves as "friends of God." They placed themselves in a privileged, preferential, inner circle of those closest to mystery itself. Late medieval monastics

---

17 I develop this argument further in my "letter" in Phyllis Tickle, ed. *Confessing Conscience: Churched Women on Abortion* (Nashville: Abingdon Press, 1990).

18 1 Corinthians 13:12.

19 James Clifford and George E. Marcus. eds, *Writing Culture* (Berkeley: California University Press, 1986), 8.

drew upon a body of literature dedicated to "spiritual friendship,"[20] and Luther would have recognized the writers and the language.

Against the horizon of friendship and brotherhood, Luther regards the other as *neighbor*, not as friend or family member. His training in the Hebrew Bible stood him in good stead, for neighbor surfaces frequently in the Levitical codes as the primary way the people of God organize their lives in community. With Luther, "neighbor" re-emerges as the primary way of regarding another person, possibly even another way of regarding another element of God's creation.[21]

This is a powerful shift away from the *blood* that binds families together and the *preference* that links friends. After all, people choose their friends, and do so according to similar likes and dislikes, shared hobbies or sports, the same backgrounds. Common preference grounds friendship. Blood binds family and tribe, knitting together people who may not choose each other, but are bound by common bloodlines.

But neither preference nor kin gathers neighbors. From different bloodlines and out of diverse tastes, neighbors simply share a common space. Proximity means they have to make a common life together— and they have to make it work. Neighbors share a public space, a civic space. Luther's language points to membership in a community larger than either the bonds of a family or the circle of friends.

Moreover, Luther develops his understanding of neighbor christologically, that is, he gives the neighbor the face of Christ. Again and again, he emphasizes that everyone bears the face of Christ to the neighbor and that the neighbor bears the face of Christ. Think of the alternatives: One could bear a face of judgment to the neighbor, a face of censure, a face of fear, even a face of invisibility. One could see in the neighbor all of these faces. But to see Christ's there—and to bear it oneself!

Increasingly, Lutheran colleges attract diverse students, faculty, and staff together into a common space, the campus. The campus quadrangle calls people from all four compass points and across a spectrum of diversities into a common space. Life together has got to work, and the sort of citizenship that develops among these diverse neighbors sparks a campus life that is often messy, but always robust.

---

20 Compare Peter Brown, *The Making of Late Antiquity* (Cambridge: Harvard University Press, 1978), particularly his chapter on saints as "friends of God," and Aelred of Rievaulx, *Spiritual Friendship*, trans. Mary Eugenia Laker (Washington, D.C.: Cistercian Publications, 1974).

21 Donald C. Ziemke, *Love for the Neighbor in Luther's Theology: The Development of His Thought, 1512-1529* (Minneapolis: Augsburg Publishing House, 1963).

The campus of Augsburg College sits next to the largest Somali community outside of Somalia. It sits in the midst of a growing Muslim community and has become keenly aware of religious and civic festivals celebrated within that community and increasingly on campus. Several years ago, music professor Bob Stacke found several Somali students in his jazz band. He started arranging works that incorporated jazz riffs into West African rhythms and harmonies. The result was a genre that can only be described as Somali/Big Band Fusion.

In contrast, a culture of fear regards the other as threat, even as enemy. Indeed, a culture of fear creates enemies—even when they are not there. Examine the aftermath of 9/11: the enormous sympathy for the United States in the immediate wake of the Twin Towers' collapse. A subsequent "War on Terror" squandered that good will, producing more terrorists than it apprehended. Consider immigration debates, which present the other as an "illegal alien," as if people could be "legal" or "illegal." Neighbor-regard recasts the debate in terms of near and distant neighbors, asking about an extended civic responsibility to those with whom we share a common space, the border zone. Neighbor-regard casts a new angle of vision on the debate.[22]

Vocational Discernment

Luther developed his understanding of "vocation" in contrast to a late medieval theology that placed on believers responsibility for salvation. Aided in varying degrees by grace, they accrued merit through good works. Priests and clerics, monks and nuns, however, had a head start in ascent to holiness. Only they were truly called; only they had a "vocation"; only they could fulfill the positive "thou shalt" commandments and counsels of perfection. Everyone else lived in the world, stuck in the works of their station (whether butcher, soldier, or mother), and bound by the minimalist requirements of the "thou shalt not" commandments.

Luther both democratized and upended medieval Catholic thinking about salvation. Because God became human, salvation had already entered the world. There was no need to aspire to holiness, because the Holy One had come and "dwelt among us" (John 1:14). All of the commandments and counsels of perfection applied equally to everyone, and people fulfilled them, not driven by fear, but moved by gratitude. They were freed *from* anxiety about the states of their soul

---

22 William C. Spohn and William O'Neill, "Rights of Passage: The Ethics of Immigration and Refugee Policy," *Theological Studies* 59 (1998): 84-106.

and freed *for* the works of their calling, which they performed in love and service to the neighbor. Everyone had a vocation or calling, and no vocation was better or worse than any other, because all were needed for God's ongoing work in the world. Through Luther's thinking on vocation, a theology of ascent became a theology of descent.[23]

Lutheran institutions are steeped in this understanding of vocation, and it permeates the work they do. In the workplace, vocation frees graduates from careerism, challenging them to use their gifts for the sake of the world. In the public realm, vocation animates citizenship, directing effort toward a common good. In the family, vocation honors domestic work, often undervalued and unremunerated. In the realm of faith, vocation lifts up worship as meeting a hardwired human need to wonder and simply be in the presence of mystery. Vocations are multiple; they span the life-cycle. When a senior came to my office, worried that she would not find her true calling, I replied: "Not to worry. Right now, your vocation is to be a good student, a committed Muslim, a loyal friend, a faithful daughter, and the president of the student body. You've already got your true calling for now."[24]

The challenge for Lutheran institutions is to put its understanding of vocation into language that its non-Lutheran constituencies can understand – without "dumbing it down" or turning a thick theological insight into "vocation-lite." One way to do this is to think of vocation as connective tissue, better elaborated by prepositions than nouns or definitions.[25] For example, people are called *by* someone or something, which some may name God, Allah, human flourishing, or a particular community that needs what they have to offer. They are called *as* people who bear distinctive gifts; they are called *into* community; they are called *for* service; they are called *from* places and people whom they have come to love and know deeply. Vocation often involves sacrifice. A few weeks ago, a gifted teacher and writer confided, "I just don't know about Pat's health. My next vocation may be a caregiver—and I'm not looking forward to that." Understanding the role as part of God's ongoing work in the world will ease the transition.

---

23 For more on the context of late medieval theology and Luther's role, see Karl Holl, *The Reconstruction of Morality* (Minneapolis: Augsburg Publishing House, 1979), and Mark Tranvik, *Martin Luther and the Called Life* (Minneapolis: Fortress Press, 2016).
24 See Chapter 14 below for development of this point.
25 See Kathleen Cahalan's book, *The Stories We Live: Finding God's Calling All Around Us* (Grand Rapids, Michigan: Wm. B. Eerdmans Publishing, 2016). Cahalan explores vocation through a series of prepositions: by, with, for, as, through, from, etc.

A culture of fear threatens this rich understanding of vocation with cynicism and powerlessness. "What can one person do?" becomes an excuse not to venture anything. More paralyzing is the distraction of self-help or self-improvement, which blunts the force of vocation by focusing it all on the individual and eliminating the possibility of sacrifice. And yet, a robust understanding of vocation grounds people in the midst of a career on hold, a relationship run aground, or a looming retirement. Rather than asking the question, "What should I do?" vocational discernment poses the question, "Where's the invitation in this?" The freedom and the responsibility to pose this question to students, staff, faculty, and institutions may be the greatest gift Lutheran institutions bring to the table of higher education in general.

Priesthood of All Believers in a World of Poverty

For Luther the language of a "priesthood of all believers" had civic import, a resonance which is hard to hear today. He used the language of "priesthood," not to confirm the various vocations, but to issue everyone an additional job description in the public realm. It conferred on all people the duties and responsibilities of the office of priest. Chief among these was care for the poor.

In his provocative *New American Blues: A Journey through Poverty to Democracy*, Earl Shorris observes: "Martin Luther practically invented the idea of welfare."[26] He had to. The sixteenth-century Reformation was simultaneously a reformation in social welfare. Institutions responsible for care of the poor were dismantled. What would take their place? Parish priests called to minister to the poor were displaced by married pastors with families of their own to feed. Who would then feed the hungry? Against the horizon of these social realities, the slogan "priesthood of all believers" had a different valence. Priests in the universal priesthood were commissioned by baptism to take on the duties and responsibilities of the clergy, one of which was to care for the poor.[27]

Reading the Reformation as a reformation in support services, one sees Luther's sensitivity to the plight of the poor. His inaugural treatise, the *95 Theses*, repeatedly names the poor. Luther's signature

---

26 Earl Shorris, *New American Blues: A Journey through Poverty to Democracy* (Boston: Norton, 1996), 205.

27 Compare Carter Lindberg, *Beyond Charity: Reformation Initiatives for the Poor* (Minneapolis: Fortress Press, 1993); Samuel Torvend, *Luther and the Hungry Poor: Gathered Fragments* (Minneapolis: Fortress Press, 2008); Martha Ellen Stortz, "'Practicing What it Means': Welfare Reform and the Lord's Supper," *Currents in Theology and Mission* 26.1 (1999): 19-32.

strategy, community chests for collecting alms, receives hefty theological argument. Luther even addresses the root causes of poverty, naming greed and avarice as chief culprits. In his catechetical writing on the Ten Commandments, Luther characteristically turns the negative "thou shalt not" commandments into positive "thou shalt" commandments, thereby increasing their range. "Thou shalt not kill" becomes a positive injunction: "Feed the hungry." Failing to do so "kills" God's creatures and violates God's command.[28]

I remember a conversation with a Syrian Orthodox Catholic businessman several years ago. He was describing the duties of the village priest. High on that list was the priest's responsibility "to know the poor. *This* is who a priest is supposed to be; *this* is what a priest is supposed to do." Luther would have completely agreed—only he passed that identity and that knowledge onto the community. Poverty becomes a civic concern.

How do institutions of higher education live into this charism to be "priests" in the "priesthood of all believers?"[29] This is part of who Lutheran institutions are. Catholic social teachings talk about a "preferential option for the poor," and they urge believers to make choices that comport with a decision to be in solidarity. It's a clear call to action in solidarity. This is what Catholics ought to do.

Yet, advocacy for and with the poor ought to cut more deeply for Lutherans. It's not so much they whom we *do* something for; it's they who we *are*. It's not so much a decision for action, as a component of identity. If these people and these institutions are to be priests, this is *who they are*. This is an element of Lutheran identity that is underexplored, not just in colleges and universities, but in congregations, synods, and churchwide offices.

How can Lutheran institutions live out this part of our charism? How can an institution be priest? Colleges and universities have various ways of doing this: service learning, cross-cultural experiences, immersions, etc. Among them, immersion trips display a particular

---

28 Luther does this consistently in his explanation of the Ten Commandments in "The Small Catechism (1529)," in *The Book of Concord,* ed. and trans. Theodore G. Tappert (Philadelphia: Fortress Press, 1959), 337-57.

29 John B. Bennett and Elizabeth A. Dreyer explore the ways institutions have a spirituality in their article, "Spiritualities of – Not at – the University," in Traub, *Jesuit Education Reader,* 113-32. They observe that most academics "have yet to attend to the spiritualities of our own academic callings and communities" (113). Lutheran institutions wouldn't call it "spirituality," but they have definitely explored their roles in terms of "calling" and "vocation."

concern for simply being with the neighbor, not doing something for the neighbor. Students go to live with, eat with, be with people in the two-thirds world. Immersion programs place their primary focus not on building wells, teaching in schools, or running shelters. The mode is receptive rather than productive. Former director of Augsburg College's Center for Global Education, Orv Gingerich, spoke of the distinction: "We encourage people to go as receivers. We want to disabuse students of the feeling that they always have something to give. We want them to receive instead."[30] And what do they receive?

Students come to know the reality of the almost two billion people in the world who struggle daily to simply stay alive. They come to know the poor. When faculty, staff, and administrators participate in the experience of immersion, it becomes part of institutional culture. Another example is from the University of San Francisco, where former President Stephen Privett S.J. took his leadership team to sites in the two-thirds world for many years. They have visited El Salvador, Tijuana, and Nicaragua, meeting with civic leaders, hearing presentations by experts, talking with local people. In Tijuana, they addressed immigration issues; in El Salvador, the role of the Jesuit university that had been an institution of resistance during the Sandanista government; in Nicaragua, the presence of grinding poverty in a garbage dump outside the nation's capital. Each evening, they reflected together on what they had seen and how it impacted concretely the university to which they would return.

In a recent article in *The Chronicle of Higher Education*, Privett observed: "I do not expect that such experiences will lead immediately to new programs and significant changes in the university requirements or policies. . . . What I do hope is that university leaders will develop an increased sensitivity to the heartbreaking struggles of the 1.89 billion people whose daily struggle is simply to stay alive."[31] As far as this university is concerned, global poverty is the context for their education.

---

30 Conversation with Orval Gingerich on July 7, 2009. While Augsburg's Center for Global Education focuses on immersion trips for students, Jesuit higher education has developed a program focusing on immersion trips for administrators. The Ignatian Colleagues Program has a five-fold approach, involving an orientation, an online learning component, a retreat on Ignatius' Spiritual Exercises, an international immersion experience, and a final capstone. See their explanation at www.ignatiancolleagues.org.

31 Stephen A. Privett, "Travel Abroad is as Eye-Opening for Administrators as It Is for Students," *The Chronicle of Higher Education*, May 28, 2009, http://chronicle.com/article/Travel-Abroad-Is-as/44418

A culture of fear plays immersion trips and service learning experiences against the backdrop of a mentality of scarcity. It regards such experiences as wasteful and unnecessary, though the team at the University of San Francisco found they cost less than an administrative retreat at a fancy conference center. A culture of fear would argue: clean up your own backyard. Yet, when institutions do, they find that the fences have been moved out significantly from where they thought they were. They may not think outside the quad, but in fact, their "backyard" now extends to Pakistan. Or Tegucigalpa. Or Cairo. Immersion trips emerge as a concrete practice of hope in a culture of fear. Lutheran colleges and universities become faith-based "seminaries," and the institution itself a "priest."

This is what it means to "know the poor"—and in so knowing discover a neighbor who bears the face of Christ.

Practicing Hope in a Culture of Fear

I've tried to identify five charisms of Lutheran higher education, gifts it brings to the table simply by virtue of who we are: In a setting where stability is prized, Lutheran higher education presents *flexible, responsive institutions*. In an academy of competing ideologies, Lutheran higher education embodies a spirit of *critical inquiry*. In a world of strangers—even enemies—Lutheran higher education regards the *other as neighbor*. In a culture hungry for meaning, Lutheran higher education offers *vocation discernment*. Finally, Lutheran higher education enters a world of poverty as a *priesthood of all believers*.

These are not the only charisms, but these seem to be the charisms needed now. These are not gifts that Lutheran institutions *used* to have or gifts that they *ought* to have, but rather gifts that they *have*—now. More sharply put, these are gifts or charisms of who they are. In ways that are both non-nostalgic and non-apologetic, these institutions simply need to be who they are.

The world needs these qualities, primarily because the world needs hope. The kind of hope these Lutheran institutions of higher learning offer is unique. We all hope *for* certain outcomes: x number of students in the entering class or x amount of dollars in the endowment. Yet, particularly in times of fear, people don't know what to hope *for*. That's when a different kind of hope surfaces: hope *in* something. For Christians, Muslims, and Jews, this hope *in* something is uniquely a hope in Someone—whether Allah or Elohim or Christ—and we find that hope in spite of ourselves. Hope *in* Someone is powerfully, and paradoxically that Someone's presence in us and for us. As the author of the epistle to the Colossians put it, "Christ in you, the hope of glory."[32]

This kind of hope does not look forward to possible outcomes, it reaches back to what is real. And what is real? Poverty is real. So is freedom, the neighbor, the solidity of the work we do together, the daily graces that swarm every moment we haven't already scheduled or fretted away. This hope in what is real anchors us in rough seas. Like any good captain we find that when the storm intensifies, we simply cast a deeper anchor.

It's like the child I watched at the pool this summer. He was terrified of the water; he couldn't even stand to get wet. But he leapt in his father's arms, suddenly bold, suddenly a swimmer. He knew he could count on his father catching him. That certainty grounded his hope.

That's what these institutions bring to the table: hope, the fruit of our charisms.

Questions for Discussion

1. Which of the three lists of marks, features, or charisms of Lutheran higher education (those by Christenson, Jodock, or Stortz) speak to your work within Lutheran higher education most directly or powerfully? How so?

2. Stortz references Augsburg College's relationship with the surrounding Somali community as inviting "neighbor-regard" over-and-against relationships based on kinship or friendship. How does your campus and its setting afford opportunities for care of neighbor?

3. The author also claims that "the challenge for Lutheran institutions is to put its understanding of vocation into language that its non-Lutheran constituencies can understand." How (well) has your institution accomplished such translations?

4. Should Lutheran colleges and universities better highlight—or enact—solidarity with the poor as one of their chief charisms? What does or would this look like on your campus?

---

32 Colossians 1:27.

Part Three

PERSPECTIVES

CHAPTER 8

WHAT IT MEANS TO BUILD THE BRIDGE
Identity and Diversity at ELCA Colleges

EBOO PATEL
Interfaith Youth Core, Chicago, Illinois

I'd like to open with the stories of two good friends of mine, women who work at senior levels at Interfaith Youth Core.[1] Both were devoted Christians when they went off to Midwestern liberal arts colleges in the 1990s, campuses that have much in common with yours in terms of size and liberal arts ideals, but do not happen to be Lutheran.

Cassie

I'll begin with Cassie's story. Cassie grew up in a largely secular household in the Seattle area and converted to Evangelical Christianity when she was in high school. She loved the closeness of the community and the fervor of the faith. When she got to college in upstate Wisconsin, she discovered that there were only enough active Christians on campus to form a single student group. It included people who grew up speaking in tongues and those more accustomed to smells-and-bells rituals. At first, Cassie had a hard time praying with Catholics; she'd been taught in her church back home that they weren't really Christian. But soon Catholics were the least of Cassie's theological worries.

One day in the library, Cassie was approached by a young man she'd been seeing around campus. He carried a notebook in his hand and asked if he could sit down. Cassie said sure, and Ahmed plunged into his purpose. He had to do a project for an Anthropology 101 class

---

1   These stories are told in full in Eboo Patel, *Sacred Ground* (Boston: Beacon Press, 2012), 129-52. This essay was originally published in *Intersections* 40 (Fall 2014): 17-25

on an exotic tribe. He'd been noticing that Cassie's Christian group had a distinct set of rituals and symbols; they even seemed to speak a special language. He was wondering if he could do the project on her.

This surprised Cassie, especially as it was coming from a dark-skinned man with an accent. From her perspective, if either of them could be described as being a member of an exotic tribe, it wasn't her. But she agreed to answer Ahmed's questions. And once she'd explained the purpose of her Wednesday night song circle and the meaning the Bible held for her, she turned the Anthropology 101 assignment on her interlocutor. She learned a little about Islam in the process. Ahmed explained that he was from Bangladesh, that observant Muslims pray five times a day and refrain from alcohol, and that the majority of the world's Muslims live in South Asia, not the Middle East.

Cassie found herself shook, in the way college ought to shake people. First of all, she was stunned that observant Muslims pray five times a day, including a pre-dawn prayer. She could barely get some of her fellow Christians out of bed by mid-morning on Sundays for church. The more Cassie thought about the encounter, the more challenged she felt. It had been deeply impressed upon Cassie by her home church that people who were not Christian were going to hell and that it was a signal duty of practicing Christians to seek to convert them. Yet she found herself a little uncomfortable with that approach in this particular scenario. It's not that she didn't believe in the truth of Christianity, it's just that she also found herself fascinated by Islam, and she realized that she both liked and admired Ahmed.

In the following weeks, as their friendship grew, Cassie experienced something of a crisis of faith. Was she being a bad Christian if she didn't view her interaction with Ahmed as primarily an opportunity to evangelize? Was she being a false friend to him if every time they were together she was looking for ways to sneak in the truth of Jesus Christ? Finally, Cassie went to see a pastor about the situation. He listened with great sympathy, but what he offered in return was almost entirely saccharine. He talked about the mystery of faith and the beauty of diversity. The message Cassie came away with was that college was a time to explore new things and that it was important to be a nice person. But honestly, she was looking for more than that. She was looking for a distinct Christian language for building a deep friendship with someone whom she admired but who did not hold the same truths that she did.

April

My second story is about April Kunze Mendez. Growing up in Minnesota, April was the poster child for church involvement. She led Bible studies and prayer circles; she participated in church camps and went on mission trips to the other side of the world. She even learned other languages so that she could proselytize more effectively. April went to a selective liberal arts college in Minnesota in the mid-1990s. The same year she was the leader of her campus Christian group, a mosque was burned down in the Twin Cities. There were claims that it was arson, a religiously-motivated hate crime. April was on a state-wide email list of religious leaders, where she received a message from the Imam asking her to attend a candlelight vigil in support of the mosque. She instinctively wrote back "yes."

The following week, at a meeting of her campus Christian group, April shared the email request and said she'd be organizing a van for people who were able to attend the vigil with her. There was some shifting in seats and some rustling in the back of the room. April asked what was up. A member of the group stood and said, "We think you are supporting devil worship." He then got out his Bible and started quoting chapter and verse about the wickedness of praying to false gods and the importance of bringing people to the true path. Other people started speaking in the same vein. Somebody said that this fire, however it might have started, was an act of God, divine punishment for those who followed the wrong religion. Another claimed that true Christian charity at this time would be to use this opportunity to invite the misguided Muslims to their church and evangelize them.

It soon became clear to April that her Christian group was not going to attend the vigil with her. When April insisted she was still going, they declared her unfit for Christian leadership and deposed her. The people who went to the candlelight vigil with April were called nice; the people who applauded the arson attack on the mosque were called Christian. April started to feel like those were not just distinct responses to this incident, but separate paths altogether. So this once-poster child for the church felt like she had to make a tragic choice—in a world of diversity, she could be nice to people from different religions or she could be Christian. She chose the former, but not without an awful lot of pain.

Fundamentalism and Relativism

What strikes me about Cassie and April's respective experiences is that they illustrate what the great social theorist Peter Berger characterized as two especially prominent religious paths today—relativism and fundamentalism.[2] April's story is, of course, an example of a form of fundamentalism. It's not violent fundamentalism—we have comparatively little of that in America, thank God—it's a fundamentalism best characterized as: Being me is based on dominating you. Cassie's story is one version of relativism—not cognitive relativism or moral relativism, but identity relativism. It can be summarized like this: I no longer know who I am when I encounter you.

We are all well aware of the dangers of fundamentalism. We read about its more violent expressions in the newspaper every day and likely deal with the dimension that April encountered (the nonviolent though quite vocal domination approach) at least occasionally. In this essay, I want to focus on the challenge posed by Cassie's experience—relativism. Certainly, relativism is less ugly and less dangerous than fundamentalism. But in my experience working on over a hundred college campuses and speaking with thousands of college students, it is far more prevalent.

The sociologist of religion Christian Smith has given this form of identity relativism a name: moralistic therapeutic deism. In his book, *Soul Searching*, the product of the most comprehensive survey of young people and religion ever undertaken, Smith talks about how the religious identities of most young Christians basically boil down to this: God exists and wants me to be a good person. Smith comments on how Christian young people are articulate about all sorts of things, from the dangers of drugs to the importance of safe sex, but have little more to say about religion than noted above. Drawing from the philosopher Charles Taylor, Smith emphasizes that "articulacy fosters reality"—in this case, the reality of identity.[3] Simply put, this means if you can't talk about Christianity, it's very hard to be Christian.

Why this inarticulacy? Smith posits that it may well be the result of being trained to be polite in a world of diversity. Here, I will quote him at length:

---

2   Peter Berger, ed., *Between Relativism and Fundamentalism: Religious Resources for a Middle Position* (Grand Rapids, Michigan: Wm. B. Eerdmans Publishing, 2010).

3   Christian Smith with Melinda Lundquist Denton, *Soul Searching: The Religious and Spiritual Lives of American Teenagers* (New York: Oxford University Press, 2005), 268.

Committed and articulate personal and congregational faith does not have to be sacrificed for the sake of public civility and respect for others who are different. Pluralism does not have to produce thinness and silence. But for it not to, people need to learn to distinguish among . . . 1) serious, articulate, confident personal and congregational faith, 2) respectful, civil discourse in the pluralistic public sphere, and 3) obnoxious, offensive faith talk that merely turns people off. . . . In efforts to be civil and accessible, it seems that many youth, and no doubt adults, are getting the wrong message that historical faith traditions do not matter, that religious beliefs are all alike, that no faith tradition possesses anything that anybody particularly needs.[4]

This is certainly the message Cassie got from the Christian minister with whom she talked about her experience with Ahmed. I've taught several seminary classes for liberal Protestants and asked them to role play the scene between Cassie and this Christian minister. They play the Cassie character exceptionally well. It's clear that they have all experienced a profound encounter with diversity that shook their faith along the lines of what happened to Cassie. But these seminarians universally had a difficult time being articulate about Christianity when playing the role of pastor. Like the pastor Cassie talked to when she was in college, they spoke the language of mystery, diversity, love, and friendship. Occasionally, they attached all this to the Holy Spirit, but that was about the limits of their faith vocabulary when it came to giving a young Christian like Cassie advice about what it meant to be both committed to the truth of Jesus and friends with a Muslim.

If there was one thing at the center for these future ministers it was attention to diversity. They cared about it in all its forms—race, ethnicity, gender, sexuality, class, religion. Thinking back to our class discussions through the lens of Christian Smith's research, I find it entirely plausible that this concern for diversity thinned out their language of Christian identity.

For Peter Berger, while relativism and fundamentalism are at opposite extremes, they are actually closely connected in that they are both

---

4   Ibid.

"products of the same process of modernization."[5] As he emphasizes in the Introduction to *Between Relativism and Fundamentalism*, frequent and intense encounters between people with different identities is the signature characteristic of the modern era—in Berger's pithy phrase, modernity pluralizes. This is a consequence of a variety of technological breakthroughs from mass communications to air travel, resulting in everything from rapid urbanization within nations to easy migration between them to knowledge of the beliefs and actions of people who live on the other side of the world. The bottom line is that more people regularly interact with people different from them today than ever before.

If modernity pluralizes, then, Berger claims, "pluralism relativizes . . . both institutionally and in the consciousness of individuals."[6] In the pre-modern era, institutions, ideas, and identities had a largely taken-for-granted status. For the vast majority of human history, the vast majority of humankind had little to no choice about which institutions they were going to participate in or what their identities were going to be. Such matters were experienced as fate. In the modern era, institutions become voluntary associations—people choose whether to participate—and identity has moved from "fate to . . . choice."[7] This puts an awful lot of pressure on moderns like us to constantly make conscious choices about what we participate in and who we are. This is pressure that our ancestors, who simply took for granted the network of institutions they grew up in and the identities they were handed, simply did not have.

One response to this pressure is to float uncomfortably in the mists of modernity, not committing to much of anything. This is the dynamic that produces relativism. But as human beings are hardwired for certainty, and because where there is a demand someone will generate a supply, the explanation for growing fundamentalism is pretty clear as well. So there you have it—a quick explanation for how the phenomenon of modernity pluralizing produces both Cassie's experience of relativism and April's encounter with fundamentalism.

From Blasé to Bridge

I believe that some version of Cassie's and April's stories are happening on a regular basis on ELCA college and university campuses.

---

5   Berger, *Between Relativism and Fundamentalism*, 2.
6   Ibid., 5.
7   Ibid., 6.

These encounters take place in classrooms and cafeterias, in dormitory conversations and on the quad, in RA training and during freshman orientation. And that is as it should be. Campuses are places where students ought to have intense interactions with deep difference and wrestle with what that means for who they are. But how frequently is the result of such encounters some form of relativism or fundamentalism? And what are the implications for campuses that seek to be both rooted in their Lutheran traditions and welcoming of diversity?

Right now some of you might be thinking about the voices in your communities who grumble about pro-active approaches to diversity. I imagine that among some of your alumni, perhaps even your donors and board, there are those who say, "A Lutheran college is where Lutherans go to become more Lutheran. What are we doing allowing Muslims and Jews and atheists and pagans in, letting them have their own student groups, accommodating their religious practices, even teaching courses about their traditions? What's up with having a Hindu chair the Department of Religion at St. Olaf?"

If Peter Berger and Christian Smith are to be believed, and if my experience with the liberal Christian seminarians above is at all telling, then such critics are far more than just cranks. Diversity does in fact undermine identity—at least it can. To complicate matters even further, the sociologist Robert Putnam has shown that diversity reduces social capital and weakens community bonds.[8] And the political scientist Samuel Huntington famously posited that increased interaction between different identities is a recipe for outright conflict—his infamous clash of civilizations thesis.[9] Simply put, diversity is not an unalloyed good.

Here's the fundamental question: Can campuses be places that do both identity and diversity? I think the answer to that is yes, and I think Lutheran campuses have an especially good shot at it.

Let me go back to the scholars for a moment. Peter Berger is not just a describer of "what is," he is also an articulator of "what ought to be." He despairs about the growth of both relativism and fundamentalism, claiming that they make a common life together impossible, even as he understands how the dynamics of our times have given rise

---

8   Robert D. Putnam, "*E Pluribus Unum*: Diversity and Community in the Twenty-first Century," *Scandinavian Political Studies* 30.2 (2007): 137–74.

9   Samuel Huntington, "The Clash of Civilizations?" *Foreign Affairs* (Summer 1993): 22-49.

to both phenomena. Berger hopes to stake out a middle position, what he refers to as "the location of those who want to be religious believers without emigrating from modernity."[10]

Christian Smith holds out this same hope, stating that:

> There is plenty of room for faith traditions to claim and emphasize confidently their own particularities and distinctions without risking religious division or conflict. Youth should be able to hear and embrace (or reject) what are the particularities of their own faith traditions and why they matter, without having to be afraid that this inevitably causes fighting and discomfort.[11]

Peter Berger also happens to be a Lutheran layperson, quite conversant both in Lutheran theology and in history. He points out that it was the Lutheran tradition that first recognized the possibility "to have faith without laying claim to certainty."[12] Moreover, Lutheran intellectuals were among the first to take the courageous step of putting modern historical scholarship in conversation with elements of faith and scripture. He expands on these notions in an essay in the book, *Between Relativism and Fundamentalism*.[13] For the purposes of this essay, I want to consider what this heritage means for ELCA college campuses.

Let me begin with a quick typology of religious identity responses to diversity: Faith can be a bubble of isolation, a barrier of division, a bomb of destruction, or a bridge of cooperation. A fifth response—the final "b"—is blasé. Faith can be something we neither care too much about nor think too much of. Barriers and bombs—the fundamentalist response—are actively destructive in a diverse democracy. Bubbles are extremely hard to build and maintain. (That's one answer to give your alum who ask why Lutheran colleges are no longer just for Lutherans seeking to be more Lutheran.) Blasé seems to be the order of the day, and the question then is how do you help shift the tide from blasé to bridge? I think the answer lies in the metaphor.

A bridge goes from here to there and has to be made of something, preferably something solid. Without a strong anchor "here," you can't bridge to "there." Furthermore, without the materials and the skills to build the bridge, it won't come into being. For Cassie to continue a

10 Berger, *Relativism and Fundamentalism*, 13.
11 Smith, *Soul Searching*, 268.
12 Berger, *Relativism and Fundamentalism*, 13.
13 Ibid., 152-63.

Christian conversation with a knowledgeable Muslim like Ahmed, she needs to know an awful lot more about Christianity than the pastor she spoke to was offering. My guess is that Ahmed was hoping for that. After all, he was standing on his "here," using the materials of his knowledge of Islam to build a bridge to Cassie's "there." For the conversation to be enriching for him—to borrow a phrase from a master—there has to be a there there.[14]

The answer to the problem of nurturing both identity and diversity—of carving out a religious location that does not flee from modernity—is not to weaken either, it is to do more of both. Brian McLaren puts this well in his recent book on Christian faith and religious diversity, *Why Did Jesus, Moses, the Buddha, and Muhammad Cross the Road?* He points out that strong Christian identity has long been associated with hostility towards others, while positive feelings towards others are connected with weak Christian identity. He wants a third alternative—strong faith identity associated with benevolence towards others. He quotes one of his mentors, "In a pluralistic world, a religion is judged by the benefits it brings to its nonmembers."[15] This is what I have started calling a theology of interfaith cooperation. It means being able to weave from your own religion's resources—its scripture, doctrines, history, theology, poetry, heroes, etc.—a coherent narrative and fundamental logic for being in positive relation with others, even though you disagree with them on some significant things. This is the substantive material from which we form the bridge that connects here and there, a bridge that can withstand bombs and break through barriers, a bridge that invites people out of their bubbles, and a bridge that provides solid footing for those floating in the blasé.

The Example of Dietrich Bonhoeffer

Many readers will know better than I the finer points of how to use the raw materials of the Lutheran tradition to build a bridge to diversity.[16] What I'd like to do right now is hold up a Lutheran figure who has deeply inspired me as a Muslim, a man who both eloquently articulated and courageously embodied a theology of interfaith cooperation, Dietrich Bonhoeffer. It is not an overstatement to say that his Christian identity was about building a bridge to diversity. Indeed, it

14 Gertrude Stein, *Everybody's Autobiography* (New York: Random House, 1937), 289.
15 Brian McLaren, *Why Did Jesus, Moses, the Buddha, and Muhammad Cross the Road?: Christian Identity in a Multi-Faith World* (New York: Jericho Books, 2012), 40.
16 See for example Chapter 6 in this book.

was the cause he died for. Consider the following scenes from Bon-hoeffer's life:

> Bonhoeffer declaring after the Nuremberg Laws were passed in 1935: "Only he who shouts for the Jews is permitted to sing Gregorian chants."[17]

> Bonhoeffer preaching at the funeral of his grandmother in 1936. A woman who—just days after Hitler ordered Germans to boycott Jewish businesses—walked into a Jewish-owned grocery store right past a group of Nazi stormtroopers, stating that she would do her shopping where she always did her shopping. Bonhoeffer eulogized, "She could not bear to see the rights of a person violated . . . her last years were darkened by the grief that she bore about the fate of the Jews in our country. . . . This heritage, for which we are grateful to her, puts us under obligation."[18]

> Bonhoeffer, returning to the United States in 1939 to teach a summer course at Union Theological Seminary and go on a lecture tour organized by Reinhold Niebuhr, realizes that he made a mistake. He boards the last ocean liner that sails east across the Atlantic during World War II, leaving Niebuhr with a letter that says: "I will have no right to participate in the reconstruction of Christian life in Germany after the war if I do not share the trials of this time with my people."[19]

> Bonhoeffer in the wan light of Cell 92, Tegel prison, writing to his friend Eberhard Bethge: "The church is only the church when it does for others."[20]

In a school house turned prison near the Nazi extermination camp at Flossenbürg on April 8, 1945, a small group of prisoners who know the inevitable has arrived asks Bonhoeffer to lead a prayer service for them. He offers a meditation on 1 Peter: "By his great mercy he has

---

17 Burton F. Nelson, "The Life of Dietrich Bonhoeffer," in *The Cambridge Companion to Dietrich Bonhoeffer*, ed. John deGrutchy (Cambridge: Cambridge University Press, 1999), 35.

18 Ibid., 26.

19 Ibid., 38.

20 Clifford Green, "Human Sociality and Christian Community," in *Cambridge Companion to Dietrich Bonhoeffer*, 130.

given us a new birth into a living hope."[21] Dietrich Bonhoeffer was assassinated by the Nazis the next day. Upon hearing of his martyrdom, Niebuhr wrote, "The story of Bonhoeffer . . . belongs to the modern acts of the apostles."[22]

Such a commitment does not emerge from the ether of relativism. In Tegel prison Bonhoeffer famously asked, "What does Jesus Christ mean for us, today?" He answered that question with his life, a life rooted in the cement of genuine conviction, a love and mastery that built out of the Lutheran tradition a bridge to everyone.

The scholar Keith Clements describes how Bonhoeffer's ecumenism is what connects his pilgrimage from peace-worker to political resister. In 1931 Bonhoeffer accepted an invitation to an ecumenical conference. In the mid-1930s he began making plans to go visit Gandhi (plans that came to an end when he was called to lead the Confessing Church's illegal seminary at Finkenwalde). He said of the Mahatma, "Christianity in other words and deeds might be discovered . . . in Gandhi and the East." Bonhoeffer's last known words before he was killed were a message for his friend and mentor in the ecumenical movement, Bishop George Bell: "Tell him . . . with him I believe in the principle of universal Christian brotherhood which rises above all national interests, and that our victory is certain."[23]

But Bonhoeffer saw problems in the ecumenical movement as well. He said in a speech at an ecumenical youth peace conference in 1932:

> Because there is no theology of the ecumenical movement, ecumenical thought has become powerless and meaningless, especially among German youth, because of the political upsurge of nationalism. And the situation is scarcely different in other countries. There is no theological anchorage which holds while the waves dash in vain. . . . Anyone concerned with ecumenical work must suffer the charges of being unconcerned with the Fatherland and unconcerned with the truth, and any attempt at an encounter is quickly cried down.[24]

As I read this critique today, nearly a century after Bonhoeffer made it, it occurs to me that the development of theology isn't the

---

21 Nelson, "Life of Dietrich Bonhoeffer," 44.
22 Ibid., 22.
23 Keith Clements, "Ecumenical Witness for Peace," in *Cambridge Companion to Dietrich Bonhoeffer*, 154-72.
24 Ibid., 160.

primary problem when it comes to bridging identity and diversity. Since Bonhoeffer we have had untold numbers of important figures who have written interfaith and ecumenical theologies—Diana Eck, Abraham Joshua Heschel, Martin Luther King Jr., Fazlur Rahman, Farid Esack, Paul Knitter, Hans Kung, Catherine Cornille, and Jonathan Sacks, to name just a few. The problem is moving this theology from seminar rooms at Harvard Divinity School and Union Theological Seminary to articulacy amongst a critical mass of a rising generation. And that is where your institutions come in.

High Impact Interfaith Practices

A religiously affiliated college is the rare institution with the natural resources to cultivate a strong, benevolent faith, to bridge identity and diversity, to help a critical mass of young people develop articulacy in a theology of interfaith cooperation. Unlike a congregation or most other church bodies, you have religious diversity in interaction. Unlike a public institution, you have a clear and strong faith heritage. Unlike the vast majority of our society, you neither infantilize young people nor treat them primarily as purchasers of your products. Instead, you ask them to inquire into their vocations and empower them to be leaders. Unique amongst all institutions, you have an intense residential community, exceptional intellectual and pastoral resources, and an ethos that prizes respect for identity, relationships between different communities, and a commitment to the common good. You are both a laboratory for interesting new ideas and a launching pad for the nation's future leaders.

So how should you take advantage of your unique environments when relativism and fundamentalism seem woven into the dynamics of the age? I think the answer is to name the challenge and face it head on, to recognize that if you are not proactive about becoming an ecology that nurtures articulacy about religious identity bridging to religious diversity, you forfeit your campus community to the overriding forces of our times.

I remember trying to find language that expressed this urgency at a lunch meeting with President Richard Torgerson of Luther College about five years ago. Luther College had chosen my book, *Acts of Faith*, as its common read, and had invited me to give the first-year convocation. I was fumbling around for words when Rick stopped me and said, "Luther recently put into its strategic plan that no student should be able to graduate from our college without wrestling with how their actions will impact the environment. It is one of the principles we have built our curriculum and co-curricular activities around. It seems to me like you are saying that interfaith cooperation ought to be at that level of significance for campuses?"

"That's exactly what I am saying," I responded.

So how does a campus do this work? Interfaith Youth Core (IFYC) will soon be putting out a list of high impact interfaith practices for campuses.[25] Let me highlight a handful right now.

Mission

The first high impact practice is to connect interfaith cooperation to the mission and values of your college and to state this clearly in the strategic documents that guide your campus. Over the past two years, we have partnered with Concordia College in this endeavor, and senior campus officials have recently put together this statement: "Concordia College practices interfaith cooperation because of its Lutheran dedication to prepare thoughtful and informed global citizens who foster wholeness and hope, cultivate peace through understanding, and serve the world together."[26] There is a high-level conversation happening at Concordia about how that statement should be connected to the mission statement of the college.

Ecology

The second high impact practice is to not see your interfaith efforts as a single program, but as integrated into your entire campus ecology. At IFYC, we think there are three parts to this:

Integrate the curricular and co-curricular. One of the advantages of colleges like yours is the barriers between your academic departments and your student affairs programs are relatively low. As interfaith leadership is about scholarly study, vocational discernment, and effective application, campus units that primarily encourage reading and writing (academic departments) and campus units that specialize in personal reflection and applied skill-building (frequently units in

25 See Eboo Patel, Katie Bringman Baxter, and Noah Silverman, "Leadership Practices for Interfaith Excellence in Higher Education," *Liberal Education* 101.1 (2015), https://www.aacu.org/liberaleducation/2015/winter-spring/patel. See also, Eboo Patel, *Interfaith Leadership: A Primer* (Boston: Beacon Press, 2016).

26 "2014 Annual Report to ELCA Synods and Congregations," Concordia College, Moorhead, Minnesota, http://www.swmnelca.org/PDF/2014%20assembly/2014concordia_college.pdf

student affairs like service-learning, university ministry, and diversity programming) should be working closely together.

Create a "horizontal." All of your students should get some robust touch with religious diversity issues (preferably in an integrated fashion, as noted above). Religious identity/diversity themes should be woven into initiatives that touch the majority of your students, such as freshman orientation, large service-learning days, and convocations. Furthermore, texts and modules on interfaith cooperation should be integrated into required general education courses. Other high priority issues like sustainability, racial diversity, and global learning have integrated horizontals that ensure most students substantively engage with them. So should interfaith issues.

Create a "vertical." For students who are inspired by their touch with interfaith issues in the horizontal, there ought to be integrated curricular/co-curricular ladders that they can climb to increase their expertise. These verticals can take the form of a course sequence where students can get a minor or a certificate in interfaith studies or leadership, or a student group that is large and well-organized enough for students to take leadership in it, to serve as officers, and to organize activities for the broader campus. One concrete benefit of having this ladder is that students in the vertical lead activities in the horizontal.

Staff and Faculty Conversations

Interfaith Youth Core did a consultation with DePaul University and in one of the interviews a staff member commented: "We love religious diversity at DePaul even though we are Catholic." When I mentioned that to the president, Father Holtschneider, he said, "When we are done with our next five year plan, every faculty and staff person will be able to say, 'We love religious diversity at DePaul *because* we are Catholic,' and will be able to tell you specific Vincentian reasons for why that is the case." In order for that to happen, the subject of interfaith engagement has to become central to your faculty and staff agenda. This means things like:

Making it the topic of your faculty convocations;

Bringing in speakers who would draw a faculty and staff crowd to their talks;

Sending faculty and staff to relevant conferences; and

Encouraging and incentivizing your faculty and staff to develop courses and programs in this area.

Measuring

One of the most important developments in the field of interfaith cooperation is the move from "let's do an interfaith something" to "let's do an interfaith something that's effective." The field is long overdue for an effectiveness discourse, and this means evaluation. Measurement should not feel suffocating and does not have to be entirely quantitative. It does require you to state your goals clearly up front, and to devise evaluations that answer two key questions: How well are our programs achieving our goals? How should we improve these programs to more effectively achieve our goals in the future? In other words, the great gift of evaluation is to encourage your strategy team to set clear goals, to devise programs that you believe will meet those goals, and to create a mechanism for continuous reflection and improvement.

Conclusion: Places Where the Light Falls

I once had a conversation with Martin Marty about Bonhoeffer and Lutheran resources for a theology of interfaith cooperation. What he said to me then applies profoundly to Lutheran colleges and universities. He spoke of Bonhoeffer and the Confessing Church and the seminary at Finkenwalde as archetypes. He pointed out: "We live by examples, and these examples define. They are like a clearing in the wood; it is where the light falls, it is where cultivation occurs."

At a time when it feels like the only faith options are relativism and fundamentalism, I think ELCA higher education institutions are examples—places that define, places where the light falls. I think this is precisely the purpose of your Lutheran colleges. As I was leaving Marty's home, he quoted Goethe to me on the task of reaching into the resources of one's tradition to advance an ethic of interfaith cooperation. I will leave you with the line he left me with:"What you have as heritage, take now as task. For thus you will make it your own."

Questions for Discussion

1. Toward which of the two predominant religious paths—relativism or fundamentalism—do students on your campus gravitate? How do they come to learn about third options or middle positions?

2. Patel suggests that Lutheran colleges and universities have "an especially good shot" at being places that "do both identity and diversity." Do you agree? What particular gifts do we bring?

3. What is the status of interfaith cooperation on your campus? Which high-impact practices—mission, ecology, staff and faculty conversations, and/or assessment—does your school most need to cultivate?

4. Is your institution able to say, "We love religious diversity here *because* we are a Lutheran school"? What would enable you to make or back up that claim?

CHAPTER 9

LEARNING TO BLOOM WHERE YOU'RE PLANTED
Adapting Vocation to the Specifics of Place

MARY J. HENOLD
Roanoke College, Salem, Virginia

In the winter of 2008 I experienced something I never expected: a vocation crisis.[1] I'm one of those folks who has everything planned out long-term. I knew I wanted to be a history professor from my first days of college. After a lifetime in the Catholic ghetto in Detroit, I knew where I would teach too: a Jesuit school—not too conservative, relatively close to my family. I allowed for the fact that I couldn't choose the exact spot; I did have a Ph.D. in the humanities after all. But there are twenty-eight Jesuit colleges and universities in the United States. Surely I would land at one of them.

But in the winter of 2008, two years out from my time as a Lilly Fellow at Valparaiso University, I wasn't at a Jesuit school, or even a Catholic school. I was at Roanoke College, a nominally Lutheran, small liberal arts college in Southwest Virginia. And I had just realized that I had not been invited to a campus interview for my dream job. I was devastated. At that point, I didn't know how I could make my vocation work in this place that seemed so unsuited to it.

Before I go any further, I want to interject here that my job is a great one by any standard. Roanoke College is vibrant, and I have great freedom in what I teach and when. It is also located in one of the most beautiful regions of the country. This isn't a cry for help; thankfully, my vocation crisis ended well. This is, instead, a story about how one lowly Christian teacher/scholar, who thought she knew everything

---

1   This essay originated as a talk given at the 2010 Lilly Postdoctoral Fellows reunion conference at Valparaiso University. Henold was a Lilly Fellow from 2003 to 2005.

there was to know about her vocation, came to realize that she didn't know jack. At the center of that story is the concept of "place."

My story starts in the winter of 2008 with my teaching. Serendipitously, at the same time as my vocation crisis, I was undertaking two new teaching projects that were separate, but related. The first was a senior research seminar with the theme, "City and Suburb." In it we traced the history of urban and suburban spaces in America, particularly nineteenth- and twentieth-century suburbanization and urban decline. At the same time, I was prepping a three-week May term course called "History Detectives," in which we explored the history of one of Roanoke's historic neighborhoods by researching the histories of individual houses and the people who had lived in them. Now, neither of these subjects are what I studied in graduate school, but they are intriguing to me, so I started to read. To teach these classes I needed to dip my toe into (what I would come to learn was) a vast literature in the fields of cultural geography, spatial history, and the history of landscape, among others. As I read and planned and taught, I saw connections between my vocation issues and this new way of looking at my discipline and, indeed, the space around me.

In my seminar we started with two very basic concepts. The first can be found in a quotation from the book, *Key Thinkers on Space and Place*: "Culture not only takes place, but makes place."[2] This quotation, from three cultural geographers, argues that human culture not only "takes place," that is, exists in time, but "makes place," that is, imprints meaning on the spaces it encounters. Our actions define what a place is, with the caveat that such definitions are relative, ever changing, and heavily influenced by the exercise of power.

The first concept, then, invites students to analyze places to reveal specific cultures and how they change over time. But the second concept offers a different challenge to students. Undoubtedly, people make places by giving meaning to the spaces they encounter and live in, but the reverse is also true: Places make us. The character of a space, the choices we make to shape a space, the meanings we impose upon spaces—ultimately, these shape our own behavior. A classic example of this is the attached garage. Created for convenience sake, the attached garage has certainly kept many a suburban commuter dry and comfortable, but that architectural choice also has contributed to a de-

---

2   Phil Hubbard, Rob Kitchin, and Gill Valentine, eds., *Key Thinkers on Space and Place* (Los Angeles: Sage Publications, 2004), 7.

cline in community. Who knew that the twenty steps from your car to your front door could be so crucial to maintaining connections with your neighbors? So one of the concepts my students and I wrestled with was the fact that constructions of place can affect behavior.

So, what does this second concept have to do with vocation? This is going to be a bit circuitous, but bear with me. When I was a Lilly Fellow at Valparaiso University, my cohort had many, many conversations about the nature of vocation. These discussions, some formal, many informal, helped me refine my own specific vocation as a teacher/scholar who hoped to teach in a Catholic institution. By necessity, these conversations were completely divorced from the concept of place. We didn't know where we were going to end up (if we were going to end up anywhere). So I did an awful lot of supposing. Not inclined to think about worse case scenarios, as this would just send me over the edge, I built up in my mind a complete picture of my vocation in a Catholic school. That was what I felt called to, and, in the absence of further information, that was what I was going to go with.

When I look back on it, I am reminded of an image described by landscape historian John Brinckerhoff Jackson in his essay, "A Sense of Place, A Sense of Time." He talks about recent efforts to reclaim downtowns and recreate a sense of place. But, he says, imagine you're in one of these downtowns late at night, and you are in your car sitting at a red light: "The dominant feature of the scene is not the cluster of magnificent forms and spaces; it is the long and empty view of evenly spaced, periodically changing red and green traffic lights. . . . The sameness of the American landscape overwhelms and liberates you from any sense of place."[3] Jackson was commenting on the generic nature of our grid system, but for me the image becomes a metaphor. The Lilly Fellows program was my red light, another stop—a welcome one, certainly—on the long open road to my vocation.

Being a Lilly post-doc fellow liberated me from the specificity of place and the complications it brings, at least temporarily. I saw in front of me a series of pauses; maybe I wouldn't get that perfect job right away, but I would get there eventually. I saw no places on the road because I didn't think they could change what I knew God wanted me to do. Wherever I landed was going to be the right place for me or it wasn't, and if that was the case, I would expect to leave it. Grant-

---

3   John Brinckerhoff Jackson, *A Sense of Place, A Sense of Time* (New Haven: Yale University Press, 1994), 152.

ed, this isn't what I *said out loud*. You can't say that out loud and get a job. What I said was: "I'll bloom where I'm planted." And I said this often, to others and to myself. But I know now that I didn't really mean it. I was sure that God was going to get me to the right place (aka the place I wanted) eventually.

The problem with this approach was made clear to me in a rather dramatic fashion when I sought some help to deal with my vocation crisis that winter. I'll have you know, it's a measure of the impact that the Lilly Fellows program had on me that I went to the college's Lutheran chaplain for help. Understand that we had never even had a long conversation, certainly not a personal one. He was coming at this having no preconceptions based on a shared history. And so I sat in his office with a box of tissues and poured forth my tale of woe. I don't remember exactly what I said, but I'm sure it went something like, "But I'm not supposed to be here! I'm supposed to be at a *Catholic* school." When I was finished he let the silence fall for a second, and then he said, "So let me get this right—you've been assuming all this time that you're going to be called home to work in the mothership." An odd metaphor, but I nodded. "But" he said, "Mary, what if you're not called to be in the mothership at all. What if you're called to be a missionary?"

I think my jaw actually dropped open. This was an insight that broke my world wide open, mainly because it hit me in the middle of my enormous blind spot about place. I knew what it meant to have a vocation in the Catholic mothership; I'd talked about that endlessly at Valparaiso. But what did it mean to be a missionary? Neither he nor I viewed it in the sense of a call to proselytize. Rather, he was inviting me to consider that God might not be calling me to do my work in a place that is familiar and comfortable, chock full of people like myself. God might be inviting me to come to my work as a stranger in a strange land—alive to a new landscape and the possibilities that come with it; forced to look for opportunities to live out my vocation and start something new, rather than settle into my expected path; invited to listen and learn from this new place and the people in it; and most important of all, *allowing this place to change me.*

I always presumed that my vocation would *fulfill* me—and those are the terms in which I thought about it—but it was an entirely new, and very risky, proposition to think that the places our vocations take us will *change us* as we grow into them, particularly if, at first glance, your new place doesn't seem to fit you. The notion that the place you land in could change your vocation may seem obvious, but it wasn't to me. I had rooted my vocation in the weakest kind of faith, based on a foundation of certainty. I knew what God wanted for me. But what I really needed as a foundation for my vocation was meditation on God's *mystery*. I wish I had been praying to welcome the unknown and unknowable, the possibility of being turned into someone I could not yet understand, by God's grace.

This was the starting point for the reassessment of my vocation. With the help of the chaplain, I felt I was ready to start adapting to Roanoke as the place where my vocation would be rooted. But I was rather at sea about how to adapt a vocation to a specific place. I'm sure there's a book somewhere that could have helped me with it, but at the time I was on my own. What do you do when you find yourself a stranger in a strange land, vocationally speaking, *and you realize that you're not going anywhere*? For the remainder of the essay I'm going to answer this question by sharing from my own experience. The easiest way to do this is to talk about the problems I faced and continue to face, and how I've worked to address each one through the process of adapting my vocation to the specifics of place.

Problem #1: The tools I need to fulfill my vocation as a Catholic teacher/scholar are not here.

Here's how I would have described my imagined vocation while I was at Valpo: I would work in a Catholic university where I'd be immersed in Catholic tradition, culture, and politics. Ever present, these would continually inform my teaching and research. The majority of my students would probably be Catholic, so we would be working from a base of shared experience. My teaching would be coming out of my abiding love of my church mixed with my deep anger and frustration with it. My goal would be to teach young Catholics, particularly Catholic women, to consider their faith and community honestly and without fear, facing what needs to be faced in pursuit of justice, while embracing what is life-giving about their faith.

In my first few years in Roanoke, one of the biggest challenges I faced was that I felt almost completely cut off from Catholic culture, or at least Catholic culture as I knew it.   I live and work in Southern Baptist country, in a Lutheran school. While religious faith certainly is present at the college, it's not a prominent aspect of campus life. Moreover, there are only four Catholic parishes in the Roanoke Valley. I have always lived in the North, where there were dozens of parishes from which to choose, allowing for Catholics to sort themselves out by politics. The four parish options in town appeared to me to range from moderately conservative to very conservative indeed. I tried not to panic.

My first strategy was to remind myself that I don't need to be in a Catholic place to pursue my vocation. After all, I was brought to Roanoke College to teach American history, which was my first love as an academic. I'm not teaching explicitly about faith most of the time, but my goals are still similar. I'm teaching young people to look more closely at their expectations and assumptions, to question what they know, to observe how people have treated each other in the past and how my students relate to others in the world now. I still teach about justice and injustice. I try to help them understand what is broken in our world and aspire to repair it, to find what is beautiful in human history and celebrate it. Spending more time thinking about what's at the center of my vocation helped.

But I still felt a desire to teach and talk about Catholicism with Catholic students. Here the solution was opening my eyes and paying attention to what was actually on my campus instead of moping. One of the first things the chaplain asked was whether I had tried to reach out to the Catholic students on campus. Although they weren't very active, Catholic students made up 19 percent of the student body at that time and represented the largest denomination on campus. Rather embarrassed, I admitted that I hadn't. In the following year, I happened to spend a day on Catholic women in a women's history class; three students seemed particularly interested. I emailed the students, all Catholic as it turned out, and asked if they'd want to meet regularly outside of class to do readings on the history of Catholic women. That tentative email led to one of the most fulfilling teaching experiences of my career thus far. I met with these three women every two weeks for three years, watching them mature, change, and grow in faith. What started as something academic morphed through their initiative into what they needed—a faith-sharing group where they could talk with me and each other about their lives and faith in the context of their education. They too were strangers in a strange land, and they needed me. I take the lesson they taught me as a gift: If I am open to the possibilities that Providence might put in my way, I will have chances to live out my vocation as a Catholic teacher/scholar at a Lutheran institution.

But this still left the question of the lack of a larger Catholic community for my family outside of the college. As it turned out, I had dismissed the Roanoke Valley's Catholic community too quickly. We spent seven years at a parish that had much to teach us about diversity and service. We then discovered that a second parish, one that we rejected as untenable after a single visit when we first arrived, was actually a pretty good fit for our family. Now that we have settled in, I've come to appreciate how the limited number of parishes forces Catholics of different mindsets to worship together. Less isolated and insular, we are called to make peace and truly enact Christian community. What at first seemed frightening, a problem of scarcity, has turned out to be a blessing.

Finally, I realized that I needed to have a lifeline to Christian teacher/scholars in the larger academic community. I am a representative to the Lilly Fellows National Network, and attending the annual conferences rejuvenates me. I also chose to get back on social media after a lengthy absence, mainly so that I could stay connected with other Catholic teacher/scholars around the country who share my interests and my vocation. When I lose focus, forgetting at times that I have my own unique call to fulfill in this place, these connections remind me who I am and what I'm about.

Problem #2: This place is Lutheran. I'm not Lutheran.

When you accept a Lilly Fellows post-doc, you are committing to being trained in a very particular skill set. Our training prepares us to go into all sorts of institutions of higher learning and be a bit of a nudge. We are to listen, ask questions, and most important, facilitate conversations. Someone in the faculty needs to keep an eye on the ball, that is, to ask *what is this institution actually doing?* Is it fulfilling its promises? Is it following its mission? Is it fostering good will and charity in its faculty, students, and staff? Is it living up to its best principles? How can we help faculty, students, and staff realize this mission better?

One of the challenges I faced, which was a factor in my vocation crisis, was that I did not know how to be that presence as a Catholic, not only at a Lutheran institution, but also at one that did not have a strong religious identity. I knew that the then president and dean saw my background as a Lilly Fellow as an asset, but that others on campus were wary of any effort they might construe as trying to make the campus "more Lutheran." This all seemed perplexing to me since I was the last person with the ability to make any campus more Lutheran; I knew next to nothing about Lutheranism. One of the great ironies of my last year at Valparaiso was that my dear friend in the program, a Lutheran theologian, landed at a Jesuit school, and I, with a Jesuit education and a specialty in Catholic history, ended up at a Lutheran school. (Where is the plan here, God?) I didn't see how I could be the kind of person that Roanoke College needed; the situation was too complicated and fraught. I didn't know how to proceed, and leaving to go to the mothership seemed much easier.

Once again, though, the new space—this Lutheran space—was going to help me adapt. Once I knew I was going to stay, I tried to pull together what I knew about being Lutheran, mainly from observing the Lutheran academics who have mentored me. It is at this point that I will disclaim any pretense of expertise in Lutheran theology. I do this on purpose, not only because I don't want to be taken to task later for anything I say, but also because I want to demonstrate that lack of knowledge cannot be a barrier to engaging in conversations about Lutheran academic communities if you find yourself in one, nor would any Lutheran I know want it to be.

In my time in Lutheran institutions I have picked up two ideas that helped me, as a Catholic, contribute to my new community. The first is about vocation. In my second and final year at Valparaiso University, I was teaching a seminar called "1970s America" in Christ College, the honors college. As is typical, on the first day I asked the students to tell me why they were in the class. The first student, a senior, said in her most jaded tone, "It was the only one without 'vocation' in the title." The whole room erupted in laughter, myself included. In Catholic culture, the word is mainly associated with the call to vowed religious life. Laypeople also have vocations, of course, but this parlance reinforces the idea that a vocation is a "higher calling," reserved for special individuals. No such restrictions could be seen at Valparaiso, where an awareness of vocation was taught not only to the Lilly Fellows, but across many levels, particularly in Christ College. All were encouraged to tease out their callings, to find the work to which they were best suited and which met the needs of the world. And while my student revealed some communal eye-rolling on the topic after four years of intense exposure, no doubt the students were deeply affected by the challenge to view their futures in the light of God's unique call. I may not have understood the intricacies of Lutheran theology, but helping others think more deeply about their vocations was a project I could support enthusiastically.

The second idea is certainly not limited to Lutheranism, but it is how I have seen the faith lived in practice as I have taken up residence in Lutheran spaces. Time and again I have been extended invitations to engage in ecumenical dialogue and form community. The Lilly Fellows Network itself was an invitation, conceived by a Lutheran over twenty-five years ago, for people of different faiths to gather in conversation and through those conversations, strengthen their own missions. I was invited, as an ecumenically-ignorant Ph.D., to enter such a conversation for two years, and it transformed me. Another Lutheran, my mentor at Valpo, invited me to teach my research on Catholics in this Lutheran setting; he himself is a Lutheran who spent his whole career in the field of Catholic studies. He showed me how to exist in multiple worlds and find bridges between them. When I had my crisis, it was Roanoke's chaplain who reminded me that my call might be to connect with people unlike myself. He was calling me to let the mothership go, and again step into ecumenical dialogue.

I realized that my call in this place was to start a Mentoring for Mission program, a program to mentor new faculty and assist other faculty members to engage with the college's mission. My status as a "stranger" was an asset in this project, not a liability. As a Catholic, I could lead discussions about the college's Lutheran heritage as an outsider, a non-threatening way to invite the other, almost entirely non-Lutheran faculty, to consider how they might connect with this tradition. We designed the program as a series of conversations, of which Lutheranism was only one component. Together we discuss questions fundamental to our work: What does it mean to educate the whole person? How can we live out our vocations as teacher/scholars? How can we forward questions of vocation for our students? Leading this program has been a way to promote meaningful conversation about work, community, and the future of our institution. And I thank the participants at the end of every year with these words: "In taking the time to talk about your own vocations, you are helping me fulfill my own."

Problem 3: I'm a stranger here, and I do not yet love this place.

I was so busy in my first three years, between working for tenure and having my first child, that I didn't have a lot of energy to explore. Consequently, I felt disconnected in Roanoke and still, literally, out of place. The solution crept up on me, and, surprisingly, it originated with my teaching. I fell in love with the history of my community, and, through that, the place became my own. It was really teaching my neighborhood history class that did it. I took students into my own neighborhood to discover its history. I didn't actually know that history myself beyond the basic outlines, so it was a journey of discovery for all of us. As my students worked in the archives, uncovering the history of the houses they'd chosen and each inhabitant, I was doing the same for my own 1925 home. I learned the story of Mae, a single teacher who had the house built, her elderly mother, and later her husband the landscaper. I learned also of the brother who moved in during the 1930s after his wife died, bringing his young daughter with him. (And I kept looking around at my three-bedroom house wondering where they all slept!) I learned all this from the census, deed cards, and city directories. Then I happened to chat about this one day with my elderly next door neighbor. "Oh, sure," she said. "I knew Mae." And then she proceeded to tell me everything I had already learned and then some. "Your peonies over there, Mae planted those. And her husband put in your giant magnolia. And the brother, Edison, he built the back stairs" (which actually explained a lot). By teaching the history of the place, I began to claim it. My love of history made this space a place in which I could do meaningful work.

Roanoke College is actually ideally suited for this to happen. It is more conscious of its history than any campus I've ever seen. Students and new faculty are given a very funny lecture and tour focusing on the college's history in orientation. All sorts of rituals exist around certain monuments on the quad, which are passed from student to student. Students and faculty actually know the words to the alma mater and sing it. This strong sense of history was one of the things that drew me to the college in the first place. I'm not suggesting that history will be the means to accomplish this for everyone. I merely suggest finding what it is that binds you to a community that might be made stronger through the act of teaching.

Finally, Problem #4: "It's only temporary."

You may think that this problem solved itself; after all, I wasn't going anywhere. But while the reality of the situation now seemed clear, psychologically my husband and I just weren't there yet. When the dream job didn't materialize, my husband and I realized that our mindset had been pretty unhealthy. We'd been living in the future, refusing to put down roots in Roanoke because we wanted to leave, answering every question about the future with, "Well, *if* we're here two, or three, or five years from now . . ." It became a secret to conceal, our refusal to commit to the community in which we lived. We had also become wrapped up in our own little family, an easy thing to do with a newborn.

We sat down and talked, deciding that we would go on from this point assuming that Roanoke would be our permanent home. That was the solution. It cost a lot to do that, not just dreams of teaching in a Catholic school, but also dreams of moving back to Rochester where we met. But the payoff was worth it. My husband could now settle into *his* teaching job, at a Catholic grade school he really liked, with the knowledge that I wouldn't drag him away from it. Again. We began reaching out to our neighbors, even the ones who, on the surface, had little in common with us. We started planting perennials in our garden and fruit vines that can't be harvested for two or three years. The act of committing made all the difference.

Four major problems, four solutions derived from the unique place I inhabit, a vocation now very much in process. By allowing my vocation to change with the specificity of place, I believe I can say—with honesty now—that I learned to bloom where I was planted.

Questions for Discussion

1. How did you come to work at a Lutheran college or university? In what ways were you drawn to it—or not? In what ways are you growing into it—or not?

2. How might (re)connecting vocation with place help the vocational discernment of your students, or your own sense of being called?

3. Henold writes of coming to appreciate her vocation "as a stranger in a strange land." What "outsider," "different," or even "strange" perspectives do you bring to Lutheran higher education? What do these perspectives enable you to see or do regarding the mission of your school or the vocation of Lutheran higher education?

4. How does your own discipline or the particular courses that you teach inform the teaching of (or your understanding of) vocation?

CHAPTER 10

HOW CAN WE KEEP FROM SINGING?

A Mennonite Responds to Lutheran Understandings of Vocation

SHIRLEY HERSHEY SHOWALTER
Goshen College, Goshen, Indiana

I keep running into Lutherans.[1] As a Mennonite professor at Goshen College in Indiana, I spent a formative year (1993-94) as senior fellow in the Lilly Fellows Program in Humanities and the Arts (LFP) at Valparaiso University. Soon thereafter I was called to become president of Goshen College where I served for eight years. The conversations with Lutherans (and others within a Lutheran setting) about vocation not only influenced my presidency, but have also stayed with me. Even though I left the academy to enter the foundation world, my vocation didn't change. I'm a learner first of all, and when I've learned something, even a little bit of something, my first impulse is to teach.

So it's not surprising that my year at Valparaiso led me to numerous conferences on vocation in higher education. Goshen College participated, along with many other church-related institutions, in the Theological Exploration of Vocation project sponsored by the Lilly Endowment, Inc. More recently I participated in a study and writing project resulting in the forthcoming book: *Vocation Across the Academy: A New Vocabulary in Higher Education.*[2]

My mentor in the 1993-94 LFP at Valparaiso University was Mark Schwehn, and our paths continue to cross. Mark spent last year with

---

1   This essay is a substantial revision of "The Literature of Spiritual Reflection and Social Action," *Intersections* 10 (Fall 2000): 21-26.
2   David S. Cunningham, ed., *Vocation Across the Academy: A New Vocabulary for Higher Education* (Oxford: Oxford University Press, 2017).

his wife Dorothy Bass at the Collegeville Institute. I will follow them to the same location this fall (2016). My topic? Jubilación: Vocation in the Third Act of Life. I can't seem to disconnect either from the topic of vocation or from the Lutherans who have influenced me!

Mennonites and Lutherans Traveling (and Singing) Together

Mennonites and Lutherans have traveled a long distance since the sixteenth century. Never have we had more cordial relationships than now. Past Lutheran persecution of Mennonites has been forgiven, movingly and publicly, at our global gatherings. Having exchanged symbols of reconciliation, we are free now to examine our differences and to recognize them for what they are: different songs in the same hymnal.[3]

Garrison Keillor would agree. He has famously described Lutherans in a way Mennonites understand:

> I have made fun of Lutherans for years—who wouldn't if you lived in Minnesota? But I have also sung with Lutherans and that is one of the main joys of life, along with hot baths and fresh sweet corn.
>
> We make fun of Lutherans for their blandness, their excessive calm, their fear of giving offense, their lack of speed, and also their secret fondness for macaroni and cheese. But nobody sings like they do.
>
> If you ask an audience in New York City, a relatively "Lutheranless" place, to sing along on the chorus of "Michael, Row the Boat Ashore," they will look daggers at you as if you had asked them to strip to their underwear. But if you do this among Lutherans they'll smile and row that boat ashore and up on the beach! And down the road!
>
> Lutherans are bred from childhood to sing in four-part harmony. It's a talent that comes from sitting on the lap of someone singing alto or tenor or bass and hearing the harmonic intervals by putting your little head against that person's rib cage. It's natural for Lutherans to sing in harmony. We're too modest to be soloists, too worldly to sing in unison. And when you are singing in the key of C and

3   See report of the 2010 study of the Lutheran-Mennonite International Study Commission, http://download.elca.org/ELCA%20Resource%20Repository/Healing_Memories_Reconciling_In_Christ.pdf.

you slide into the A7th and D7th chords, all two hundred of you, it's an emotionally fulfilling moment. . . .

I do believe this: People who love to sing in harmony are the sort of people you could call up when you're in deep distress. If you're dying, they will comfort you. If you're lonely, they'll talk to you. If you're hungry, they'll give you tuna salad![4]

Any Mennonite reading those words feels them deep in the bones, connecting harmony in music to peace in body and spirit. Not surprisingly, Garrison Keillor discovered Mennonites also. He visited Goshen College three times and broadcast one of his last Prairie Home Companion shows from there, posting these words on his blog after his second visit: "I think maybe I did the best show of my life Tuesday night and all thanks to the audience, a thousand Mennonites and their neighbors in a small town in Indiana."[5]

During the 1993-1994 academic year I spent among Lutherans at Valparaiso University, I was often amused to discover denominational similarities. When Lutherans started contrasting the Norwegians to the Germans, I knew exactly how to play the game, since Mennonites divide into two large ethnic groups also: the Swiss-German and the Dutch-Russian. It was a little disconcerting, however, to discover that some of the traits I thought were strictly Mennonite turned out to be shared with German Lutherans!

One specific memory from that memorable year with the Lutherans at Valparaiso: As senior fellow, I planned our Monday afternoon colloquium meetings. I asked Mary K. Oyer, emerita professor of music at two Mennonite institutions, to explain the role of music in Mennonite life. She nodded in respect to great Lutheran chorales and to the great Bach tradition, and then walked us through recordings of Amish people singing from the *Ausbund,* the collection of dirge-like hymns dating from the sixteenth century. In each song one could hear suffering and survival, surrender to God's will. She then described her transformation as a classically-trained musician who went to Africa and discovered entirely different rhythms, styles, instruments, and ways to worship there. That personal transformation then became a

---

4   Garrison Keillor, "Singing with the Lutherans," https://sites.google.com/site/sr-wsite/Home/lutheran-music.
5   "A Look Back at Garrison Keillor's Visits to Goshen College," https://www.goshen.edu/news/2016/06/30/garrison-keillor-goshen-college.

denominational one as she selected hymns in the *Mennonite Hymnal*, not only from Bach or Martin Luther or Menno Simons but also from the Cheyenne and other Native American nations, Japan, and many countries in Africa. Whereas Mary's vocation in her early years of teaching could be described as introducing untutored farm kids to the great canon of the fine arts, her later years became much more inclusive, experimental, and global, like the Mennonite Church itself. In many ways, Lutheran history and hymnody follow a similar path.

We live in an ecumenical era in which old religious wounds are being healed and many commonalities of faith are being discovered. Yet each tradition also struggles to name its own history and heritage. It may be instructive to look backward as we seek faithful ways forward. Walter Sundberg recognized that Lutheran identity from the beginning placed itself in a position of being both not-Catholic and not-radical (Anabaptist). In his essay, "What does it mean to be Lutheran?" he says:

> In the earliest years of the Reformation, Luther found himself in conflict not only with Rome but also with "radical reformers" who taught that the true community of faith is made up of believers who experience personal conversion, These reformers taught a wide variety of doctrines, the effect of which was to exhort Christians to make a self-conscious commitment to Christ that expresses itself in outward behavior. Some insisted that baptism is for adults, not infants, because only an adult can make a responsible decision for Christ. . . . Some stressed that moral discipline is not only the fruit of faith, but the necessary proof that faith is genuine. Luther argued that the general effect of these teachings is to bind faith to certain works. These works become the "angels" of authority.[6]

Today's Mennonites were one group of the radical reformers in this description. Our ancestors dared to baptize each other as adults and thereby challenged the authority of both church and state. We expected that conversion would result in a life of obedience to the cross, even unto death. For thousands of Anabaptists who fled Catholics and Calvinists and Lutherans alike, this sense of radical commitment led to

---

6   Walter Sundberg, "What Does It Mean to Be Lutheran?" in *Called to Serve: St. Olaf and the Vocation of a Church College*, ed. Pamela Schwandt, L. DeAne Lagerquist, and Gary De Krey (Northfield, Minnesota: St. Olaf College, 1999), 6.

martyrdom, a fact that has shaped our community as much as or more than our theology has.

If we were sixteenth-century disputants today, heresy hunters, we would each be advocating for one horn of a dilemma. To vastly oversimplify, let us call these the horn of grace and the horn of discipleship. Mennonites have maintained that discipleship is different from "works righteousness" and have their own terms of derision for the opposite problem: "cheap grace." The signs of conversion most highly valued historically have been pacifism, service, and community—all ways of submission of the individual to the will of the church and the welfare of others.

Yet the Mennonite Church, like the ELCA, is undergoing great change. You and your Catholic brothers and sisters have signed the 1999 Augsburg Accord after three decades of ecumenical dialogue, indicating that the reciprocal condemnations both groups made of the other in the sixteenth century no longer apply to the crucial doctrine of justification. Similarly, Lutherans and Mennonites have examined their conflicts in the past and have reached unprecedented levels of trust and forgiveness.[7] Remaining issues of difference over baptism and the role of civil authority hold little of the charge they had in the sixteenth century.

The Vocation of Mennonite Higher Education

If we have been growing closer over time, do we have anything to learn from each other in higher education? In particular, as Mennonites examine the idea of vocation in their institutional settings, what can they contribute to Lutheran and other Christian traditions?

Keith Graber Miller, Goshen College professor of Bible, religion, and philosophy, has written most extensively on this subject, especially in his book, *Living Faith: Embracing God's Callings*.[8] He traces three historical influences on Anabaptist ideas of vocation: (1) in Europe governing authorities prohibited Anabaptists from entering some crafts and professions, seeking to limit their influence; (2) Anabaptists themselves excluded work that aligned with the state's interest in using force; and (3) suspicion about the role of corrupt pastors and

---

7   See footnote 3 above. See also the moving reports of recent continuing connections such as this June 2016 meeting in Ft. Wayne, Indiana: https://themennonite.org/daily-news/lutherans-mennonites-celebrate-covenant-peace.

8   Keith Graber Miller, *Living Faith: Embracing God's Callings* (Telford, Pennsylvania: Cascadia Publishing House, 2012).

priests, combined with the martyrdom of their own early leaders, led to anti-clericalism.[9]

These three historical factors not only restricted the idea of vocation to a smaller space than Catholics or Lutherans or Calvinists, they also delayed the entry of Mennonites into higher education, even after they had escaped persecution in Europe by coming to America.

Long after fellow Christians had set up colleges in order to educate clergy and other professionals, Mennonites still largely followed the calling that had shielded them from persecution: agriculture. Only at the very end of the nineteenth century did Mennonites recognize the need for their own version of higher education. Under the influence of progressivism and revivalism, the Mennonite church began explorations into building colleges. One of the chief motivators behind this inquiry was fear of losing youth who were beginning to leave the farm. Oral tradition describes Goshen College in its early days as the place necessary to prevent Mennonites from going to the University of Chicago. But it was also an institution filled with hope that Mennonites might make a special contribution to education. Educational pioneer and Mennonite evangelist John S. Coffman's 1896 speech, "The Spirit of Progress," traces a line of radical Christian thought from the medieval Waldensians to the present day Mennonites and urges the next generation to extend this spirit into the future: "Had the [Mennonite] church . . . cultivated the spirit of learning which her people originally possessed we might be a people famed for learning; and our congregations might number thousands where now count only hundreds."[10]

Coffman's essay tracing a countervailing spirit throughout time was a method on which later leaders would also rely. Since Mennonites have a history of persecution and few creeds, we pass the torch from generation to generation largely through stories and songs and a few central images. We are a people of narrative.

For us, church history has been as influential as theology or even biblical studies in shaping our identity. In Mennonite colleges, the study of Anabaptist history and Mennonite history has ignited Mennonite intellectuals, lay members, and clergy with a sense of their identity and central questions ever since 1944 when Goshen Dean Harold S. Bender's "The Anabaptist Vision" appeared in *Church History*. But

---

9   Graber Miller, *Living Faith*, Kindle Location 226-46.
10 John S. Coffman, "The Spirit of Progress," 1896 speech, https://en.wikipedia.org/wiki/John_S._Coffman.

even more formative has been experience. Some of these experiences include being conscientious objectors to war, seeking to demonstrate commitment through international relief work, and going into cities to try to alleviate the pains of poverty. Today, poets and painters have expanded and sometimes challenged the historical identity project. Finding consensus among all these claims to faithful identity is elusive. Many Mennonites have come to embrace ambiguity and paradox, but we also have a history of schism, of trying to unite, and then of dividing again.

Within Mennonite higher education, however, there may be more unity now than in previous generations. The Mennonite model of both "calling" and " service" is rooted in a theology of suffering and humility, which is passed on most effectively through narrative, singing, and other experiential forms. At its best, it aspires to nothing less than the formation of a communal conduit for God's grace so that "healing and hope" in the form of peacemaking and service "flow through us to the world."[11]

One would expect that a church formed in this vision would create colleges with a distinctive understanding of vocation. And it has. A quick glance at the college catalogs of all five Mennonite colleges[12] illustrates the centrality of peace studies, global studies, and environmental studies in addition to excellent programs in pre-med, nursing, and education (the primary service vocations encouraged since the beginning of Mennonite higher education).

Keith Graber Miller highlights the centrality of discipleship in his examination of Mennonite scholarship and experience on the subject of vocation, settling upon three themes:

- Calling should be understood primarily and fundamentally as being a follower of Jesus Christ.
- A Christian theology of vocation in Mennonite perspective honors and blesses the ways followers of Jesus live out their faith in their occupational, professional, and worldly roles.
- A commitment to being Jesus' disciples ought to shape and transform occupational, business, and professional roles. In its

---

11 From the vision statement crafted in 1995 as two Mennonite denominations were merging and becoming Mennonite Church—USA., http://www.anabaptistwiki. org/mediawiki/index.php/Vision:_Healing_and_Hope_(Mennonite_Church,_General_Conference_Mennonite_Church_,_1995).

12 In order of their founding: Bethel College (Kansas), Goshen College (Indiana), Bluffton University (Ohio), Hesston College (Kansas), and Eastern Mennonite University (Virginia).

ideal form, the call to discipleship drives paid work more than the typical demands of the role or the occupation itself.[13]

How does this philosophy of vocation manifest in the classroom? Professors in Mennonite colleges and universities have no uniform answer to this question, but they should be able to articulate a personal response. Here are a few of my own experiences as illustration.

Stories In and Out of Class

In the mid-1990s, when I chaired the English department at Goshen College, I taught a course called the Senior Seminar. To prepare, I was searching for methods that would help our students use their literary analytical skills, reflect on their learning after four years, bond with each other and with Goshen College, and prepare to enter the world. Most liberal arts colleges have "capstone" courses like this one in the major. When bookended with an introduction to college course, the class provides a good way to frame a four-year experience of higher education. My favorite class period was always the last one in which my students and I shared short essays called, "My Personal Hermeneutic," in which we described the values by which we wanted to judge not only the literature we read but also our lives.[14]

I was called to the presidency in 1996. During the final on-campus interviews, I met with students who asked if I would continue to teach a class as president. I promised to do so and went on to teach a one-hour class every second year. I selected the course title,"The Literature of Spiritual Reflection and Social Action," an homage to the course Robert Coles designed at Harvard. The premise for this course was simple. I asked three people I respect for their learning and their Christian faith to tell me about the book that made the most significant change in their lives. Amazingly, each person could tell me immediately what the book was and what happened when he or she read it. To the books they picked, I added one of my own.

One of those books, and the first one we read, was *Man's Search for Meaning* by Viktor Frankl, a survivor of Auschwitz, Dachau, and two other concentration camps.[15] The sixteen students who elected to add

---

13 Graber Miller, *Living Faith*, Kindle location 1016-52.
14 Beginnings and endings within courses and within the college experience are wonderful opportunities to imprint and extract ideas about vocation. See my essay, "Called to Tell Our Stories: The Narrative Structure of Vocation," in *Vocation Across the Academy*.
15 Viktor Frankl, *Man's Search for Meaning* (Boston: Beacon Press, 1964).

this one-hour class on top of a regular load were all Mennonites. Two Chinese professors who were exchange scholars in our international service-learning program, the Study-Service Term (SST), audited the class. They were interested in Mennonite faith and offered points where they saw agreement or disagreement with Eastern thought. The person who chose the Viktor Frankl text, and who came to class to talk about its impact on his life, is a Methodist-turned-Presbyterian. He is also wheelchair-bound, having been diagnosed with multiple sclerosis a decade ago.

The idea for the course came as a flash of inspiration. People walked into my life at the right moment. The course did not so much develop along pre-planned lines as it unfolded as a series of relationships between texts, guests, professor, and students. I am still awed by what took place in those winter afternoon presentations and discussions.

I did not plan it consciously, but the class took up many of the themes of Anabaptism. Our first book was about suffering, terrible suffering, meaningless suffering. We never used the word "martyr," as we would have done if we had been studying about the 4000 Anabaptists who were drowned or torched in the sixteenth century instead of six million Jews exterminated in the twentieth century. But there were passages of this book that resonated with Mennonite students in special ways, often without their knowing why. Frankl described his purpose: "I had wanted simply to convey to the reader by way of a concrete example that life holds a potential meaning under any conditions even the most miserable ones."[16]

Throughout the book the author's tone is remarkable. Such humility. Such love of life itself. Frankl writes for the living, but he carries the memory of those who died. He begins his book with this statement, "We who have come back, by the aid of many lucky chances or miracles—whatever one may choose to call them—we know: The best of us did not return."[17] Mennonites of the sixteenth century might have said the same. In a chapter called, "The Case for Tragic Optimism," Frankl gives what could be called an apology for the course itself: "All we can do is study the lives of people who seem to have found their answers to the questions of what ultimately human life is about as against those

16 Ibid., 12.
17 Ibid., 19.

who have not."[18] In the end, is this not the meaning of vocation to all of us? Mennonites, Lutherans, Jews, Buddhists?

Mennonites, of course, study more than life stories. We also study chemistry, math, poetry, computer science, art, history, etc. Individual classes in a random sample of courses would probably not differ drastically from those of any other good liberal arts college. But we do have a special place in worship and in our academic life for the narrative—especially the life narrative or spiritual autobiography—and we encourage our faculty to tell their own and other's stories in order to testify.

I came to Goshen College expecting to stay three years in 1976. Instead, I stayed for twenty-eight. What drew me and held me were powerful stories. I can recall, from among scores of personal narratives I know well, the story of Carl Kreider, dean and president emeritus, who told the audience in a 1978 chapel service that he chose to borrow money in the 1930s in order to attend Goshen rather than take a full scholarship to Oberlin because "he did not want to break his parents' hearts." He went on to describe a journey of the highest intellectual and spiritual challenges in a way that was so beautiful, both in its use of simple yet eloquent language and through gentle tone of voice and body language, that I found myself saying, "There's something here they never heard of in graduate school. And I want to find it."

I found one deep source of vocational commitment when my husband Stuart and I co-led international service-learning experiences for students in Haiti and later in the Ivory Coast, West Africa. The program behind these narratives, the Study-Service Term (SST), was instituted almost fifty years ago as part of the general education package. Since then, thousands of students have spent thirteen or fourteen weeks in a "significantly different" (usually "third world") culture and have spent half of that time in a service assignment. Hundreds of faculty members have led units of students in this powerful form of experiential education. Almost everyone who participates tells others about ways his or her life was changed, sometimes dramatically.

Goshen, Indiana, is a town of more than 30,000 in the middle of America, and the students on campus, like most residential college students, are mostly white, mostly middle-class students.[19] Yet

18 Ibid., 146.
19 In the past decade the student body of Goshen College has become more diverse, especially with Hispanic students, now at 18 percent of the total.

if the dormitory walls were to give up their secrets, they would ring with stories of suffering and ecstasy that come from such places as Chengdu, Abidjan, Jakarta, Port au Prince, San Jose, Tegucigalpa, Jena, Santo Domingo, and hundreds of villages from all parts of the globe. Students make meaning out of these experiences. They watch the "president for life" of Haiti roar past beggars and poor peddlers lined up on both sides of the street, tossing small coins out the window of his Mercedes. They walk through beautiful-but-threatened rainforests, dig wells, worship in mud huts and then in spectacular cathedrals. Or they recognize the privilege Americans carry with their passports and the resentment privilege breeds.

The most touching stories, however, usually come from the families with whom students live and from the generosity of their hospitality. Students return back home with softer, more sensitive, hearts and stronger minds. On SST, hearts and minds are connected because the stories require the engagement of both. If a student reads about some cultural fact first and then sees a version of the practice or value described, there is either an "aha" moment or a moment of cognitive dissonance due to either the perception or the reality differing from the expected. The experience is more than clinical, as observation in a laboratory might be. It usually matters in some visceral way to a student. It may come at a moment of physical pain or exertion or homesickness or hunger. It may induce guilt, fear, a flood of tears, quiet musing, or a surge of adrenaline. Even people who want to be objective or detached cannot avoid the subjective on SST. But those who gravitate to the subjective are not safe either. If they are to make meaning, they must draw back far enough to see and seek information outside themselves.

The narratives of SST, though different in every case, often bear the mark of the redemption narratives of the Bible, whether or not our students (and even faculty) always recognize these marks. Read these words from student David Roth after returning to the Dominican Republic following four days in Haiti:

> I'm going to bed tonight tired, but a good tired that has come from thoroughly extending myself in every intellectual, emotional, and physical way during the Haiti trip. I am spent intellectually—I pushed so hard to soak up every word from every speaker, pushed my brain constantly for three days, examining/connecting/critiquing ideas presented to me. I spent myself in staying up late all the

nights to talk among wonderful people in fascinating subject areas. And I've never learned so much in three days, never. I think my life/views/opinions have been altered permanently in some areas, like thinking about poverty, and about dependence/service issues, and about entering a culture you have little knowledge of. And it feels good to be spent. The rush I got from all the input has given me so much to ponder in a long-term sense.[20]

Both the deliberate placement of the student in a disorienting situation and assigning him to learn via the reflective mode of journaling are part of the pedagogy and part of the deeply imbedded and too often unarticulated philosophical-theological structure of the SST curriculum. The form the student gravitates toward naturally is the narrative.

Robert Frost has said that poetry begins in wonder and ends in wisdom. In this case, the narrator begins in exhaustion and ends in a "rush" that he recognizes will be the stockpile of memory on which he will draw—"ponder" for the rest of his life. If I were writing comments on this entry, I would point out to David that he has written in these sentences his own psalm, with the usual structure of great exertion mixed with pain leading to deep satisfaction from what Anabaptists called *gelassenheit* or yielded-ness. He has therefore discovered something profound about his own name, "David." He is a singer and dancer before the Lord. He has also wrestled, like Jacob, for a blessing. Now he will ponder these things in his heart, like Mary.

Naming and Being Named

I do not consider such observations to be "mere piety"—a patina of religiosity over an experience not presented as religious by the student. Rather, I see this as an opportunity simultaneously to deepen learning (Has he ever thought about the structure of the Psalms?) and deepen faith (Does he recognize the biblical power of naming to his own calling in life? Is he aware that he has used biblical allusions?).

The author Madeleine L'Engle has a great following among Mennonites. She visited the Goshen campus three times. I have read her trilogy to both my children. Inside a dog-eared copy of her book,

---

20 David Roth journal, quoted with permission by Keith Graber Miller, "Crossing Cultures: Transforming Lives," *Vision: A Journal for Church and Theology* (Fall 2001), http://www.mennovision.org/Vol%202%20No%202/Graber-Miller_Crossing-cultures-transforming-lives.pdf.

A Wind in the Door, is her admonition, in her own handwriting, to my son Anthony: "Be a namer." Ever since L'Engle's first visit to Goshen, wherein she named the process of naming for me, and ever since I read the passage in that same book about Progo the angel, whose job it is to name all the stars, I have had a deep appreciation for the power of naming in education, especially church-related education.

What would happen to the world if every one of the students who left our campuses were truly and deeply named? L'Engle herself would say that war and violence would subside, and the world would reflect more clearly God's design in creation. The secret to building a redemptive community is to lavish love and attention on each of its members, as God has lavished love on us. What is a more profound way to do that than to help each member discover meaning in his or her name, either literally or metaphorically? We become peacemakers as we ourselves are filled with the peace that passes understanding. That peace comes from knowing who we are. From self-knowledge comes vocation.

When each member of a community comes to know the meaning of his or her own name, another kind of naming occurs—the naming of the powers and principalities that dominate the political and social worlds around us. Theologian Walter Wink is well-known for his treatment of powers and principalities in a secular age. Less well known is his idea that institutions, as well as individuals, may be able to have vocations. Noting that in the book of Revelation the New Testament churches of various cities were addressed not by the name of their cities, but by the names of the angels who defend the church from the powers and principalities, Wink asks us to consider the possibility of taking seriously what kind of angels our institutions might have or recover.[21]

In the case of Mennonite institutions, the answers might be peace, or discipleship, or the environment, or global studies. In Catholic parlance, these might be called our "founding charisms." Nothing brings out a charism better than the opportunity to explain it to another part of the Christian church, one with a different founding charism, one with whom disputations in the past have created wider views of God's mercy.

---

21 Vocation Conference for College Leadership, sponsored by Lilly Endowment, Inc. 1996. Held at the Fetzer Institute, http://www.resourcingchristianity.org/grant-project/vocation-conference-for-college-leadership.

One of my venerable predecessors in the presidency at Goshen College described so well the relationship of Lutherans and Mennonites to each other. And just for good measure, he threw in a nod to the Calvinists. I think most of us understand completely this kind of daily life vocation: "I begin my day full of Christian intentionality as would an Anabaptist, devote myself to administration as would a Calvinist, and close the day asking for forgiveness as would a Lutheran." If I have erred in my description of Lutheran history and theology, I do indeed ask forgiveness.

I hope to continue to run into Lutherans. How can either of us keep from singing?[22]

Questions for Discussion

1. How do Mennonite understandings of vocation and the vocation of Mennonite higher education compare to those of Lutheran higher education? What can each network of church-related colleges/universities learn from the other?

2. What stories—from your religious tradition, your institution, or your own life—might help you or your students deepen their sense of calling?

3. In your experience, how does study off campus—especially within a "significantly different" culture—help support lives of meaning and purpose?

---

22 At the conclusion of the concluding worship session on reconciliation with Mennonites at the ELCA annual assembly of the Indiana-Kentucky Synod, June 9-11, 2016, a choir of volunteer singers from several Mennonite churches near Ft. Wayne, Indiana, sang a hymn written by Menno Simons in the sixteenth century. The Lutheran audience rose to join them in *a capella* four-part harmony. "We are people of God's peace," they sang. Grace and peace abounded. What a combination! See http://livestream.com/accounts/8056179/events/5562660.

CHAPTER 11

INTEGRITY AND FRAGMENTATION
Can the Lutheran Center Hold?

ROBERT BENNE
Roanoke College, Salem, Virginia

Will our Lutheran colleges of the future have anything recognizably Lutheran or Christian about them?[1] Or will they gradually turn into generic—but sometimes highly ranked—liberal arts colleges of a distinctly secular bent? As an observer of Christian higher education for nearly forty years now, I have seen some church-related colleges firmly maintain—and in some cases strengthen—the public relevance of their Christian tradition to the ongoing life of their schools. Baylor University is a school that has actually strengthened its connection to the Christian heritage. I wrote about those positive examples in *Quality with Soul: How Six Premier Colleges and Universities Keep Faith with their Christian Traditions*.[2] On the other hand, I have witnessed more examples of colleges losing their "souls" to the secularization process than I have those "keeping the faith." I fear that most of our Lutheran colleges will gradually succumb to that process.

So, contrary to the mostly positive essays in this volume, my view is more pessimistic and, I think, more accurate and realistic. My short answer to the above question is: No. The Lutheran center cannot hold in many, if not most of our colleges, because it was never there in an articulated form in the first place. To quote James Burtchaell, "How

---

1   This essay was originally published in *Intersections* 8 (Winter 2000): 4-10.
2   Robert Benne, *Quality with Soul: How Six Premier Colleges and Universities Keep Faith with Their Religious Traditions* (Grand Rapids, Michigan: Wm. B. Eerdmans Publishing Co., Inc., 2001).

can those colleges miss what they never had?"[3] How can they hold now what they never held in the first place? But such a hard and stark answer needs some nuances, which I will offer shortly.

A few of our colleges have been able to articulate and hold a Lutheran center that has shaped and organized their lives as colleges. In my *Quality with Soul*, published fifteen years ago, I identified Valparaiso and St. Olaf as positive examples.[4] At that time others could also have been mentioned. However, I am less sanguine about them now. In a Ph.D. project that became the book entitled *College Identity Sagas*, Eric Childers found that none of the ELCA-related colleges kept track of how many Lutherans were on their faculties.[5] If such carelessness—or the naïve assumption that observant Lutherans would automatically appear—is indicative of how seriously Lutheran colleges "hire for mission," then they face grave danger in the future. Such heedlessness simply means that the "Lutheran factor" is not that important in the make-up of the faculty. It is quite a stretch to think that one can have a robust Lutheran college without a significant portion of observant Lutherans.

In the following I wish to: (1) give a brief account of those colleges that had no articulated center followed by another brief account of those who had one; (2) articulate what I think the Lutheran center is; and (3) close with practical suggestions about how to keep intact such a center for those colleges who have one and then some suggestions for those that don't have a Lutheran center at all.

But before I move on to those tasks, it is important to define at least provisionally and formally what I mean by "center." I would argue that the center for Lutheran liberal arts colleges ought to be religiously defined. That is, a religious vision of higher education should provide the organizing center for their lives as academic institutions. This Christian religious vision has some important characteristics: It is comprehensive, central, and unsurpassable.

By *comprehensive*, I mean that it casts a canopy of meaning over all of life, one that is biblically and theologically grounded. It is a holistic and comprehensive worldview. That doesn't mean that it provides all

---

3   James Burtchaell, *The Dying of the Light: The Disengagement of Colleges and Universities from Their Christian Churches* (Grand Rapids, Michigan: Wm. B. Eerdmans Publishing Co., Inc.), 838.

4   Benne, *Quality with Soul*, 126-44.

5   Eric Childers, *College Identity Sagas: Investigating Organizational Identity Preservation and Diminishment at Lutheran Colleges* (Eugene, Oregon: Wipf and Stock, 2012), 169-96.

the meaning and truth in a college; that would be an absurd claim. Nor does it mean that the religious vision simply trumps secular claims of truth and meaning. Rather, it honors them and engages them in a dialectical process. Second, the Christian vision addresses *central* issues: where we come from, where we are going, what our human nature consists of, as well as the nature of nature itself, what our human predicament is and how we are freed or liberated from it, what gives purpose to life, and how we shall conduct ourselves. Finally, the vision is *unsurpassable*. We claim it is most meaningful and truest vision of ultimate reality, and we pledge our lives to the truth and meaning to which it points. In a robust Christian college this vision would provide the paradigm of meaning that governs the college. It would be publically relevant to all facets of academic life. (This provision, of course, eliminates a lot of our colleges who would currently find it quite embarrassing to admit that their mission was religiously defined.)

The religious vision comes from a living religious tradition. Alasdair MacIntyre has famously argued that a living tradition is "a historically extended, socially embodied argument about the goods which constitute that tradition."[6] Traditions extend through many generations. The argument—the tradition's intellectual dimension—is also expressed in practices that constitute its ethos. Worship and moral practices are examples of practices that make up an ethos. Lutheranism is such a tradition—or better, such a constellation of traditions—and it has sponsored the colleges and universities from which we come.

In giving a rationale for its involvement in higher education, Lutheranism has never exhibited unanimity. But its religious commitments led it to establish colleges that had an educational purpose consonant with its perceived mission. Something in these Lutheran bodies impelled them to establish colleges.

Lutheran by Confession or Cultural Habit?

Now, the problem for many of our colleges is that they were not conceptually clear about what they were doing. The impulse was there but the sharp rationale—particularly a theological rationale—was not. These colleges were "Christ-of-culture" colleges.

What do I mean by that? H. Richard Niebuhr, in his renowned book, *Christ and Culture*, identified five classic ways that Christian

---

6 Alasdair MacIntyre, *God, Philosophy, and Universities: A Selective History of the Catholic Philosophical Tradition* (Lanham, Maryland: Rowan and Littlefield, 2009), 223.

traditions have related Christ (the Christian vision) to culture. One of those, the Christ-of-culture tradition, identifies Christianity with the best of high culture.[7] For example, during the Enlightenment many of the elite identified Christ as a sublime teacher of morality. He was a hero of culture along the lines of a Socrates. The way I am using the Christ-of-culture category is a bit different. I mean that for many Lutheran groups that established colleges, the Christian vision was deeply and unconsciously entwined with their particular ethno-religious culture. They were fairly homogenous groups that wanted their young to be educated within the ethno-religious culture that they prized. They wanted their laity-to-be to be immersed in the "atmosphere" of their culture. Moreover, they wanted that culture to encourage candidates for the ordained ministry who would then go on to seminaries of that tradition.

The Midland Lutheran College (now Midland University) of my college days was such a college. We were children of the German and Scandinavian Lutheran immigrations to the Midwest. Most of our parents hadn't gone to college but they and our local parishes encouraged us to go to "our" school. We were taught by faculty generally of that same ethno-religious culture. Ninety-some percent of us were from those backgrounds. How could such education not be Lutheran? Almost everyone at the college was Lutheran. Similar statements could be made about a Gettysburg and a Muhlenberg several generations or so earlier. Many of our colleges exhibited these characteristics.

Was there anything more specifically Lutheran about that Midland of yore? Not a whole lot. Religion was a pretty inward, non-intellectual matter. We had pietist behavioral standards that prohibited premarital sex and alcohol. We had Bible courses offered at a low level of sophistication. We had required chapel of a distinctly non-liturgical sort. We had faculty who had committed their lives to the college and who now and then would connect their Christian perspective with their teaching. By and large the faculty and administration encouraged us as young Christians.

But there was no articulated center that sharply delineated the mission of the college. The theological acuity to do that was simply absent, or was not felt to be needed. Lutheran theology and ethics were not taught. Lutheran history was nowhere to be found. The Lutheran

---

7   H. Richard Niebuhr, *Christ and Culture* (New York: Harper and Row, 1975).

idea of calling was not explicitly taught to young people who had had it bred into them in their parishes. There was no concerted intellectual effort to interrelate the Christian vision with other fields of learning. We were simply Lutheran by cultural habit. We were immersed in a Christ-of-culture educational enterprise.

When the colleges expanded their student bodies and faculties in the late 50s and 60s, students and faculties were recruited who were no longer part of that culture. Indeed, the Lutheran culture itself was melting into the general American culture. Since the colleges had no articulated center, the colleges lost whatever integrity and unity they had. Soon faculty appeared who were not only apathetic about the tradition that originally sponsored them, but actually hostile to it. Raising any question about a religious center disturbed and offended them. The culture that was once friendly to Christ became one that either ignored or rejected him, and the college went with that culture.

Now the loss of such a religious, Christ-of-culture, orientation did not mean death for the colleges. Some of them found new ways to define themselves. Some, like Gettysburg, went for high quality and high selectivity pre-professional education. They have a certain kind of integrity and unity, but it is not religiously defined. At most, religion is a grace note, a flavor in the mix, a social ornament--but certainly not the organizing center. It remains to be seen whether such an identity is satisfying enough to either college or church to maintain it.

Other Lutheran colleges, which Burtchaell calls the "confessional colleges," did have a more articulated center. That is, the religious vision that sprang from their religious tradition was more specific, often theologically stated. They didn't mind being viewed as "sectarian," an appellation from which the Christ-of-culture colleges fled. This theological distillation of the religious vision served as the paradigm around which was organized the whole life of the college—its academic, social, organizational, and extracurricular facets.

These colleges exemplified a Lutheran version of Christian humanism. Their theology departments taught Lutheran theology and ethics as well as Bible and church history. Their faculty made a point of interrelating the Christian vision and other fields of secular learning. Often this was strongest in the fields of literature and the arts. The notion of calling was explicitly taught as a way to shape one's life before God. The moral ethos of the campus was guided by explicitly

Christian principles. Lutheran worship was provided in an impressive chapel at a set-apart time.

All this was led by people who had a clear rationale for what they were doing. And it sprang from their religious tradition and was theologically articulated. It was supported by a board that explicitly supported and prized that tradition. Above all, the college had the courage to select faculty who supported such a notion of Lutheran humanism.

Such Lutheran colleges still exist, I believe, but have an uphill battle to maintain themselves. Some had a clear rationale but are losing it. A number of reasons for that are obvious. Some colleges fight for survival and are willing to adapt to market conditions even if it means giving up their religious center. Others are seduced to give up their religious center by a glorious worldly success that goes far beyond mere survival. Some have increasing numbers of administrators and faculty who simply do not see the point in trying to operate from a religious center. They do not believe that the Christian vision is any longer an adequate vision for organizing the life of a college. For many of those administrators and faculty, religion is a private, interior matter that should not be publicly relevant to the educational enterprise. For some, classic Christianity is retrograde, intolerant, and perhaps even bigoted.[8] Some colleges can no longer agree on the center and fall into a kind of chaotic pluralism. They cannot summon the clarity and courage to hire faculty that support Lutheran humanism in higher education.

A number of our colleges fall between these two depictions. They are a bit more intentional than the Christ-of-culture types but less defined than the Lutheran humanist types. I do not wish to set up exclusive categories. But it does us no good to go on congratulating ourselves about our fidelity to a Lutheran center when so many of us have little or no semblance of one.

---

8   As national academic life becomes increasingly dominated by "secular progressives" who resist the public expression of classic or "conservative" Christianity, it is difficult to see how Lutheran colleges will resist this powerful trend. They will be tempted to adapt to a new Christ-of-culture Christianity that will shrink from classic Christian teachings about the uniqueness and decisiveness of Christ and Christian sexual ethics, to offer just two examples. The only Christians to survive on such faculties will be those who agree with the "secular progressive" agenda of religious pluralism and sexual liberation. Others will not be hired in the first place or will remain silent if they perchance are hired.

Centering the Lutheran Christian Vision

That brings us to the question: What is an adequate Lutheran "center"? Let me say that a Lutheran center is first of all a Christian center. We share with other major Christian traditions a common Christian narrative—the Bible and the long history of the church. From those narratives emerged early on what we could call the apostolic or trinitarian faith, defined in the classic ecumenical creeds. In the long history of the church much theological reflection took place; a Christian intellectual tradition was shaped. This intellectual tradition is, as I mentioned before, comprehensive, central, and unsurpassable. This Christian tradition also bears Christian practices such as worship, marriage, hospitality, charity, etc.

The Lutheran Reformation and its ensuing history arose from and expressed a Lutheran construal of this general Christian tradition. Many of the facets of that construal are ensconced in the Lutheran Confessions. Some of the more particular elements of that Lutheran construal will be discussed a bit later as I further delineate the Lutheran center for Christian higher education.

This Lutheran Christian vision of reality, particularly in its intellectual form, constitutes the center. But how will it work out practically in the life of a college? How will it provide the organizing paradigm for the identity and mission of a college? How will it make a difference? What difference will it make?

Mark Schwehn, in an address at the University of Chicago, gives us a wonderful starting point.[9] In it he attempts to define the characteristics of a Christian university, one that, as I put it, employs the Christian vision as the organizing paradigm for its life and mission. Schwehn talks generically about "Christian" institutions, but I will transpose his language for specifically Lutheran colleges. Also, I will abbreviate the rich elaboration of each of his characteristics.

Schwehn first lists what he calls "constitutional requirements." A Lutheran college must have a board of trustees composed of a substantial majority of Lutheran persons, clergy and lay, whose primary task is to ensure the continuity of its Lutheran Christian character. This will mean appointing a majority of Lutheran leaders who are committed to the idea of a Lutheran Christian college.

---

9   Mark Schwhen, "A Christian University: Defining the Difference," *First Things* 93 (1999): 25-31.

These leaders will in turn see to it that all of the following things are present within the life of the institution: first, a department of theology that offers courses required of all students in both biblical studies and the Christian intellectual tradition; second, an active chapel ministry that offers worship services in the tradition of the faith community that supports the school (Lutheran) but also makes provision for worship by those of other faiths; third, a critical mass of faculty members who, in addition to being excellent teacher-scholars, carry in and among themselves the DNA of the school, care for the perpetuation of its mission as a Christian community of inquiry, and understand their own callings as importantly bound up with the well-being of the immediate community; and fourth, a curriculum that includes a large number of courses, required of all students, that are compellingly construed as parts of a larger whole and that taken together constitute a liberal education.[10]

Next, Schwehn develops three qualities that ought to be present in a Lutheran Christian college that flow directly from its theological commitments. The first is *unity.* By that he means the conviction that, since God is One and Creator, all reality and all truth finally cohere in him. Thus, the Christian college quests for the unity that follows from this theological principle. The second quality is *universality,* the understanding that all humans are beloved of the God who has created and redeemed them. All humans must be treated with dignity and respect. The third is *integrity,* which involves the belief "that there is an integral connection among the intellectual, moral, and spiritual dimensions of human life, and that these therefore ought where possible to be addressed concurrently within a single institution rather than parceled out into separate and often conflicting realms."[11] While these qualities may be grounded in other views of life, they are thoroughly grounded for a Christian college in trinitarian theological principles.

His fourth principle deserves more attention because it gets at, at least for this essay, the particularly Lutheran qualities of a Christian college. Schwehn argues that a "Christian university privileges and seeks to transmit, through its theology department, its official rhetoric, the corporate worship it sponsors, and in myriad other ways, a particular tradition of thought, feeling, and practice."[12]

---

10   Ibid., 26-27.
11   Ibid., 28.
12   Ibid., 29.

Resisting "Autonomous" Reason

While one could spend a good deal of time on a Lutheran college's "feeling"—its aesthetic tone and "practices," as well as its worship, arts, and sense of corporate and institutional calling—I would rather focus on its tradition of thought, its approach to higher learning. This is shaped by the particular way that Lutherans relate Christ and culture, gospel and law, the right-hand kingdom and the left. And since the Lutheran approach is complex and dialectical, it is highly vulnerable to distortion.

The first thing to say is that Lutheran colleges respect the independence, creativity, and contributions of the many "worldly" ways of knowing. The disciplines are prized in their full splendor. Luther roared, "How dare you not know what you can know!" He also argued that Christians have to be competent in their secular callings; a Christian cobbler makes good shoes, not poor shoes with little crosses on them. Lutheran teacher-scholars teach and write well; their piety will not excuse incompetence.

However, the disciplines are not given idolatrous autonomy, for they, too, are under the dominion of finitude and sin, and they often claim too much for themselves. Rather, the disciplines are to be engaged from the point of the view of the gospel, and here "gospel" is meant to refer to the whole trinitarian perspective on the world, not just the doctrine of the forgiveness of sins. That is, a Lutheran college aims at an ongoing dialogue between the Christian intellectual tradition—Lutheranly construed—and the secular disciplines. This is what is meant by a lively tension and interaction between Christ and culture, the gospel and the law, and the two ways that God reigns in the world.

A genuinely Lutheran college will aim at such an engagement, rejoicing in the areas of overlap and agreement that may take place, continuing a mutual critique where there are divergences and disagreements, anticipating that in the eschaton these differing views will come together in God's own truth, but in the meantime being willing to live with many questions unresolved. Thus, in some areas of inquiry, a Lutheran college will recognize paradox, ambiguity, and irresolvability. But this recognition takes place at the end of a creative process of engagement, not at the beginning, where some of the proponents of "paradox" would like to put it. Those proponents then simply avoid real engagement by declaring "paradox" at the very beginning, essentially allowing everyone to go their own way and do their own thing.

Let me enter a caveat here. This sort of engagement does not go on all the time and by everyone in every classroom. A good deal of the time of a Lutheran college is given over to transmitting the "normal knowledge" of the field or the freight of the liberal arts core. But in probing the depths of every discipline, in addressing perennial and contemporary issues, in shaping a curriculum, in the kind of teaching and scholarship it prizes, and, above all, in the kind of faculty it hires, it nurtures this ongoing engagement between the Christian intellectual tradition and other ways of knowing.

Contrary to the Reformed approach, it does not give an automatic privilege to the Christian worldview which in the end can "trump" the other ways of knowing. Contrary to the Catholic approach, which sees all knowledge rising to a synthesis organized by Catholic wisdom, it lives with more messiness. And yet, it respects those models of Christian humanism and finds itself closer to them than to the modern secular tendency to marginalize and then sequester into irrelevancy the Christian view of life and reality.

This genuine Lutheran approach also guards against its own Lutheran distortions, the prime one being the separation of Christ and culture, gospel and law, and of the two ways that God reigns. This separation takes place in this way. The gospel is narrowly defined as the doctrine of justification. This gospel is preached in the chapel and taught by the theology department. But it is not the full-blown, comprehensive vision of life explicit in the trinitarian faith. It does not have the intellectual content of the full Christian vision.

In this flawed view, the law (culture or the left hand of God) embraces everything else. All disciplines are under the law, and reason is the instrument for understanding them. Indeed, Luther's understanding of reason is often appealed to in support of such dichotomies. His understanding at first sounds like an affirmation of autonomous reason set free from Christian assumptions. But if that is the case, then a Lutheran college simply allows all inquiries shaped by reason to proceed freely. The results of these inquiries are respected and left pretty much unchallenged. The best available faculty can be hired for this exercise of autonomous reason without regard to their religious convictions or their interest in the theological dialogue I outlined above.

A Lutheran college, in this view, is simply one that encourages the exercise of autonomous reason. Or, in postmodern terms, it respects the various perspectives that people bring to learning from their social locations. The postmodern approach now seems to be winning out over the modern.

There are enormous problems with this approach. For one thing, it assumes that Luther meant the same thing by reason that we do. On the contrary, the reason that Luther respected was thoroughly ensconced in a Christian worldview. It was a reason that could affirm the good, the true, and the beautiful in a way that was consistent with Christian presuppositions. But such a view of reason is long gone. Reason has been removed from the religious traditions within which it worked and now operates from very different assumptions, usually characterized by a pervasive philosophical naturalism (the modern) or by an arbitrary epistemological tribalism (the postmodern).

Allowing the claims of such epistemologies to go unchallenged in a Lutheran school is irresponsible. It leads to bifurcations of the minds of students and faculty alike. Christian faculty who worship God on Sunday teach a view of the world that shuts out God and human freedom on Monday. Students live their faith and intellectual lives in two separate compartments. To combat this unhappy situation, the disciplines must be engaged by the Gospel, i.e. the Christian vision with its comprehensive claims to truth. However, the Christian vision is not immune from challenge. The disciplines engage the Christian vision. In any genuine conversation there is the chance that both conversation partners' views may be changed. What's more, Christian claims are often of high generality; the claims of discipline more detailed and concrete. One often needs the other. Engagement is not always conflictual; it is often complementary.

The distorted Lutheran approach I have depicted above splits Christ (the Christian vision) from culture (the academic enterprise), or the gospel (in its full elaboration) from the law (the exercise of reason). This separation of the Christian intellectual tradition from secular learning is as dangerous to Lutheran colleges as the separation of the gospel from politics was to the Germany of Nazi times. Certainly the stakes are quite different, but such a separation will lead to a situation in which secular education with all its idolatrous pretentions is unchallenged by the Christian vision.

Such an approach, which often is used as a rationalization to disguise the prior lapse into secularization, can then well appeal to paradox, ambiguity, and uncertainty since it will have nothing but a cacophony of voices each claiming their little corner of the college. Such a condition, which is not too far from the one prevailing at many of our colleges, led one of our graduate students who attended a Lutheran college summer conference a few years back to say: "Gee, from what I gathered there, a Lutheran college is a wonderful place because everyone can think and do whatever they wish. It's a free-for-all."

Re-centering: Practical Considerations

A Lutheran college at its best fosters a genuine engagement of Christ and culture. It encourages a creative dialectic between gospel and law by giving the gospel in its fullest sense intellectual standing. Such a college stands at the lively junction between the two ways that God reigns. All of this flows from the Lutheran Christian center that guides the college. Such a college is willing to make the hard institutional decisions that ensure that such a vision lives on. It will hire an administration and faculty who not only tolerate such a vision, but support and participate in it. Indeed, they will feel called to it. Such a college will recruit students who are open to such an enterprise. And if it executes such an enterprise well, it will have something special to offer the church and world. It will become more than just a pretty good generic liberal arts college with a Lutheran gloss.

Those colleges that approximate such a view of Lutheran higher education—Lutheran humanism, if you will—will have a good idea of what to aim at. The practical aspects of that task will be difficult and challenging, but the principles are pretty clear. In actual fact, a few of our colleges have a fighting chance to move closer to the ideal. I wish them well and godspeed.

But what of the many colleges who have long lost a Lutheran center, a religious vision that shapes the life of the college? What of the many readers who find my ideal Lutheran vision simply impossible. You say: We can't put Humpty-Dumpty together again. We can't unscramble the eggs in our omelet. We simply have little chance of regaining such a robust center. Some of you might be saying silently: We shouldn't do that even if we could.

To you—and I include myself in this group—I say that we should aim at an *intentional, robust pluralism,* a pluralism in which the college guarantees that the perspectives of Lutheran Christianity are represented in all the departments and divisions of the college. The Lutheran vision may no longer be the paradigm that organizes the college's life, if it ever was, but it can be intentionally represented among the many voices representing other perspectives.[13]

Could we not ensure that Christian public intellectuals--those who in their teaching and scholarship embody the dialogical model I elaborated above--are intentionally sprinkled among the departments? Could we not ensure that the Christian perspective on our life together be represented in student affairs along with the more secular ones? Could our leaders not articulate a Christian rationale for our involvement in service as well as the more generic ones?

It seems only honest to press for such an intentional pluralism—affirmative action for Christians generally and Lutherans specifically—in a college that still claims a relationship to the Lutheran tradition. If we would make provision for such a pluralism, our appeal to Lutheran donors and Lutheran students would have more plausibility. We would avoid the kind of hypocrisy which takes Lutheran money for projects that lead to further secularization of the college. We could at least guarantee to our Lutheran constituencies that we have made provision for the Lutheran voice to be heard, even if it is part of a small minority.

Certainly boards of trustees, presidents, deans, department heads, and faculty could be persuaded to see the cogency of such a proposal. If being related to a religious tradition means anything significant, it must mean that that tradition can speak within its "own" institution. If we can't muster at least that commitment, why in heaven's name should we continue the relationship?

---

13 In *Quality with Soul*, I developed a typology that delineated "orthodox," "critical mass," and "intentional pluralist" colleges that could meaningfully claim to be related to the Christian tradition. "Orthodox" schools insist that all faculty be observant members of a particular religious tradition. There are no such schools among the ELCA colleges and universities. In the preceding part of this essay I have described the "critical mass" type, which both Valparaiso and St. Olaf seemed to exemplify at the turn of the century. My hunch is that they are more likely now to fit the "intentional pluralist" category. My own college, Roanoke College, fits the intentional pluralist type well, though it will have to take bold measures in the future if even such a relationship to its Christian heritage will be maintained. In 2017 my major study of the "soul" of Roanoke College—from its inception to the present—will be published by Eerdmans with the tentative title: *The Quest for Soul at Roanoke College: Learnings from its 175-year Venture in Christian Higher Education.*

Questions for Discussion

1. Do you agree with Benne that having a robust Lutheran college or university depends at least in part on "hiring for mission" or otherwise ensuring that Lutherans make up a significant portion of the faculty or administration? Why or why not?

2. How would you narrate the history and trajectory of your institution when it comes to being Lutheran by confession, by cultural osmosis, by intentional pluralism, and so forth?

3. Where in your institution's curriculum or in your own pedagogy do you find ongoing engagement—or even mutual critique—between the Christian intellectual tradition and other ways of knowing?

4. Some would interpret Benne as in direct disagreement with Wilhelm (over "institutional markers" or mandating a certain percentage of Lutherans on campus) or with Christenson (over the value or temptations of secular reason and academic freedom). What underlying concerns do these authors share? Are there other ways to construe their differences?

Part Four

TRAJECTORIES

CHAPTER 12

WHY INTERFAITH UNDERSTANDING IS INTEGRAL TO THE LUTHERAN TRADITION

JASON A. MAHN
Augustana College, Rock Island, Illinois

This essay seeks to help fundamentally rethink very standard, seemingly "normal" ways of making sense of the different religious traditions that we practice as they intersect with the Lutheran tradition that we share by virtue of our work within the twenty-six ELCA colleges and universities.[1] Some will assume that claiming one's institutional identity as Christian or Lutheran necessarily dampers diversity and prohibits interfaith cooperation—or inversely, that cultivating interfaith cooperation depends on secularizing the context of that work. These assumptions must be called into question in order to develop institutional perspectives that are *both* committed to their religious traditions *and* hospitable to others. Indeed, we must reconsider the very idea that identity and hospitality, commitment and openness, are counter forces that must be balanced somehow—as if the more robustly Lutheran means the less engaged with and challenged by the traditions of others, and vice-versa. Perhaps identity and openness are more like two sides of the same coin. Or better, perhaps they are connected like cultivating one's own Buddha-nature depends on cultivating nonattachment to that nature. Such re-thinking is a *radical* enterprise.

---

1   This essay first appeared in *Intersections* 40 (Fall 2014): 7-16; an expanded and revised version was later included in *Becoming a Christian in Christendom: Radical Discipleship and the Way of the Cross in American's "Christian" Culture* (Minneapolis: Fortress Press, 2016), chapter 9.

I here return to the *root* or *radix* (from which we get *radical*) of the Lutheran tradition to show how interfaith encounter, understanding, and cooperation are integral to it. By the "Lutheran tradition" I mean three things. We can speak of Lutheranism as a church, where membership is typically considered incompatible with membership elsewhere. Lutheran theology is a broader designation; it refers to a 500 year-old reform movement within the church catholic (lowercase *c*)—a grouping of *particular* and *distinctive* (but not absolutely unique) ways of encountering God in light of Jesus and of cultivating Christian faithfulness and human flourishing. Finally, we can speak of Lutheran higher education, a designation that can and should remain irreducible to the other two without thereby meaning anything and everything. Lutheran education or Lutheran pedagogy has its own particularity—it is a distinctive approach to educating whole persons in mind, body, and spirit with the goal of fulfilling one's calling by responding to the deep needs of the world. How does interfaith understanding and action crisscross with these three spheres of the Lutheran church, Lutheran theology, and Lutheran education? How might interfaith engagement be seen not as the vanishing point—a last receding concentric circle—of Lutheran identity, but something central to Lutheranism from its inception?

Lutheranism As Church

As I write of how Lutheranism pushes people beyond their fold to recognize God in other peoples and to work together toward the common good, I am *painfully* aware of Martin Luther's dramatic shortcomings when it came to understanding and working with people of other religions. The sixteenth-century reformer had only a cursory knowledge of "the Turks" (as he called Muslims south and east of Saxony), and he displayed a good deal of ambivalence about them. On the one hand, the expanding Ottoman Empire extended much more religious tolerance than did the church against which Luther was dissenting, and Luther knew it; he wondered whether the Sultan might not become a tactical ally. He also writes, in a sort of double-critique, that "a smart Turk makes a better ruler than a dumb Christian."[2] On the other hand, Luther could describe a "clash of civilizations" between the Christian West and Turks from the East with enough good-versus-evil imagery as to make Samuel Huntington blush. When Luther pens

---

2   Lewis W. Spitz, *The Protestant Reformation 1517-1559* (New York: Harper and Row, 1985), 330.

his famous "A Mighty Fortress is Our God" around 1527, it was probably first used as a battle song to inspire soldiers to rise up against those encroaching Muslims.[3] When in the fourth verse Luther writes, "Were they to take our house, goods, honor, child, or spouse, though life be wrenched away, they cannot win the day. The kingdom's ours forever," the "they" may in fact be Muslims and the "kingdom" over which they battle may in fact be Western Europe, even if the song also refers to other forces and powers, both visible and invisible, then and today.

Luther's anxieties about and caricatures of other traditions gets more treacherous when it comes to Judaism. As is well known, Luther had hoped that once his own evangelical reforms did away with "papist" distortions, Jewish people would finally see that their own Hebrew scriptures pointed toward their fulfillment in the gospel, and thus would start lining up for Christian baptism. Early in his career, he writes "That Jesus was Born a Jew" (1523), condemning the fear-tactics and baptism by sword used by earlier Christians and encouraging his contemporaries to "treat the Jews in a brotherly manner." They are the "blood relatives" of Jesus, insists Luther; we Gentile Christians are only "aliens and in-laws."[4]

When, despite Luther's soft-sell, most Jews continued to politely decline the invitation to convert, Luther became outraged. Writing "On the Jews and Their Lies" twenty years later (1543), Luther mounts a violent invective against the Jews. Where earlier he called Jews the blood relatives of Jesus, he now calls them poisoners, ritual murderers, and parasites.[5] In his last sermon, delivered just days before his death, Luther calls for the expulsion of Jews from Germany altogether. Luckily, the influence of these invectives was not very great in Luther's time. Yet German Nazis did not need such texts waiting to be picked up and used for ideological justification 400 years after the fact. Luther's writings have not only led to deep anti-Judaism, the defamation of Jews on theological grounds, but also have been appropriated in support of anti-Semitic racist ideology, scapegoating, fear-mongering, and murder.

I say this first of all simply to be honest and to name the elephant in the room whenever one speaks of the Lutheran tradition and in-

---

3 John Merriman, *A History of Modern Europe: From the Renaissance to the Age of Napoleon*, 3rd ed. (New York: W. W. Norton, 2010), 101.
4 Martin Luther, "That Jesus Christ Was Born a Jew," in *Luther's Works*, American ed., vol. 45 (Philadelphia: Fortress Press, 1962).
5 Martin Luther, "On the Jews and Their Lies," in *Luther's Works*, American ed., vol. 47 (Philadelphia: Fortress Press, 1971).

terfaith cooperation. I also say it because the *confession* of Lutheran complicity in the stereotyping and scapegoating of others must be the starting place for any candid commitment to interfaith cooperation.

In this light, one of the most significant contributions Lutherans have made to interfaith is the statement on Lutheran-Jewish relations that the church council of the Evangelical Lutheran Church in America adopted in 1994. This document underscores the importance of Luther's central confession of faith: "Honoring [Luther's] name in our own, we recall his bold stand for truth, his earthy and sublime words of wisdom, and above all his witness to God's saving Word. Luther proclaimed a gospel for people as we really are. . . ."[6] But at this point, as Lutherans confess God's saving Word and sufficient grace, they also confess their sin, how that "grace [must reach] our deepest shames and address the most tragic truths." The document continues:

> In the spirit of that truth-telling, we who bear his name and heritage must with pain acknowledge also Luther's anti-Judaic diatribes and the violent recommendations of his later writings against the Jews. . . . [W]e reject this violent invective, and yet more do we express our deep and abiding sorrow over its tragic effects on subsequent generations. . . .
>
> Grieving the complicity of our own tradition within this history of hatred, moreover, we express our urgent desire to live out our faith in Jesus Christ with love and respect for the Jewish people. We recognize in anti-Semitism a contradiction and an affront to the Gospel, a violation of our hope and calling. . . .[7]

Confession of sin is central to Lutheran identity—Lutherans typically don't start worship without it. So, too, with interfaith encounter. Such confession—of what we have done badly and failed to do altogether—*is* one of the gifts that Lutherans bring to the table when meeting our brothers and sisters from other traditions.[8]

---

6   "Declaration of ELCA to Jewish Community," Evangelical Lutheran Church of America, 1994, http://download.elca.org/ELCA%20Resource%20Repository/Declaration_Of_The_ELCA_To_The_Jewish_Community.pdf.

7   Ibid.

8   For other foundations upon which ELCA interfaith relations build, see Kathryn Lohre, "Building on a Firm Foundation: ELCA Inter-Religious Relations, *Intersections* 40 (Fall 2014): 27-30, http://digitalcommons.augustana.edu/cgi/viewcontent.cgi?article=1006&context=intersections.

Philosophical Interlude

As I transition from speaking of the Lutheran church to Lutheran theology, I want first to rehearse some fairly well-worn categories for interpreting and regarding different religions. As far as I can tell, these categories were invented, or at least formalized, with the publication in 1987 of *The Myth of Christian Uniqueness.* In the Introduction, the editors lay out a typology that has structured interfaith understanding since. They write of the "exclusivist" position, the understanding that one's own religion has a monopoly on truth or is the only road to salvation. The line between my way of true faith and devotion and those heretical and idolatrous beliefs and practices *over there* is clear and stark. The editors then describe a second, "inclusivist" position, comprised of the idea that while my religion has the fullest manifestation of truth or gives it proper name, other traditions also glimpse this truth and designate it with their own analogous terms. In many ways this mindset remains more open to listening to and learning from others; still, it remains supremely confident that Christ, for example, is the *full* and *final* revelation of God; other traditions are affirmed only insofar as they *resonate* with that final truth.

Third and finally, we get the position called "pluralism." We should emphasize with Diana Eck that pluralism is distinct from the sheer fact of religious plurality or diversity.[9] It entails an interpretation of that diversity and an affirmation of multiple religions for contributing to an understanding of God (or "the Ultimate," or "the Real") or for joining in efforts for social justice. The editors of *The Myth of Christian Uniqueness* describe the passage from inclusivism to pluralism as crossing the Rubicon towards recognizing the independent validity of other religious approaches.[10] Even more suggestive is this earlier imagery: Going from inclusivism—where it is still *my* tradition that provides the norms and sets the terms of inclusivity—to pluralism is like going from a Ptolemaic understanding of the universe to a Copernican model, where each of our traditions is but circling around something that is beyond the sphere of each.[11]

---

9   Diana L. Eck, *Encountering God: A Spiritual Journey from Bozeman to Banaras* (Boston: Beacon Press, 2003), 191.
10 John Hick and Paul F. Knitter, eds, *The Myth of Christian Uniqueness: Toward a Pluralist Theology of Religions* (Maryknoll, New York: Orbis Books, 1987), viii.
11 John Hick, *God and the Universe of Faiths* (Oxford: Oneworld Publications, 1973), 133-47.

Now, this typology of exclusivism, inclusivism, and pluralism can be incredibly helpful for reminding religious folks that God is not contained within any of their traditions, that God (or Buddha-nature, or Dharma, or "the Real") always transcends the terms and stories that we have for Her (or Him, or It). According to a famous Jataka Tale of Buddhism, we should not confuse the finger that points to the moon for the moon itself. Each tradition points to the truth, but none of them contains it.

At the same time, however, the categories are limited and sometimes unhelpful.[12] To start with, notice the way that the account of *plurality* that you find in the *pluralist* position subtly relegates religions into different versions *of the same thing.* Once one understands that all religions are like planets circling around the same sun, are like different paths leading up the same mountain, one has just portrayed them as essentially or functionally equivalent, as versions of the same kind of thing. "Salvation," "enlightenment," "moksha" and "paradise" get relegated to specific versions of a more abstract and overarching "final end." "Yahweh," "the Triune God,"' "Allah," and "Dharma" all become different ways to describe "the Ultimate" or "the Real." At worst, then, differences can appear so shallow and unimportant that the traditions begin to resemble brand names: You prefer your New Age iPhone and I'm still clinging to my Doctrinal Blackberry, but either gets the job done and the wiring is about the same once we peel off the plastic.

Ironically, then, "pluralism" *as a category* can undercut the plurality it is meant to affirm. Related to this problem is this: Many self-proclaimed pluralists end up introducing a philosophical framework that is meant to mediate differences between religious "frameworks," but simply adds an additional framework in need of mediation. To return to our earlier metaphor, we could say that the Copernican model of the universe is also just a model of, an earthly perspective on, the universe—*itself* no more heliocentric than other perspectives. Or again: Seeing that each tradition's finger only points to the moon gets one no closer to standing on the moon. In fact you can only indicate *that* truth with yet another finger that points to the fingers pointing, and so on.

---

12 Compare Mark S. Heim, *Salvations: Truth and Difference in Religion* (Maryknoll, New York: Orbis Books, 1995) and Muhammad Legenhausen, *Islam and Religious Pluralism* (London: Al-Hoda, 1999).

Let me go at the difficulty related to pluralism as a category in a different way by suggesting that it answers a problem that may not in fact be our most pressing one. Certainly the tactics of "othering" employed by the exclusivist—her proclivity to stereotype, scapegoat, and even demonize those outside her own fold—have been and are a major concern of Christianity, in particular, with its too-long history of baptism under duress, of pogroms, and of "holy wars." But does that too-clear understanding that I possess absolute truth and you do not characterize the majority of Christians in this time and place? According to a well-known National Study on Youth and Religion, the vast majority of teenagers who call themselves Christian actually have little to no idea what Christianity entails aside from the idea that they are supposed to be nice and that God will reward them and protect them if they are. Propounding a religion more accurately called "Moralistic, Therapeutic Deism," these Christian kids believe in a pretty hands-off God, an ethereal Big Daddy in the sky, who just wants them to be good, which often means nonjudgmental, and, most of all, to be happy.[13]

The researches make clear that this is not just a teenager problem; youth have been thoroughly schooled into this indeterminate faith through the equally abstract "religiosity" of their parents.[14] Perhaps then an overly-stark separation of me and my tradition from you and yours is not the primary obstacle to interfaith understanding today. Perhaps the primary challenge is how to recognize and cultivate difference in the first place—to notice that you and I see the world differently, and that these differences are good.

One final qualification about these philosophical categories before returning to Luther: Notice the way that positioning "inclusivism" along a spectrum spanning from the narrowest forms of "exclusivism" to the widest embrace of "pluralism" tends to reduce it to a kind of half-way house position. To the pluralist, it looks not as good as pluralism but a whole lot better than exclusion. To the critic of pluralism, inclusivism seems like a happy medium—not as closed-minded as the exclusivists but also not as abstract and all-accommodating as the pluralists—like Goldilocks preferring the middle bed: not too hard, not soft. I happen to think that describing inclusivism in this way actually obscures the *unique* set of challenges that arise when people under-

13 Christian Smith and Melinda Lundquist Denton, *Soul Searching: The Religious and Spiritual Lives of American Teenagers* (New York: Oxford University Press, 2005), 118-71.
14 Ibid., 191.

stand other religions as constituting analogues or shadows of their own. These challenges are especially prevalent in traditions that share histories and texts—as when Christianity interprets Judaism as having part of its full truth, or when Islam thinks in a similar way about the other "religions of the book."

This is the specific problem of supersessionism—the idea that one's faith, as newer and more complete, surpasses and supplants that which has gone before.[15] Notice that the problem of supersessionism is not the problem of relegating the other as completely "other," as strange and unique, but rather the temptation to include her under terms that are really my own. Perhaps then Luther's first, seemingly more benign interpretation of Jews as "almost Christian" was just as mistaken and dangerous as his final, exclusivist rant when they claimed their own uniqueness. If inclusivism can be toxic, and history shows that it can, then the remedy must come by underscoring differences and by keeping them from becoming divisive by cultivating gratitude and even holy wonder for them. I want now to show how some core themes in Luther's theology help cultivate such gratitude and wonder for the particularity and uniqueness of our traditions.

Lutheranism As Theology

The Lutheran emphasis on justification by grace through faith apart from the work of the law is about Christian identity, about who humans *are* as they stand before a God made known in Christ and before their neighbors in need. It is important to say this because so much popular religious sentiment takes "justification" and "grace" as things that get you other things, as an admission ticket for eternal life. For Luther, justification—being made right in the gracious eyes of God—is not the way one gets to salvation. It is salvation.

The way that Luther and Lutherans speak of salvation (including justification or righteousness, grace, faith, and freedom) matters for how they regard Christian identity as it relates to the identity of others. We could say that justification is about encountering others and that such encounters necessarily stem from justification—at least for Christians. Being justified by grace through faith matters because "my" graced identity *is never truly mine* as a security or possession. Rather,

---

15 See R. Kendall Soulen, *The God of Israel and Christian Theology* (Minneapolis: Fortress Press, 1996), 1-12; Michael Wyschogrod, *Abraham's Promise: Judaism and Jewish-Christian Relations*, ed. R. Kendall Soulen (Grand Rapids, Michigan: Wm. B. Eerdmans Publishing, 2004), 183-84.

I am graced with my identity as loved, healed, and capable of service only insofar as I receive it, share it, and have it drawn out by others. It is only before others—the capital *O* Other and then other others—that I become the one I am.

Now, Lutherans are rather good at witnessing to the necessary relationship with God and God's unmerited grace in determining their Christian identities. One is justified before God, by God's loving regard, or not at all. But they should remember, too, that for Luther Christian righteousness and freedom are "secured" only insofar as they are lived out before other human beings, regardless of whether those others share Christian understandings. Early in the reforming movement Luther writes of "Two Kinds of Righteousness" (1519) and, a year later, of two kinds of freedom in "The Freedom of a Christian" (1520). First is the righteousness "instilled from without," whereby Christ "is entirely ours with all his benefits"[16] and where we are entirely freed *from* having to construct our own holiness. The second is the Christian's "proper righteousness" which comprises "that manner of life spent profitably in good works"[17] and the freedom *for* humble service to any and every neighbor in need.[18] Once God's gift of righteousness becomes "ours" in faith, we can and should be willing to grasp it less tightly, so to speak. In Luther's words, once a person hears Christ the Bridegroom declare "I am yours," and she answers, "I am yours," "then the soul no longer seeks to be righteous in and for itself, but it has Christ as its righteousness *and therefore seeks only the welfare of others.*"[19] Having been opened to the self-giving Christ, the Christian almost ineluctably passes on whatever he or she can in order to meet the needs of others.

Luther imagined that Christian "encounters" with others happened primarily by serving them. In imagining interfaith engagement, we must of course imagine more reciprocal, symmetrical exchanges as all participants "come to the table" with their own stories and gifts as well as their needs and receptivity. But note just how constitutive standing before other humans, open both to their need and to their gifts, is for Christian righteousness and freedom, according to Luther.

---

16 Martin Luther, "Two Kinds of Righteousness," in *Luther's Works*, American ed., vol. 31 (Philadelphia: Muhlenberg Press, 1957), 297-98.

17 Ibid, 299.

18 Martin Luther, "The Freedom of a Christian," in *Luther's Works*, American ed., vol. 31 (Philadelphia: Muhlenberg Press, 1957), 370-77.

19 Luther, "Two Kinds of Righteousness," 30, my emphasis.

It is not as if Christians become fully Christian and then happen to share that identity (and a little bit of time and money) with others or decide to keep it to themselves, afraid that they'll lose it with too much openness. Rather, becoming open to the other—to God and other others—*is* what Christian identity is all about. The Christian becomes properly righteous only when that righteousness is lived out before others. The Christian becomes fully free only when freely binding herself or himself to others in service for the common good. Or, somewhat anachronistically, we could say that *Lutherans* become fully *Lutheran* only as they participate in dialogue and service for and with people who are *not*.

The subtext for these early Lutheran texts is the "Christ hymn," a bit of verse probably sung or recited by the earliest Christians, which Paul quotes in Philippians 2. Paul there beckons fellow Christians in Philippi to look to the interests of others above and beyond their own, and to "have the same mind in you" that was in Christ Jesus,

> who, though he was in the form of God,
> > did not regard equality with God
> > as something to be exploited,
> but emptied himself,
> > taking the form of a slave,
> > being born in human likeness.
> And being found in human form,
> > he humbled himself
> > and became obedient to the point of death—
> > even death on a cross.[20]

In this so-called kenotic or self-emptying Christ, Christians have an example of one who resists clinging to the identity he has through equality with God. Christ chooses instead to humble himself, receiving his identity through friendship, solidarity, and communion with those who are radically—*radically*—"other." Christians pattern their lives after this kenotic Christ when they, too, meet religious others in all their otherness not *despite* being Christian but *because* they are Christian and *in order to* be more fully Christian.

Recalling those philosophical terms, I want also to show how Luther's framework might couple seemingly exclusivist claims with openness to honest interfaith exchange. Early in his career, Luther

---

20   Philippians 2: 6-8.

distinguished theologians of glory—whom he critiqued for having all-too-cozy understandings of God—from theologians of the cross—those who rightly know and serve the God revealed through the suffering of Jesus. In his famous Heidelberg Disputation (1518), Luther puts it this way: "A theologian of glory calls evil good and good evil. A theologian of the cross calls the thing what it actually is."[21] Luther then explains:

> This is clear: He [the theologian of glory] who does not know Christ does not know God hidden in suffering. Therefore he prefers works to suffering, glow to the cross, strength to weakness, wisdom to folly, and, in general, good to evil. These [however] are the people whom the apostle calls "enemies of the cross of Christ" [Philippians 3:18], for they hate the cross and suffering and love works and the glory of works. . . . [But] *God can be found* only *in suffering and the cross.* . . .[22]

Certainly these are exclusivist claims, including a clear distinction between "the friends of the cross" and "enemies of the cross of Christ." To claim that God can be found *only* in suffering and the cross is enough to make almost any non-Christian uncomfortable. Muslims and others with an understanding of the absolute indivisibility and impassibility of God may here downright cringe. But we should be careful to note what exactly Luther's exclusivist claims exclude. The theologian of glory is one who looks around to whatever has value in our dominant society and projects them onto God: God is like the power of domination—only stronger. God is like a kingly authority—only more unquestionable. God is like the Unmoved Mover—only more invulnerable. It is over-and-against these seemingly obvious, self-assured, and typically *ideological* understandings of "the divine" (in other words, ones that function to secure our own power and authority) that Luther posits the God who freely discloses Godself in the most unusual places—in a barn in Bethlehem and on a cross outside Jerusalem. Luther thus underscores the *particularity* and *peculiarity* of a God who fully revealed Godself in such unlikely places and the necessary peculiarity of Christians who follow this God.

How might particular and seemingly exclusivist claims such as these help foster authentic interfaith encounter? First, theologians of

---

21 Martin Luther, "Heidelberg Disputation," in *Luther's Works*, American ed., vol. 31 (Philadelphia: Muhlenberg Press, 1957), thesis 21.
22 Ibid., emphasis mine.

the cross—if they take this peculiar self-revelation of God seriously—are formed to see God in unlikely places. The One revealed "outside the camp"[23] is utterly free to be revealed outside Christian circles as well. Christians will be ready to find God in unusual places, and so enter into interfaith exchange with eyes wide open.

Second, embracing their own scandalous particularity, Christians allow space for others to inhabit their own stubborn particularity. Without a sense of the tradition's particularity and limits, without ample witness to a God who eludes their own grasp, theologians of glory are bound to mistake their particular glimpse of God with full and final comprehension. When others can't or won't see it the same way, they will get exasperated, as Luther himself became with the unconverted Jews around him. A theologian of the cross, by contrast, knows the limits of her sight of God. Or, to put it positively: Appreciating the fact that her God is strangely, wonder-fully revealed in this peculiar way, she allows space for other revelations, each of which are no more graspable and incontestable—and no less wonderful—than her own.

Lutheranism As Pedagogy

We turn finally from the Lutheran church and Lutheran theology to our Lutheran colleges and universities. How do they—how might they—provide the place and space for interfaith encounter, understanding, and shared service for the common good? I will name three more gifts (and tasks) that Lutheran higher education brings to interfaith understanding.

Religious Formation and Interfaith

Many who write about the distinctive third path or set of charisms characterizing Lutheran higher education today[24] connect the best of its pedagogy to Luther's proclivity toward "both/and" thinking, toward abiding tensions or even paradoxes. Luther wrote that "a Christian is perfectly free lord of all, subject to none" *and* that "a Christian is a perfectly dutiful servant of all, subject to none."[25] A person before the law is bound to sin *and yet* wholly responsible for doing the sin that does her. And perhaps most paradoxical of all, a person before the redeeming God is "*simultaneously* sinner and saint"—not half and half, but entirely sinful and yet entirely virtuous in the eyes of God. Embodying

---

23 Hebrews 13:13.
24 See especially Part Two of this book.
25 Luther, "Freedom," 344.

this tensive outlook in new ways, Lutheran colleges and universities become places where the reforming tradition is empathically taught *and yet also* places where academic freedom still reigns supreme. They are places that honor the scientific method and empirical research *and yet also* address questions of ultimate meanings, purpose, and value.

One more tension intrinsic to Lutheran education is this: Colleges and universities of the Lutheran Church are assuming the role of the Christian faith formation of young people in unprecedented ways, and yet this is best done not prior to or instead of encountering people of other faiths, but by facing them in conversation and joining them in pursuing justice. Certainly there was a time when first year students arrived on our campuses already well catechized in their faith tradition. Nowadays, college has become the place of many students' first serious formative encounter with the meaning and values of the Christian faith. We must now help them not only critically reflect *on* their faith, but also to grow *into* it. The question then becomes: Does teaching other faith traditions, does fostering conversation and joint service projects among students of different religions, do even some experiments in interfaith worship foster or undermine the faith formation of a college student?

I am convinced by the work of Eboo Patel and the Interfaith Youth Core, Dianna Eck and the Pluralism Project, and by my own experiences with Augustana students that a person comes to know and embody her own tradition more fully and gracefully when working with others as they embody theirs.

Suspicion and Trust

The second gift that Lutheran higher education brings to interfaith work is its institutional willingness to straddle the sometime ambiguous line between the academic study of religion and more personal and pastoral approaches to religious faith and meaning. All of our colleges have both religion departments and chaplaincy offices, centers for vocational reflection, and the like. While a distinction between these curricular and co-curricular offices is needed and helpful, I would guess that only in rare cases has the distinction become an absolute divide. Our campus pastors teach the Christian tradition and other traditions as they lead Christians, Jews, Muslims, "whateverists," and seekers into deeper lives of meaning and conviction. Our religion professors, too, though they may need to clarify that courses in religion are not the same as Sunday school, do help students name their burning questions and sometimes walk them across the hot coals. Our campus pastors disabuse students of uncritical faith, and our professors often model ways of remaining faithful to the tradition they are critiquing. On both sides of the curricular/co-curricular distinction, then, Christianity and other religions are both criticized and claimed, investigated and entrusted.

This distinctive ability to treat religion with both a hermeneutic (or interpretative lens) of suspicion and a hermeneutic of trust stems directly from the Lutheran Reformation as a re-forming tradition. Unlike some other reformers, Lutherans did not want to do away with 1,600 years of Christian history in order to start from scratch. Rather, they critiqued the church as faithful members of it. Yet unlike those ecclesial powers that resisted every reform, Luther and Lutherans were not and are not afraid to name all the ways that the church they love falls into idolatry and perpetuates ideology. One of the deep mores of Lutheran education is this ability to critique the faith that you love—precisely because you love it.

If Lutherans are called to call their own tradition into question so that they can inhabit it more fully, then conversations with people of other religions provide the primary vehicle for them to do so. Unlike empty skepticism or something that we assume to be "purely secular reason," the differing beliefs, practices, and abiding virtues of other faiths provide the footing, so to speak, as Christian step back and forth from their own, just as the committed Christian provides the opportunity for the Hindu or Jew to reconsider and re-inhabit her or his own faith. Learning about Avalokitesvara, the Bodhisattva of Compassion, from the committed Mahayana Buddhist might help a Christian consider whether his own self-sacrificial love hasn't been too self-serving, a round-about strategy to get into heaven. Listening to the committed Muslim speak of God's radical oneness and transcendence might help the Christian to consider whether her Christ doesn't look too much like the Buddy Christ from the satirical film *Dogma*. Finally, even listening to the committed atheist—or even the sophomoric atheist who has read his first bit of Nietzsche and goes around proclaiming to his churchy friends that "God is dead"—even this one might help the Christian consider how her own tradition might repeat the same truth in a different register. Yes, God is dead—fully revealed in the cross of Christ—and yet still ruling the world with that vulnerable, suffering love.

Vocation

Finally, then, we come to *sine qua non* of Lutheran education—namely, that education is not *primarily* a financial investment, a privileged cultivation of the life of the mind, or access to upward mobility, *but the development of and reflection on one's giftedness so that one can capably respond to God's calling and the deep needs of the world.* In shortest form: Lutheran education is education as and for vocation.

Now, when Lutheran theologians are talking among themselves, it matters where one places understandings of vocation within Lutheran intellectual schemata. Most assert that to answer God's call belongs to what Lutherans call a first use of the law, the law as applicable to all and as guiding civil society toward a semblance of peace and order. I happen to think that Luther's language of calling is best understood as a second use of the Gospel, as that second form that grace and righteousness take when put into play among the neighbors and strangers and enemies that Christians are called to love. I think, in other words, that Christians living out their callings should take a deeply christological shape as they begin to have the same mind in them that was in Christ Jesus. But note well—even if vocation properly construed is decidedly Christian in name and shape for the Christian—the *enactment* of it can be shared by many folds of religious and non-religious types. Thus, while Christians come to humble service because their Lord humbly serves, they shouldn't be surprised to find Jews engaged in the same service, who come in the spirit of the Jewish prayer *tikkum olam*—from the hope that by doing small acts that contribute to God's ongoing creation humans can "heal the world."[26] And they shouldn't be surprised to find Muslims so engaged, perhaps responding to the Qur'an's exhortation to believers to "strive in the way of God with a service worthy of Him."[27] When Buddhists participate in shared service with the Heart Sutra on their lips, or when lovers of the Bhagavad Gita come with intentions to act for good simply and purely, "without attachment to the fruits of their actions," Christians, again, should not be surprised.

We can thank national leaders of interfaith work for underscoring the importance of moving beyond dialogue alone and actually *acting* together, across religious boundaries, to combat poverty, bigotry, in-

---

26 Kristen Johnston Largen, *Finding God Among our Neighbors: An Interfaith Systematic Theology* (Minneapolis: Fortress Press, 2013), 235-37.

27 Qur'an, 22:78.

justice, and environmental degradation. The colleges and universities of the ELCA will continue to train their religious and nonreligious students to come to this work expecting to see their own and other lives transformed. We will continue to train Christian students to look for Christ hidden in those they serve and in those that they serve beside. But we need also to provide the institutional support—places to gather, time to reflect, even curriculums to be followed—that enable diverse people to better hear and respond to their callings. Lutheran educators have a particular yet versatile understanding of vocation, of radical, cooperative service for a needy world. Let that, too, become what draws many together as peoples of God and healers of a broken, and redeemable, world.

Questions for Discussion

1. What is the state of interfaith cooperation or dialogue on your campus? How does it relate to the living-out of your institution's Lutheran identity?

2. Assuming that a foundation for interfaith encounter can come from the Christian story and Lutheran theology, what dimensions of religious or nonreligious traditions with which you are familiar might also bring people to interfaith encounter?

3. How is religious diversity interpreted on your campus, by students and/or by educators? With pride? Suspicion? Indifference? Hope? As a potential problem to be managed? As opportunity? As gift?

CHAPTER 13

SEMPER REFORMANDA
Lutheran Higher Education in the Anthropocene

ERNEST SIMMONS
Concordia College, Moorhead, Minnesota.

> I believe that God has created me together with all that exists.
>
> —Martin Luther, *Small Catechism*

> A constituency able and willing to fight for the long-term human prospect must be educated into existence.
>
> —David Orr, *Earth in Mind*

Identity is a process, not a possession.[1] It is always undergoing dynamic change because of conditions in space and time. Traditions and institutions are no exception. Luther and Melanchthon understood this well. That is why one of the watch phrases of the Reformation was *semper reformanda*—to always be reforming—whether that be in the church, society, or education. Change, then, is not something to be mourned or simply obstructed, but rather embraced so that a trajectory may be channeled and developed in consonance with tradition.

This has been the challenge and opportunity to be found in Lutheran higher education, especially over the last twenty years. While acknowledging the changes in society, learning styles, administrative structures, and faculty preparation, the ELCA has also been inten-

---

1   This essay was published in *Intersections* 43 (Spring 2016): 33-38; some of it appeared earlier as "Lutheran Education in the Anthropocene," in *Dialog: A Journal of Theology*, 55.1 (March 2016): 2-5; and as "Liberal Arts for Sustainability: Lutheran Higher Education in the Anthropocene," in *Eco-Reformation: Grace and Hope for a Planet in Peril*, ed. Jim Martin-Schramm and Lisa Dahill (Eugene, Oregon: Wipf and Stock, 2016).

tionally involved in supporting programs to reform the Lutheran expression of higher education alongside all the other changes in higher education. This effort has not simply been a retrieval or repristination process, for that would ignore the intrinsic changes of our time. Rather, Lutheran higher education has brought current academic life into dialogical interaction with the Lutheran tradition. Among such interaction has been an intentional effort to interpret higher education as preparation for the expression of vocation in the context of Christian freedom. It has been an effort to differentiate vocation from vocational training and to place career preparation within the wider context of service to society, world, and self.

This essay begins by briefly enumerating the initiatives that the ELCA has undertaken over the last twenty years to retrieve the Christian understanding of vocation in higher education. It then turns to the future and the directions that Lutheran higher education might (must?) take in the coming decades. Indeed, Lutheran higher education has been reforming, as the following sections will bear out. It must continue to do so if it is to have any constructive contributions to make to our rapidly changing world. Our focus question will be: "In what ways should Lutheran higher education on vocation be revised (or re-formed) to include the fact that we are living in a natural world massively impacted by human behavior?" The contention of this article is that Lutheran liberal arts education should become environmental and sustainability education in addition to education in whatever major a student selects. Through the theological and ethical exploration of vocation, Lutheran colleges and universities can help prepare students to become sustainability leaders in the critical areas of society, ethics, ecology, and economics. They must do so in a geological age in which the climate and environment are dominated by human influence and control—an epoch that geologists call the Anthropocene.

Re-Rooting Lutheran Higher Ed

Starting in the early 1990s, Dr. Robert Sorenson and later Dr. Leonard Schultz, executive directors of the Division for Higher Education and Schools, and Dr. Jim Unglaube, director of Higher Education in the ELCA, began a series of initiatives to address the retirement of a major segment of college faculty who had entered teaching during the sixties. By and large these persons had been the pillars of the college's identity and spokespersons for the church-related tradition of the college, and they were now leaving. An intentional effort was needed, therefore, to help educate the new ranks of faculty, administration, and staff into the tradition. Over the next several years, and with the additional encouragement of presidents Dr. Paul Dovre of Concordia College and Dr. Mel George of St. Olaf College, a number of nationwide programs were launched to address this need. These initiatives included:

- **The Vocation of a Lutheran College Conference.** This annual summer conference helped introduce new faculty and administrative staff to the Lutheran tradition in higher education. It continues to the present, meeting in recent years at Augsburg College in Minneapolis.

- **Lutheran Academy of Scholars Summer Seminar**. Patterned after NEH summer seminars, these two week summer seminars (typically at Harvard University and chaired by Ron Thiemann), assisted faculty in connecting faith and learning in their respective academic fields and in producing publishable articles and books. (Because of budget and other considerations, this program was discontinued in 2012.)

- *Intersections*. The establishment of this journal encouraged reflection on Lutheran higher education and disseminated informative essays on conference and additional themes.

- **Other scholarship on Lutheran Higher Education.** Among others, two books directly sought to lift up the intellectual tradition informing Lutheran colleges and universities. *Lutheran Higher Education: An Introduction* by Ernest Simmons (Augsburg Fortress, 1998), provided historical, theological, and pedagogical background of the Lutheran tradition of higher education to assist faculty, board members, and other interested parties. *The Gift and Task of Lutheran Higher Education* by Tom Christenson (Augsburg Fortress, 2004), addressed issues of why a college or university should be "Lutheran" and what the continued robustness of Lutheran higher education has to contribute to the church and broader public arena.

- **Faith and Learning Centers**. Many colleges, starting with Concordia College in Moorhead, Minnesota, with the Dovre Center for Faith and Learning, established faculty/staff development centers to direct mentoring programs as well as research and writing projects, conferences, heritage travel seminars, and workshops in faith and learning in order to stimulate campus-wide discussions on vocation.

- **Lilly Endowment Grants**. Large grants from the Lilly Endowment critically assisted many ELCA campuses in their "exploration of vocation." These significant grants raised awareness, discussion, and preparation for and reflection on vocation, the impacts of which continue to this day.

- **Thrivent Fellows for Administrative Leadership.** Begun in 2002 under the leadership of Paul Dovre with sponsorship by the ELCA Council of College Presidents and financial support by Lutheran Brotherhood/Thrivent, this week-long training seminar informed future academic administrators about academic management within the context of Lutheran higher education. There are now over 150 fellows serving in a variety of roles and places.

What we have seen over the last twenty years, then, is a concerted effort to bring the richness of the Lutheran tradition to bear on the changing circumstances of higher education. Such changes have only accelerated with globalization, dispersed learning, social media and other new technologies, increased assessment, changing demographics, and economic realities. One change, however, is so significant that it threatens to subsume and render insignificant all these other changes, as well as the concerted efforts of Lutheran colleges and universities to respond to them creatively and collaboratively. I have in mind the potentially catastrophic environmental changes that human societies are and will be facing with ever greater intensity.

Repurposing the Liberal Arts and Lutheran Learning

Several of the world's leading geologists and climatologists coauthored "The Anthropocene: Conceptual and Historical Perspectives." It begins thus: "The human imprint on the global environment has now become so large and active that it rivals some of the great forces of Nature in its impact on the functioning of the Earth system."[2] The article assesses the appropriateness of naming our current geo-

---

2   Will Steffen, et al, "The Anthropocene: Conceptual and Historical Perspectives," *Philosophical Transactions of the Royal Society*, A369, 1938 (2011): 842.

logical epoch the "Anthropocene" to signify such human impact. The anthropological is now having as much impact on the planet as the geological and meteorological. The planet is no longer dark at night, just one indication of global human impact. Our focus question, "In what ways should Lutheran higher education on vocation be revised to include the fact that we are living in a natural world massively impacted by human behavior?" can now be broken down into two more explicit questions: "What is the role of liberal arts education in such a changed context?" and "What resources in the Lutheran tradition can contribute to preparing our students to become effective sustainability leaders?" Let us turn to the first question.

What is the role of liberal arts education in such a changed context?

Here I think re-envisagement of the classical purpose of liberal arts education will serve us well. In the Greek city-state, the purpose of such education was to prepare a person for thoughtful and responsible citizenship in the polis. This meant having knowledge of the fundamental "liberating" arts of grammar, logic, and rhetoric, which during the Middle Ages became known as the *Trivium*, literally, "where the three roads meet." Whereas grammar teaches the mechanics of language, logic is the "mechanics" of deliberation and analysis as well as the process of identifying erroneous arguments. Rhetoric is the application of language in order to persuade the listener or the reader. While the *Trivium* is later supplemented by the *Quadrivium* of arithmetic, geometry, music, and astronomy, for our purposes these three basic "liberating arts" are the most important.

One need only look at the recent dissembling discussions of climate change to see the importance of these three arts. To be able to name something clearly and to ferret out the illogical and fallacious arguments that have been made are survival skills for society, especially today. We have to prepare our students to be able to critique and dismantle obstructionist thinking and call out the powers that have a vested interest in promoting such arguments. In their book *Merchants of Doubt,* Naomi Oreskes and Erik Conway indicate that by supporting fringe scientific research, the energy industry has engaged in the same tactics of sowing uncertainty about climate change that the cigarette industry did for decades concerning the carcinogenic character of cigarette smoking and nicotine addiction.[3] As horrible as the loss of

---

3   Naomi Oreskes and Erik Conway, *Merchants of Doubt* (New York: Bloomsbury Publishing, 2010).

life from smoking is, it is still on an individual basis. Climate change, however, is not. Whole cultures and nations are at stake, as well as the viability of human civilization itself. We no longer have time for such distracting and fallacious arguments. We must prepare our students to think clearly and critically in order to cut through obfuscation and disinformation as well as to creatively formulate viable responses. We must enable them to communicate clearly, effectively, and persuasively in their social context. Along with grammar and logic, the art of rhetoric is as needed today as in the ancient polis. All this is to say that a liberal arts education is one of the best educations to prepare students for sustainability leadership in the coming decades. As the liberating arts were once used to prepare persons for citizenship in the Greek polis, we must now prepare our students for citizenship on the planet, that is, for planetary citizenship.

We turn now to the second question:

What resources in the Lutheran tradition can contribute to preparing our students to become effective sustainability leaders?

For Luther, the purpose of education was to preserve the gospel and equip the priesthood of all believers for vocations of serving others within the world. Today this understanding of vocation must be enlarged to also include the natural environment. In the first article of his Small Catechism, Luther observed, "I believe that God has created me together with all that exists." Luther understood our own experience of createdness to be our most intimate experience of creation and a window onto all the rest. He had a deep love for creation and often referred to the divine presence within it—ourselves included—as *larvae Dei*, the masks of God.

For Luther, God is present in, with, under, and through the natural world. The world is full of God and God fills it, yet God is not limited or circumscribed by it. In essence, this is a panentheistic position where God is in the world but more than the world. Such an understanding provides an excellent theological foundation for the development of an ecological and sustainable understanding of vocation on our campuses. While much of the Lutheran ecclesial tradition has tended to emphasize christology in regard to justification and human salvation (particularly during the period of Lutheran scholasticism), Luther himself also saw the justifying grace of God as acting to restore nature and the nature-human relationship. Humans stand before God (*coram Deo*) by grace through faith and before humanity and the world (*coram hominibus* and *coram mundo*) through loving service, making one's faith active in love, as St. Paul enjoins in Galatians 5:6. Just as human relationships are subject to distortion, as persons become *incurvatus in se* (curved in upon themselves), so too can humanity's relation with nature become so distorted. Humans have too often seen nature merely as a natural resource for human use. This curves nature into our own sinful self-preoccupation and promotion of self.

Fast forward a couple hundred years: From the beginning of the Enlightenment through most of the twentieth century, it was common to speak of a separation between fact and value, science and religion, nature and history. Nature, as object, had no intrinsic development but was understood through scientific analysis as an objective, value-free inquiry where both human and religious purposes were considered to be irrelevant. History, on the other hand, was the realm of subjective human purpose and religious value in which civilizations rose and fell, charting their course in dominating an impersonal world. While there are many scholars today who still affirm such a separation, many if not most have come to understand it as a false dichotomy. In *Exiles from Eden*, Mark Schwhen discusses what Parker Palmer perceives as the Enlightenment scheme of "objectivism." Palmer observes that epistemologies (ways of knowing) have moral trajectories; they are not morally neutral but morally directive.[4] Ways of knowing necessarily include ways of valuing, and so a complete separation of fact and value is not possible. The challenge today is to retain the achievements of objective reflection without perpetuating its limitations. Nature need not be defined simply as "natural resources" for human use, but rather as having its own intrinsic integrity.

Religion has a particular view of the world; it is not limited to "subjective" value. On the other side, science requires values for the consideration of its applications. History would not exist without nature; nature itself has a history. In *Earth in the Balance*, Albert Gore asserts that humanity has always connected history to nature through technology and its impact upon the surrounding environment.[5] Many civilizations have fallen because of the environmental destruction they wreaked upon their supporting nature.[6] Technology is a prime exam-

---

4   Mark R. Schwhen, *Exiles from Eden: Religion and the Academic Vocation in America* (Oxford: Oxford University Press, 1993), 25.

5   Albert Gore, *Earth in the Balance* (New York: Houghton Mifflin, 1992).

6   See Jared Diamond, *Collapse: How Societies Choose to Fail or Succeed*, revised ed. (New York: Penguin Books, 2011).

ple of the intentional connecting of fact and value. The values intrinsic in scientific research are given embodied expression through technological application.[7] Today we see this with unprecedented clarity. With this clarity comes an increased responsibility to reconnect fact and value and steward the relation. Such a reconnection would go a long way toward preparing for sustainability leadership.

Divine Entanglement and Hope

When one studies the scholarly literature on the diverse changes taking place during our time, it is easy to become apocalyptic and feel that we may be living in the "final days" when nothing can be done. Such belief is stultifying and undermines the very will to change that is necessary for human and planetary survival. Make no mistake, the planet and some form of nature will go on for billions of years to come. The question is whether that will be with or without human presence. The planet has already existed far longer without humanity than it has with it, and, given human impact, some suggest that it may be better off without it. If we succeed in making the planet uninhabitable for our species as well as many others, will that have demonstrated that the great brain was not a positive survival characteristic? In the face of such negativity one needs to find a basis for hope that can inspire constructive and creative change. One of the gifts of Christian faith is hope in the face of suffering and death. Environmental education must be supplemented with religious and ethical education that provides hope in the face of impending cultural and climatological change. Fostering hope and feasible practical responses will provide a foundation for our graduates to become sustainability leaders in their future communities.

It is precisely here that I think theology has a global role to play. I will speak briefly from the Christian, trinitarian understanding of the nature of God, but other theistic and nontheistic traditions have critical roles to play in their respective geographies and cultures.

Within a Christian framework, human hope, along with salvation, ultimately rests upon the grace of God alone. This places human response and action in a transcendent context which does not rely entirely upon human motivation. Indeed, as I have argued in my recent book, *The Entangled Trinity: Quantum Physics and Theology*, God is "entangled" with creation in general and humanity in particular through the work of Christ and the animating power of the Holy Spirit. In

---

7   Frederick Ferre, *Hellfire and Lightening Rods* (Maryknoll, New York: Orbis, 1994).

quantum physics, research has demonstrated that two particles (such as paired photons) are entangled once they have interacted. When one is measured, the condition of the other is immediately known. Particles are still connected at the level of the quantum vacuum no matter how far apart they are separated in the physical universe. This means that at a deep, ontological level there is interrelationality and connectivity throughout the universe.[8] Appropriating this understanding for theology affirms that God is interrelated to everything in the cosmos and that there is a reciprocity of affect. What we do affects God as well as God affecting us. We are in a reciprocal, if unequal, ontological relationship with God. The divine is present in everything (radically immanent) and everything is present in the divine, while God still transcends it—thus the "panentheism" described above. Theologically, Luther would affirm such a dynamic, interdependent relationship. This entangled intimacy can be the ground for hope. It provides a more inclusive vision as well as animated action for constructive change.

Conclusion

Our students come to us formed by mass media merchandizing, social media patterning, and material consumption and waste. Our contemporary society encourages a person to be preoccupied with the self and the satisfaction of its desires. To be liberated from such a condition is one of the main objectives of a liberal arts education. Only with a changed vision can we begin to talk about a viable foundation for a sustainable future. It is in light of what might be that one can become empowered to challenge and change what is. The green grace of creation intersects the red grace of redemption upon the wood of the cross, making possible the blue grace of hope in the Spirit. We need a grace from beyond the self to reform the self and provide both forgiveness and hope. Judgment is easy, and cynicism breeds self-defeat. What is needed is reconciliation that motivates beyond the despair and hopelessness that inevitably result when coming to terms with one's own responsibility for destructive actions. We are becoming aware of our collective environmental responsibility and now need a forgiving, motivational grace to transcend self-interest for constructive change.

The Christian tradition, among others, can provide such grace-filled hope that can sustain one in the face of enormous challenges. As Viktor Frankl observed in his classic work, *Man's Search for Meaning*,

---

8   Ernest Simmons, *The Entangled Trinity: Quantum Physics and Theology* (Minneapolis: Fortress Press, 2014).

"Everything can be taken from a man but one thing: the last of human freedoms—to choose one's attitude in any given set of circumstances, to choose one's own way."[9] Lutheran higher education must foster a realistic but hopeful attitude towards the future and the systemic changes that we are all facing. Accordingly, environmental education for sustainability must be supplemented with religious and ethical education that provides hope in the face of impending cultural and climatological change. As the quotation by David Orr at the beginning of this article states, we must "educate into existence" leaders for sustainability that can undertake this task with grace and hope as well as knowledge and conviction.[10] Lutheran liberal arts education—a tradition founded on change and encouraging continued reform—is up to such a task if we undertake it as educators and administrators. Fostering hope and feasible practical responses, Lutheran higher education could provide a foundation for our graduates to become sustainability leaders in their future communities and engage the challenges of the twenty-first century, the epoch of the Anthropocene. This would be education *semper reformanda*!

Questions for Discussion

1. Of the seven ELCA initiatives within higher education listed at the start of this essay, in which have members of your campus participated? What effect has this had on the church-relatedness or Lutheran identity of your school?

2. Do you agree that environmental education must be supplemented with religious and ethical education in order to provide hope in the face of ecological degradation? Why or why not?

3. What particular resources does the Christian or even the Lutheran tradition bring to "education for sustainability leadership"?

9   Viktor Frankl. *Man's Search for Meaning* (Boston: Beacon Press, 2006), 66.
10 David W. Orr, *Earth in Mind: On Education, Environment, and the Human Prospect*, 10th Anniversary ed. (Washington D.C.: Island Press, 2004), 126.

CHAPTER 14

CALLED FORWARD
Educating for Vocation in the Twenty-first Century

KATHRYN A. KLEINHANS
Wartburg College, Waverly, Iowa

Lutherans and Lutheran theology have a complex relationship with the idea of "work."[1] At the heart of Lutheran theology stands the bold claim that Christians are justified by grace, for Christ's sake, through faith alone, apart from works of the law. And yet, coupled with this central theological claim is the equally bold assertion that good works necessarily follow faith as naturally as a tree bears fruit. Holding these two claims together can be a tough balancing act, especially in areas that call for concrete application. Focus too much on works as the necessary fruits of faith and risk being labeled a "legalist." Focus too little on these works and risk being called, at best, lazy and, at worst, an "antinomian," one who is against "the law." So how do Christians talk about work faithfully? More importantly, how do people *actually work faithfully*—whether they be Christian, Jewish, Muslim, Hindu, Buddhist, atheist, or "none of the above"?

Martin Luther's 1520 treatise "The Freedom of a Christian" is one of the clearest explications of Luther's view of the relationship between faith and work. Fundamental to Luther's understanding is a distinction between the inner and outer person. The inner person "is justified by faith alone and not any works"[2] and is intimately united

---

1   This essay draws from "The Work of a Christian: Vocation in Lutheran Perspective," *Word and World* 25.4 (Fall 2005): 394-402 (used with permission), as well as from "Distinctive Lutheran Contributions to the Conversation about Vocation," *Intersections* 43 (Spring 2016): 24-28.

2   Martin Luther, "The Freedom of a Christian" (1520), in *Luther's Works*, 55 vols., ed. Jaroslav Pelikan and Helmut Lehmann (Philadelphia and St. Louis: Fortress Press and Concordia Publishing House, 1955-1986), 31:346. All references to the American Edition of Luther's works will hereafter use the abbreviation LW followed by volume number.

with Christ through faith. But Christians understand humans to be incarnate beings, both spiritual and bodily, who live in the world. The outer person has to *do* something and thus occupies himself or herself with works, both for the purpose of self-discipline (like an athlete in training) and for the service of others.

One cannot overemphasize the fact that, for Luther, the distinction between the inner and outer person is not a dualistic separation in which an inner spirit is simply housed in an outer and relatively expendable package. Luther's anthropology is holistic. The language of "inner person" and "outer person" does not describe two separate components of the human being; rather it describes the whole Christian person from two different perspectives. In the relationship with God (*coram Deo*), faith alone matters. In our relationships with others (*coram hominibus*), however, we are evaluated on the basis of actions and results. Luther expresses this succinctly in "The Babylonian Captivity of the Church," written earlier in 1520, when he says, "We . . . cannot deal with God otherwise than through faith in the Word of his promise. He does not desire works, nor has he need of them; rather *we deal with [others] and with ourselves on the basis of works.*"[3]

Revitalizing Vocation

The language of vocation has become a useful lens for Lutherans—and others—to consider Christian life and work in response to God's gracious initiative. Its role within Lutheran higher education has been particularly pronounced and generative. Church reformer and university professor Martin Luther is generally credited with the recovery of the word "vocation" for general Christian (and now extra-Christian) use. Indeed, theologian Jürgen Moltmann identifies vocation as "the third great insight of the Lutheran Reformation," after word and sacrament.[4]

The word "vocation" literally means "calling." Prior to Luther, vocation typically referred to a special calling to religious life, as a priest or as a member of a vowed order. Such a vocation was understood as

---

3 Luther, "The Babylonian Captivity of the Church" (1520), LW 36:42, emphasis added.
4 Jürgen Moltmann, "Reformation and Revolution," in *Martin Luther and the Modern Mind*, Toronto Studies in Theology, v. 22, ed. Manfred Hoffmann (Lewiston, New York: Edwin Mellen, 1985), 186; cited in D. Michael Bennethum, *Listen! God is Calling! Luther Speaks of Vocation, Faith, and Work* (Minneapolis: Augsburg Fortress, 2003), 41. Another excellent resource is Douglas J. Schuurman, *Vocation: Discerning Our Callings in Life* (Grand Rapids, Michigan: Wm. B. Eerdmans Publishing, 2004). Schuurman examines both the Lutheran and Reformed understandings of vocation.

a higher calling, set over against life in the household and in civil society. Luther's understanding of the gospel as God's free gift led him to reject monastic life as an expression of a higher and more meritorious calling. He also rejected the division between sacred and secular spheres on which the medieval church's understanding of calling was predicated. In so doing, Luther broadened the concept of vocation from a narrow ecclesiastical focus to describe the life and work of all people in response to God's call. Luther insisted that "every occupation has its own honor before God, as well as its own requirements and duties."[5] Or again: "Just as individuals are different, so their duties are different; and in accordance with the diversity of their callings, God demands diverse works of them."[6]

Luther's so-called "two kingdoms" doctrine is illustrative here. In its mature form, it refers not to two separate, mutually exclusive spheres, but rather to two distinct ways in which God exercises divine authority: God is at work through the gospel, offering forgiveness and new life, and God is at work through the law, bringing order to the world. This twofold understanding of God's activity is the background for the distinct Reformation understanding of vocation as God's call to service in and for the world. The "secular" world is also God's world and is a suitable realm for divine service—not by serving God directly (since God does not need human works) but insofar as one serves the God-given neighbor. Seen through the lens of vocation, all human work becomes a means to participate in God's creating and sustaining activity on earth.

This Lutheran understanding of vocation is distinct not only from the Catholic understanding but also from the Anabaptist understanding.[7] The Schleitheim Confession, adopted by the Swiss Brethren in 1527, explicitly rejected the participation of Christians in "civic affairs," since worldly government and punishment are necessary only for those "outside the perfection of Christ." The Augsburg Confession, in turn, just as explicitly rejected the Anabaptist position, defending the legitimate participation of Christians in civil and military matters. One might say that Lutheranism rejected the "call to be apart from" the world in favor of a "call to be a part of" the world. It was not the nature of a work itself that was determinative for the Lutheran under-

---

5   Luther, "A Sermon on Keeping Children in School" (1530), LW 46:246.

6   Luther, "Lectures on Genesis [Genesis 8:17]" (1535), LW 2:113.

7   See also Chapter 10 in this book.

standing of vocation, either as affirmation of a special spiritual work or as rejection of a particularly secular work. What was determinative was responding in faith to God's call to be of service. According to Luther, the Christian "should be guided in all his works by this thought and contemplate this one thing alone, that he may serve and benefit others in all that he does, considering nothing except the need and the advantage of his neighbor."[8] Christians may even be soldiers and executioners without sin when they use their authority to protect and preserve and not for their own advantage.

Luther's understanding of vocation as service to the God-given neighbor was revolutionary in Luther's day, but in the years since Luther it has been too often domesticated or ignored. Over thirty years ago, theologian Marc Kolden called for a revitalization of Luther's idea of Christian vocation, grounded deeply in a law/gospel dialectic. More than a generation after Gustav Wingren's ground-breaking work on vocation, Kolden observed that Luther's dynamic understanding of vocation had made relatively little impact on North American Lutheranism.[9]

In recent years, Lutheran theologians have answered the call to revitalize Lutheran understandings of vocation.[10] Some of the best revitalization has been from within Lutheran colleges and universities, who have put the concept "to work" in forming and educating students for service of neighbor. For twenty years, in the journal *Intersections* as well as within the broader "vocation movement" within Lutheran higher education,[11] educators at Lutheran institutions have not only debated and lifted up Lutheran understandings of vocation, but also used the concept as a framing metaphor for their daily work and that of their students.

Taking Vocation to School

In recent years, two developments have helped shape a wider conversation about vocation in the United States. First, explicit talk of vocation has resurfaced noticeably in both church and the academy thanks to Frederick Buechner's assertion that "the place God calls you to is the place where your deep gladness and the world's deep hunger

---

8   Luther, "The Freedom of a Christian," 365.
9   Marc Kolden, "Luther on Vocation," *Word & World* 3.4 (1983): 382-90.
10 See, for example, the recent book by Mark D. Tranvik of Augsburg College: *Martin Luther and the Called Life* (Minneapolis: Fortress Press, 2016).
11 See especially Chapter 4 for the birth and development of what Mark Wilhelm calls the "vocation movement."

meet."[12] Second, and more important for higher education, was the Lilly Endowment's Programs for the Theological Exploration of Vocation (PTEV), and the subsequent Network for Vocation in Undergraduate Education (NetVUE). Through these programs, the Lilly Endowment encouraged institutions to define and explore vocation within their own contexts, informed by their particular theological and historical identities.

As a result of these two developments, there has been a noticeable resurgence of a rich language of vocation in many church-related schools. However, much of the conversation about vocation has been shaped by a somewhat generalized emphasis on finding meaning and purpose in one's career. What is more, while there is meaning and power in his articulation of vocation, Buechner's language is easily romanticized and thus trivialized in an age that focuses as heavily as ours on personal fulfillment. Even more problematic is that affirmation of work as a divine calling may devolve into a passive justification of the status quo or even an active cover for injustice. Does emphasizing the dignity inherent in the humblest work make it easier for a society not to raise its minimum wage, for example? And when does doing a job well become the "just following orders" of Auschwitz or Abu Ghraib? Faced with these challenges, a recovery of the distinctive characteristics of the deeper Lutheran understanding of vocation has much to offer.

In fact, the Lutheran understanding of vocation is also inseparable from the historic Lutheran commitment to education. In his 1524 address, "To the Councilmen of All Cities in Germany," Luther called for the establishment of schools to educate both boys and girls in order to equip them to serve the needs of a changing society. Regardless of whether their primary responsibilities were in the workplace, in the public sector, or in the home, young people needed a strong foundation in languages, history, and the liberal arts so that they would be prepared to "take their own place in the stream of human events."[13] Luther's criticism of parents who prefer to set their offspring up with a good living rather than providing them with a general education is perhaps worth reviving today when a college diploma is frequently

---

12 Frederick Buechner, *Wishful Thinking: A Theological ABC* (San Francisco: HarperSanFrancisco, 1993), 119.

13 Luther, "To the Councilmen of All Cities in Germany that They Establish and Maintain Christian Schools" (1524), LW 45:369.

viewed as a short-term investment strategy that will eventually pay off in a better job and a bigger paycheck.

What are the distinctive characteristics that the Lutheran tradition brings to vocation? As we have already seen, for Luther, all human work is equally valued, not only specifically religious work. Moreover, the purpose of human work is not primarily to please God but to serve the neighbor. Lutheran colleges and universities have made good use of a distinctive Lutheran concept of vocation in two additional ways: (1) Lutherans understand that the call to live faithfully in service of the neighbor is not limited to Christians but is part of God's intent for the whole creation; and (2) Lutherans understand people to have multiple vocations—over a lifetime, of course, but also within multiple dimensions of human life at the same time. We take each of these understandings in turn.

Vocation for All

While most of our ELCA colleges and universities were founded to educate members of the founding religious and/or ethnic community, today our campuses are characterized by a wide diversity of students. We have students of all faiths and none. Among the "nones," there are students who are actively asking religious and spiritual questions apart from any organized religious community, as well as those who dismiss religious and spiritual concerns as irrelevant. Does a non-Christian student have a calling? If so, from what or whom? When one cannot assume a shared faith, Luther is (perhaps surprisingly) a helpful resource, because he grounds vocation in *created life* rather than the *life of faith*.

In fact, Luther's sense of vocation is rooted in a dynamic doctrine of creation. For Luther, to confess God as creator is to acknowledge not only God's original work but that God continually (daily!) sustains the creation by providing that which is necessary for life. Luther understands the necessities of life quite broadly, defining "daily bread" to include food, clothing, and shelter; physical health; family, friends, and neighbors; fiscal resources; and stable government—"in short, everything that pertains to the regulation of our domestic and our civil or political affairs."[14]

---

14 Luther, Large Catechism (1529), in *The Book of Concord*, ed. and trans. Theodore G. Tappert (Philadelphia: Fortress Press, 1959), 430.

Given this broad understanding of the scope of God's concern as creator, it should come as no surprise that God's sustaining activity on behalf of the creation is mediated. Just as God's saving grace is conveyed through word and sacrament as means of grace, so God's providential care of the world also occurs through tangible means—including not only natural structures (sun, moon, and stars; the laws of gravity, entropy, etc.) but also the work of God's human creatures. According to Luther, God "wants to act through His creatures, whom He does not want to be idle."[15] God now gives food through human labor, rather than through the miraculous appearance of manna, and God now creates human beings through sexual union rather than out of dust. As Wingren explains it, "With persons as his 'hands' or 'coworkers,' God gives his gifts through the earthly vocations (food through farmers, fishermen and hunters; external peace through princes, judges, and orderly powers; knowledge and education through teachers and parents, etc.)."[16]

It is also important to recognize that God works through humans not only through their individual efforts but also through their social and political structures. Luther frequently describes life in three "orders" or arenas of activity—the household, the state, and the church—each of which he understands as having been established by God for the common good. God's will for the creation can thus be expressed through socially constructed laws as well as through the laws of nature, and humans are subject to God's regulating activity in both of these ways. From the point of view of the Lutheran reformers, to withdraw from civic affairs, as did both monks and Anabaptists, was to deny the legitimacy of God's created orders. Indeed, to withdraw from civic affairs was to abandon the neighbor rather than to serve the neighbor.[17]

But most important for our diverse institutions is this: God, as creator, calls *all* people to live responsibly in the world God has made. Because God works in the created world indirectly, through natural

---

15 Luther, "Lectures on Genesis [Genesis 19:14]," LW 3:274.

16 Gustav Wingren, *Luther on Vocation*, trans. Carl C. Rasmussen (Philadelphia: Muhlenberg Press, 1957), 27. This is the perspective that grounds theologian Philip Hefner's description of humans as "created co-creators." As Luther himself says, "Through faith a Christian becomes a creator." Martin Luther, *Luthers Werke, Weimar Ausgabe* (Weimar: Boehlau, 1883ff), 27:400, as cited in Bennethum, *Listen! God Is Calling!*, 51.

17 See Chapter 10 for updates and further nuance when comparing Mennonites and Lutherans on vocation.

and human agency, this is true regardless of whether or not the people themselves "hear" or acknowledge this call as coming from God.

How do the custodians of an institution's heritage talk about religious or spiritual values in ways that are faithful to their own particularity without excluding those whose views differ? Can shared human and religious commitments to the common good create relationships and conversations through which students, faculty, and staff come to a deeper appreciation for the church-relatedness of their institutions? A Lutheran understanding of vocation within the context of creaturely existence offers our colleges, universities, and campus ministries an important base from which to reach out to students of other religions or students with no religion at all. We can state without hesitation that all people have callings, not only Christians. All people are called to lives of responsible service within the realms of family, economic, and civic life.

Regardless of the labels our students espouse or eschew, the broad Lutheran understanding of vocation is a way of engaging all of our students with questions of meaning and purpose in life. As our students choose majors and prepare for future occupations or professions, we have an opening to talk about what author Sharon Daloz Parks has termed "big questions, worthy dreams."[18] The notion of vocation as how we steward life on our shared planetary home is a way of challenging our students to locate meaning and purpose outside themselves and their immediate environs.

The Vocations of Students: Always Present and Plural

I have been arguing that the distinctive Lutheran understanding of vocation has served higher education well in recent years. But can it take us into the future? Is vocation really durable enough for education today, given all the present anxieties about the cost of higher education, rapidly shifting job opportunities, the loss of human work to the work of machines, and the emergence of "emerging adulthood," which has elongated the transition to "the real world" and has changed what young adults want and expect to find therein? Anxieties about work and purpose are very real.

Vocation in the context of a broad liberal arts education dedicated to forming whole persons continues to be ideally suited to meet these

18 Sharon Daloz Parks, *Big Questions, Worthy Dreams: Mentoring Emerging Adults in Their Search for Meaning, Purpose, and Faith*, 2nd ed. (San Francisico: Jossy-Bass, 2011).

anxieties. At the heart of a liberal arts education is the goal of equipping students to think and to act both critically and nimbly. These skills and habits of mind are essential in our fast-paced, ever-changing world. The Lutheran understanding of vocation offers a lens that values all areas of work and all forms of study, even those not yet identified. For example, no one working today as a sustainability manager, a patient advocate, or a social media strategist could have chosen—or even found—a pre-professional major twenty years ago to prepare them for the job they now hold, since these jobs did not yet exist. But even more important, the understanding of human work as directed toward service of neighbor and toward the stewardship of the earth requires students to learn about a world much bigger than their own neighborhoods and communities. The lens of vocation offers a view of the world that is both wider and more generous than many of the prevailing worldviews our students encounter elsewhere.

The durability and adaptability of liberal arts education itself owes something to Luther's understanding of vocation, given his affirmation of the plurality of callings in the individual's life. The arenas of worldly activity identified by Luther are not mutually exclusive: one can be a family member, an employer or an employee, a citizen, and a member of the Christian community simultaneously. We have multiple callings—multiple "places of responsibility"—because we participate simultaneously through multiple roles in multiple communities.[19] Colleges and universities are no exception.

Of course, many students still assume that their vocation is something of the future, and always singular in nature. Here again, Buechner's popular description of vocation as "the place where your deep gladness and the world's deep hunger meet" carries the implication that vocational discernment is about finding one's personal "sweet spot." It can also foster a perspective that one stands somehow outside of vocation until one identifies and takes up one's calling. In other words, if vocation is God's call, there are too many Christians who expect that call to be difficult to understand. It is not uncommon to hear the assertion that God has a "personal plan for my life." From such a perspective, the individual's responsibility is both to find and to follow that unique, mysterious plan. One almost conjures up images of

---

19 I have developed this point in "Places of Responsibility: Educating for Multiple Callings in Multiple Communities," in *At This Time and in This Place: Vocation and Higher Education*, ed. David C. Cunningham (Oxford: Oxford University Press, 2016), 99-121.

God on a cell phone, moving from place to place asking "Can you hear me now?" with the person on the receiving end of the call desperate to find the one right place where a clear signal is possible.

The Lutheran understanding of vocation offers an important corrective to this all-or-nothing, hit-or-miss mentality by focusing on how God is already at work in one's everyday life here and now. Within this framework, the "now" of "Can you hear me now?" suggests an incarnational (embodied) commitment to any place and every place that people find themselves. One does not move farther away from God or closer to God depending on the choices one makes; rather each person's task is to act responsibly in each concrete role or situation.

While Luther affirmed human freedom to make choices within the framework of our earthly lives and relationships, much about his understanding of vocation in his own context was simply a given. For Luther, all people have callings within the areas of family/household, religious community, and civil society. (Later Lutherans distinguished the workplace as a fourth area, although Luther himself understood economic work as part of one's household responsibilities.)

In the realm of family, I may choose whether and whom to marry and whether to have children. However, my relationships as daughter, granddaughter, and sister are simply given—and existed long before I was aware of them. Having chosen to marry, my relationships as daughter-in-law and sister-in-law came as givens with my choice of spouse. At issue is not whether I am called to these relationships but how I live faithfully within these callings, even (and especially when) they conflict. How do I love the neighbors who are given to me within these family relationships? Luther's understanding of vocation in service of neighbor reminds me that I am called to do so for their own sake, regardless of whether it contributes to "my deep gladness."

This recognition of the given-ness of our vocations within our individual contexts calls our attention to vocation as a present reality, not a future one. This emphasis is particularly important for the work we do as educators. Indeed, educators at Lutheran colleges and universities need to claim the bold affirmation that residential, liberal arts, and church-related colleges are perhaps uniquely equipped for acknowledging and fostering the multiple vocations of our students. In particular, if we take seriously our own call to educate "the whole student," we are challenged to recognize that our students' callings outside the classroom also have value. Many students struggle between the demands of school and family. In my experience, this is particularly so for first-generation college students. Much as we rightly call our students to take seriously their present calling as students, we need to recognize that their legitimate callings as son or daughter, sibling, etc. do not cease for the years they are enrolled in college or university. Insisting that academic coursework trumps all other obligations is neither helpful nor likely to be effective.

Even on our campuses, our students have roles and responsibilities outside the classroom, as student athletes, student employees, members of musical ensembles, in the residence halls, and more. Our colleges offer these opportunities because of the understanding that they contribute to the educational experience of our students. Educating the whole person entails the recognition that learning extends beyond the classroom and thus that faculty are not the only resources in educating for vocation. Administrators, student life professionals, coaches, and others all play important roles in student education and formation. Educating students to live as whole (holy?) persons and responsible selves requires the resources of the entire college community. How do we equip all members of the college community to help students see the many aspects of their lives through the lens of vocation?

The affirmation of both the particularity and multiplicity of one's callings clearly demonstrates the Lutheran conviction that one need not—and indeed should not—abandon one's existing circumstances in order to pursue a supposedly higher and more spiritual calling. Luther is fond of saying that one's own roles and relationships surely give one more than enough God-pleasing work to do without having to look for more. In Luther's time these roles and relationships were often given rather than individually chosen. Nevertheless, the Pauline injunction to "remain in the condition in which you were called" (1 Corinthians 7:20) need not result in an acceptance of social determinism at the expense of freedom of choice in daily life. Luther's point is not that one *may* not change one's station or office but than one *need* not do so in order to serve God.

Luther intended this recognition of our existing responsibilities as vocation to be reassuring. Unfortunately, the multiplicity of roles is often experienced in modern times as overwhelming. Competing demands result in feelings of fragmentation and, on a practical level, in the compartmentalization of work, home, and community life for many of us, just as our students often compartmentalize academics, co-curricular activities, student employment, and "fun."

Much of the marketing of higher education, in tune with the consumer expectations of students and their parents, focuses on the future: What does a college or university education prepare you to do? What kinds of jobs does a particular course of study open for you? As real as those future callings will one day be for our students, many of us challenge our students to recognize and embrace the reality that one of their primary vocations here and now is the vocation of student. College students are called to be students here and now, in addition to being called to be friends, roommates, student workers, teammates, family members, citizens, faithful followers of their religions, and so on.

The developmental task for our students is to learn how to negotiate these overlapping and conflicting responsibilities in new ways as their life circumstances change. As educators committed to a broad understanding of vocation, we have the opportunity to support them in this work. We need to recognize that the academic vocation of students does not negate their other callings in domestic, economic, and communal life. We need to help them identify and affirm these roles and relationships as legitimate callings, and we need to help them learn to think and to act responsibly, as whole persons, within the complex intersections of lived human experience.

Lutheran colleges, universities, and campus ministries understand that the undergraduate years are not only about education, but also about formation. Even in these challenging times for higher education, our calling is to help students to articulate and to claim their own callings, for today and for whatever new challenges tomorrow will hold.

Questions for Discussion

1. Kleinhans claims that a Lutheran understanding of vocation, as grounded in "created life" rather than "the life of faith," is able to reach students of different faiths or of no faith. Has vocation been a versatile, while still meaningful, focus on your campus? What ongoing challenges in this regard does your institution face?

2. Among the various anxieties about work and purpose facing our students/graduates, which do you find to be most significant? Which of these challenge traditional understandings of vocation most directly? What resources in Lutheran higher education do we possess for facing such anxieties?

3. In what ways have you come to know students' present, multiple, and sometimes conflicting callings? How have you supported them—and how might you better support them—as they responsibly negotiate and live out those callings?

EPILOGUE

EXPANDING THE VISION
The Vocation of Church-Related Colleges

DARRELL JODOCK AND MARK WILHELM

This book as a whole has offered a history of "the vocation movement" within Lutheran higher education, identified some of its defining marks, voiced critical questions about this intellectual and pedagogical tradition (especially from those on the outside looking in), and located sample trajectories for important issues and ongoing conversations. The chapters here have responded to questions that educators at Lutheran colleges and universities have learned to ask and debate. Chief among them are these: What does it mean to be a Lutheran college or university especially now that non-Lutherans sometimes far outnumber Lutherans among students and faculty? What difference does our church-relatedness make for the way we administer our schools and teach our students? In short, what is Lutheran higher education *for?*

Church-related colleges from other denominations certainly ask similar questions about their own histories, defining characteristics, and relationships with church bodies. And yet, we are bold to suggest that ELCA colleges and universities are particularly practiced in asking these questions and deliberating carefully about their shared mission and defining characteristics. Given this experience, and the distinctiveness and generativity of "education for vocation," the ELCA higher education community should invite leaders in church-sponsored higher education outside the ELCA to join the vocation movement. Despite differences in the interpretation of the Christian doctrine of vocation, all these traditions share the concept as a central feature of Christian practice. Could they not also embrace the redefinition of church-sponsored higher education as described in the essays of this volume? Might they not also re-appropriate the doctrine of vocation *as* the mission of their college?

Any and every church-related college might begin to consider our invitation to join the vocation movement by asking: What is the goal of a church-related college, whatever its denominational connection?

Many will answer this question by saying that its goal is to provide the church with educated leadership. Some of these leaders will be clergy, but the vast majority will be laity. They will serve on congregational councils, participate in choirs, and teach in educational programs. Providing leaders for the church is, indeed, a partial answer to the question. Church-related colleges do serve the church in this way.

Others might respond by saying that the goal of church-related education is to prepare students with the knowledge and skills necessary to find the kind of employment reserved for college graduates. This, again, is a partial answer to the question. Church-related colleges do this admirably well. Some focus on high achieving students, while others assist marginal and non-traditional students who need remedial work and/or alternative educational arrangements in order to succeed. In either case, students are being prepared for work in a variety of fields.

But a fuller answer begins to emerge when we affirm that the goal of a church-related college is to serve the larger society. In this sense *the college itself has a vocation, a calling.* While including the two partial answers already mentioned, this calling involves other goals.

The vocation of a church-related college includes fostering a robust sense of vocation among its students, faculty, and staff that extends into every area of life—work, marriage, family, community involvement—and equips persons to challenge the mainstream as well as to function in it.

The vocation of a church-related college also involves deepening the education mission of its faculty and students to include the cultivation of wisdom in addition to the acquisition of knowledge and skills. Such wisdom enhances a person's ability to bring out the best in others, to identify and work for the common good, and to foster a healthy community. Such wisdom is needed to guide a person's vocationally-oriented actions—to help him or her determine what will or will not actually benefit the neighbor and the community. When wisdom is the overarching educational goal, education becomes a communal enterprise. It is communal, because multiple insights are necessary in order to identify the common good and discern how to advance it.

This affects how classes are conducted, how assignments are designed, and how exams are constructed.

The vocation of a church-related college includes encouraging significant art and music in order to enhance the lives of people in the larger community. By adding beauty, most art and music can enrich human life. However, some art and music also call attention to transcendence, explore the complexity of the human situation, and, in so doing, contribute even more. Such art and music expand horizons. They challenge narrow perspectives and open new possibilities. They celebrate and explore mystery. They break open the ordinary to reveal the presence of the sacred within all of life. When viewed as a vocation, art and music, while including self-expression, can contribute to the common good in an uncommon way.

The vocation of a church-related college also involves fostering the capacity for and commitment to civil discourse so necessary for a democracy to flourish. This capacity is particularly urgent in our day in order to overcome the overheated rhetoric that contributes to political polarization and political paralysis. Given the religious diversity of our nation, the capacity for civil discourse includes a readiness to seek interreligious understanding.

The vocation of a church-related college involves fostering a lively sense of justice and a commitment to achieve it. This involves attending to structural injustice and to those groups who are marginalized and harmed by the present social, political, and economic order.

Finally, the vocation of a church-related college involves inspiring a sense of agency (the conviction that a person can make a difference in the world) and a sense of hope based on God's activity in the world. Such agency and hope counteract the anxiety and fear that contribute to overly-simplistic ideologies, culture wars, and military conflicts.

All of this involves fostering a commitment to a deeper sense of meaning and purpose than is provided by the relatively superficial values of a consumerist society. And all of this can be described as seeking shalom (whole, healthy relationships among humans, between humans and God, and between humans and the rest of creation) or as "mending the world"—to borrow a phrase from the Jewish tradition.

The vocation of a church-related college is advanced more effectively when the college community practices and models its vocation by engaging its own neighborhood. Its classes and extra-curricular activities can involve students, faculty, and staff in such things as reducing a community's reliance on fossil fuels, assisting with the instruction of underprivileged children, recommending financial or managerial improvements for a non-profit, bringing diverse segments of the community into conversation with each other, helping to re-settle refugees and immigrants, and so on.

Of course, each particular denomination will understand vocation with different emphases and will narrate the history, defining marks, weaknesses, and trajectories of its own vocation differently. Still, by defining church-relatedness through vocation, church-related higher education in the United States can begin to cut through conflicting and divisive assumptions about what constitutes "Christian education."

For more than fifty years, church-related institutions in the United States have been stuck in futile debates about "authenticity,"framed by the division of church-sponsored higher education into "Christian" and "church-related" camps.[1] Despite this division, both groups continue to assume that church-sponsored higher education must be sectarian, in great contrast to the vocation movement's identification of service to others (as sketched above) as its purpose. The two groups have differed only over the extent that sectarian commitments must determine the identity and academic mission of a college or university, with "Christian" colleges requiring a more rigorous embrace of sectarian commitments than "church-related" colleges. Both groups thus have assumed the terms of the same questions: How far can a school move toward sectarianism and still be a credible academic institution? How far can a school move toward secularism and still be authentically Christian? To this day an all-too-stable continuum with "sectarian" on one end and "secular" on the other, and the supposed location of all schools on that continuum, frames the culturally-dominant conversations about the mission and authenticity of church-sponsored higher education. It is precisely these assumptions and divisions that the vocation movement within Lutheran higher education rejects. The vocation movement follows instead a "third path"[2]—one that lies

---

1   The beginning of the Christian/church-related division in higher education is probably best marked by *Church-Sponsored Education in the United States: Report of the Danforth Commission*, ed. Manning M. Pattillo, Jr. and Donald M. Mackenzie (Washington, D.C.: American Council on Education, 1966). The division was reinforced by the publically recognizable transformation of the fundamentalist movement in the Reformed/Holiness tradition into neo-evangelicalism at about the same time.

2   See especially Chapter 6.

alongside sectarianism and secularism, one that promises to guide us *around* fruitless debates.

Should not educators at Lutheran colleges and universities encourage others in church-sponsored higher education to join us in the vocation movement? Should we not invite them to join us in rejecting the sectarian-secular continuum, along with its assumptions and questions, as the measure of "authentic" Christian practice in higher education? More positively, can we not invite them into the conversation about how the vocation movement calls us to serve the neighbor, to cultivate wisdom, to encourage art, to foster civil discourse, to work toward justice, to seek shalom, and to promote a sense of agency, hope, meaning, and purpose? Should we not stop asking whether the veneer of parochial control at a college or university is thick enough to guide and inspire, without stifling, scholarly work? Should we not instead redirect questions to the insights gained from the wisdom fostered by the exploration of vocation, as described in this volume? Part of the vocation of Lutheran higher education may very well be to invite other church-sponsored higher education leaders to consider how higher education can be authentically, faithfully Christian, even though its practices are not parochial and may even appear secular.

Of course, the Lutheran tradition has its particular interests and emphases in the doctrine of vocation. And yet—as an implication of the gospel itself—the concept of vocation is held in common with other Christian traditions. Lutheran educators should invite others into a broader discussion about the vocation movement. The invitation certainly must be extended in a spirit that allows Lutheran educators to learn from other traditions, and yet we, too, have something to teach and share. Let us make this expanded conversation our new agenda.

RESOURCES FOR CONTINUED CONVERSATIONS

On the Vocation of Lutheran Higher Education

Ahlstrom, Sydney. "What's Lutheran about Higher Education?—A Critique," in *Papers and Proceedings of the 60th Annual Convention.* Washington, D.C.: LECNA, 1974. 8-16.

Ashmon, Scott A., ed. *The Idea and Practice of a Christian University: A Lutheran Approach.* St. Louis: Concordia Publishing House, 2015.

Appold, Kenneth G. "Academic Life and Teaching in Post-Reformation Lutheranism." *Lutheran Ecclesiastical Culture, 1550-1675.* Ed. Robert Kolb. Leiden, Boston: Brill, 2008. 65-115.

Benne, Robert. *Quality with Soul: How Six Premier Colleges and Universities Keep Faith with Their Religious Traditions.* Grand Rapids, Michigan: Wm. B. Eerdmans Publishing, 2001.

Childers, Eric. *College Identity Sagas: Investigating Organizational Identity Preservation and Diminishment at Lutheran Colleges and Universities.* Eugene, Oregon: Pickwick, 2012.

Christenson, Tom. *The Gift and Task of Lutheran Higher Education.* Minneapolis: Augsburg Fortress, 2004.

_____. *Who Needs a Lutheran College? Values, Vision, Vocation.* Minneapolis: Lutheran University Press, 2011.

Dovre, Paul J. *The Cross and the Academy: Occasional Papers and Addresses 1975-   2009.* Minneapolis: Lutheran University Press, 2011.

Evangelical Lutheran Church in America (ELCA). *Our Calling in Education: A Social Statement of the Evangelical Lutheran Church in America* (2007). Web http://download.elca.org/ELCA%20Resource%20Repository/EducationSS.pdf

Frame, William V. *The Dialogue of Faith and Reason: The Speeches and Papers of the Tenth President of Augsburg College.* Minneapolis: Lutheran University Press, 2006.

LaHurd, Carol Schersten, Darrell Jodock, and Kathryn Mary Lohre, eds. *Engaging Others, Knowing Ourselves: A Lutheran Calling in a Multi-Religious World.* Minneapolis: Lutheran University Press, 2016.

Noll, Mark A. "Early Protestants and the Reformation of Education." *Westminster Theological Journal* 43:1 (Fall 1980): 97-131.

Schwehn, Kaethe and L. DeAne Lagerquist, *Claiming our Callings: Toward a New Understanding of Vocation in the Liberal Arts.* Oxford: Oxford University Press, 2014.

Schwhen, Mark R. *Exiles from Eden: Religion and the Academic Vocation in America.* Oxford: Oxford University Press, 1993.

———. "Lutheranism and the Future of the University." *The Cresset* 73.2 (Advent-Christmas 2009): 6-14.

Simmons, Ernest L. *Lutheran Higher Education: An Introduction for Faculty.* Minneapolis: Augsburg Fortress, 1998.

Solberg. Richard W. *Lutheran Higher Education in North America.* Minneapolis: Augsburg Publishing House, 1985.

Relevant Works by or about Martin Luther

Bennethem, Michael D. *Listen! God Is Calling!: Luther Speaks of Vocation, Faith, and Work.* Minneapolis: Fortress Press, 2003.

Gritsch, Eric W. *A History of Lutheranism.* Minneapolis: Fortress Press, 2002.

Grosshans, Hans-Peter. "Luther on Faith and Reason: The Light of Reason at the Twilight of the World." *The Global Luther: A Theologian for Modern Times.* Ed. Christine Helmer. Minneapolis: Fortress Press, 2009. 173-85.

Harran, Marilyn. *Luther and Learning.* London: Associated University Presses, 1985.

Kittleson, James. *Luther the Reformer: The Story of the Man and His Career.* Minneapolis: Fortress Press, 2003.

Kleinhans, Kathryn. "The Work of a Christian: Vocation in Lutheran Perspective." *Word & World* 25.4 (Fall 2005): 394-402.

Lindberg, Carter. *Beyond Charity: Reformation Initiatives for the Poor.* Minneapolis: Fortress Press, 1993.

Luther, Martin. "The Freedom of a Christian," *Luther's Works* (American Edition), volume 31. Philadelphia: Muhlenberg Press, 1957.

_____. "Sermon on Keeping Children in School," *Luther's Works* (American Edition), volume 46. Philadelphia: Muhlenberg Press, 1961.

_____. "To the Councilmen of All Cities in Germany That They Establish and Maintain Christian Schools," *Luther's Works* (American Edition), volume 45. Philadelphia: Muhlenberg Press, 1962.

_____. "Two Kinds of Righteousness," *Luther's Works* (American Edition), volume 31. Philadelphia: Muhlenberg Press, 1957.

Mahn, Jason, ed. *Radical Lutherans/Lutheran Radicals*. Eugene, Oregon: Cascade, forthcoming.

Marty, Martin. *Martin Luther: A Life*. New York: Penguin, 2004.

Torvend, Samuel. *Luther and the Hungry Poor: Gathered Fragments*. Minneapolis: Fortress Press, 2008.

Tranvik, Mark D. *Martin Luther and the Called Life*. Minneapolis: Fortress Press, 2016.

Westhelle, Vítor. *Transfiguring Luther: The Planetary Promise of Luther's Theology*. Eugene, Oregon: Cascade, 2016.

Wingren, Gustaf. *Luther on Vocation*. Trans. Carl C. Rasmussen. Eugene, Oregon: Wipf and Stock, 1957.

Scholarship on Vocation

Benne, Robert. *Ordinary Saints: An Introduction to the Christian Life*. Minneapolis: Fortress Press, 2003.

Buechner, Frederick. *Wishful Thinking: A Theological ABC*. San Francisco: HarperSanFrancisco, 1993.

Clydesdale, Tim. *The Purposeful Graduate: Why Colleges Must Talk to Students about Vocation*. Chicago: University of Chicago Press, 2015.

Cunningham, David S., ed. *At This Time and In This Place: Vocation and Higher Education*. Oxford: Oxford University Press, 2016.

_____., ed. *Vocation Across the Academy: A New Vocabulary for Higher Education*. Oxford: Oxford University Press, 2017.

Hahnenberg, Edward P. *Awakening Vocation: A Theology of Christian Call*. Collegeville, Minnesota: Liturgical Press, 2010.

Kolden, Mark. *Christian's Calling in the World*. St. Paul, Minnesota: CenteredLife, 2002.

Palmer, Parker J. *Let Your Life Speak: Listening for the Voice of Vocation*. San Francisco: Jossey-Bass, 2000.

Parks, Sharon Daloz. *Big Questions, Worthy Dreams: Mentoring Emerging Adults in Their Search for Meaning, Purpose, and Faith*. 2nd ed. San Francisco: Jossey-Bass, 2011.

Placher, William C. *Callings: Twenty Centuries of Christian Wisdom on Vocation*. Grand Rapids, Michigan: Wm. B. Eerdmans Publishing, 2005.

Schuurman, Douglas J. *Vocation: Discerning Our Callings in Life*. Grand Rapids, Michigan: Wm. B. Eerdmans Publishing Co., Inc., 2004.

Schwehn, Mark R. and Dorothy C. Bass, eds. *Leading Lives that Matter: What We Should Do and Who We Should Be*. Grand Rapids, Michigan: Wm. B. Eerdmans Publishing, 2006.

Related Resources

Arum, Richard and JosipaRoksa. *Academically Adrift: Limited Learning on College Campuses*. Chicago: University of Chicago Press, 2010.

Berger, Peter, ed. *Between Relativism and Fundamentalism: Religious Resources for a Middle Position*. Grand Rapids, Michigan: Wm. B. Eerdmans Publishing, 2010.

Bok, Derek. *Our Underachieving Colleges: A Candid Look at How Much Students Learn and Why They Should Be Learning More*. Princeton: Princeton University Press, 2006.

Burtchaell, James Tunstead. *The Dying of the Light: The Disengagement of Colleges and Universities from their Christian Churches*. Grand Rapids, Michigan: Wm. B. Eerdmans Publishing, 1998.

Carpenter, Joel, Perry Glanzer, and Nicholas Lantinga, eds. *Christian Higher Education: A Global Reconnaissance*. Grand Rapids, Michigan: Wm. B. Eerdmans Publishing, 2014.

Delbanco, Andrew. *College: What it Was, Is, and Should Be*. Princeton: Princeton University Press, 2012.

Dovre, Paul, ed. *The Future of Religious Colleges: The Proceedings of the Harvard Conference on the Future of Religious Colleges, October 6-7, 2000.* Grand Rapids, Michigan: Wm. B. Eerdmans Publishing, 2002.

Farrell, James J. *The Nature of College: How a New Understanding of Campus Life Can Change the World.* Minneapolis: Milkweed Editions, 2010.

Hughes, Richard T. *How Christian Faith Can Sustain the Life of the Mind.* Grand Rapids, Michigan: Wm. B. Eerdmans Publishing, 2001.

Hughes, Richard T. and William B. Adrian. *Models of Christian Higher Education.* Grand Rapids, Michigan: Wm. B. Eerdmans Publishing, 1997.

Jacobsen, Douglas and Rhonda Hustedt Jacobsen, eds. *The American University in a Postsecular Age.* Oxford: Oxford University Press, 2008.

_____. *No Longer Invisible: Religion in University Education.* Oxford: Oxford University Press, 2012.

Jodock, Darrell, ed. *Covenantal Conversations: Christians in Dialogue with Jews and Judaism.* Minneapolis: Fortress Press, 2008.

Kimball, Bruce A. *Orators and Philosophers: A History of the Ideal of Liberal Education.* New York: Teachers College Press, 1986.

Madsen, Susan R. *On Becoming a Woman Leader: Learning from the Experiences of University Presidents.* San Francisco: Jossey-Bass, 2008.

Marsden, George. *The Outrageous Idea of Christian Scholarship.* Oxford: Oxford University Press, 1997.

_____. *The Soul of the American University: From Protestant Establishment to Established Nonbelief.* Oxford: Oxford University Press, 1994.

Marty, Martin E. *The One and the Many: America's Struggle for the Common Good.* Boston: Harvard University Press, 1998.

Niebuhr, Richard. *Christ and Culture.* New York: Harper and Row, 1975.

Nussbaum, Martha. *Not for Profit: Why Democracy Needs the Humanities.* Princeton: Princeton University Press, 2010.

Orr, David W. *Earth in Mind: On Education, Environment, and the Human Prospect.* 10th anniversary edition. Washington D.C.: Island, 2004.

Palmer, Parker, *Healing the Heart of Democracy: The Courage to Create a Politics Worthy of the Human Spirit.* San Francisco: Jossey-Bass, 2011.

Palmer, Parker J. and Arthur Zajonc, *The Heart of Higher Education: A Call for Renewal, Transforming the Academy through Collegial Conversations.* San Francisco: Jossey-Bass, 2010.

Parks, Sharon. *Leadership Can be Taught.* Boston: Harvard Business School Press, 2005.

Patel, Eboo. *Interfaith Leadership: A Primer.* Boston: Beacon, 2016.

Patel, Eboo, Katie Bringman Baxter, and Noah Silverman."Leadership Practices for InterfaithExcellence in Higher Education."*Liberal Education* 101.1 (2015): Web <https://www.aacu.org/liberaleducation/2015/winter-spring/patel>.

Putnam, Robert D. "E Pluribus Unum: Diversity and Community in the Twenty-first Century." The 2006 Johan Skytte Prize Lecture. *Scandinavian Political Studies* 30.2 (2007): 137–74.

Ringenberg, William. *The Christian College: A History of Protestant Education in America.* 2nd Edition. Grand Rapids, Michigan: Baker Academic, 2006.

Selingo, Jeffrey J. *College (Un)bound: The Future of Higher Education and What It Means for Students.* New York: Houghton Mifflin Harcourt, 2013.

Smith, Christian with Melinda Lundquist Denton. *Soul Searching: The Religious and Spiritual Lives of American Teenagers.* New York: Oxford University Press, 2005.

Smith, Christian, Kari Christoffersen, Hilary Davidson, and Patricia Snell Herzog. *Lost in Transition: The Dark Side of Emerging Adulthood.* New York: Oxford University Press, 2011.

Stortz, Martha E. "Beyond Service: What Justice Requires." *Currents in Theology and Mission* 37:3 (June 2010): 230-37.

Schwhen, Mark. "A Christian University: Defining the Difference." *First Things* 93 (1999): 25-31.

Traub, George W., ed. *A Jesuit Education Reader: Contemporary Writings on the Jesuit Mission in Education, Principles, the Issue of Catholic Identity, Practical Applications of the Ignatian Way, and More.* Chicago: Loyola, 2008.

VanZanten, Susan. *Joining the Mission: A Guide for (Mainly) New College Faculty.* Grand Rapids, Michigan: Wm. B. Eerdmans Publishing, 2011.

The Twenty-six ELCA Colleges and Universities: Articulations of their Lutheran Identities

Augsburg College
www.augsburg.edu/about/history/

Augustana College (Illinois)
www.augustana.edu/general-information/mission-and-history

Augustana University (South Dakota)
www.augie.edu/mission-values-and-vision

Bethany College
www.bethanylb.edu/about/lutheran-identity/

California Lutheran University
www.callutheran.edu/about/lutheran-experience.html

Capital University
www.capital.edu/About-Capital/Mission-and-Vision/

Carthage College
www.carthage.edu/about/

Concordia College
www.concordiacollege.edu/about/our-mission/

Finlandia University
www.finlandia.edu/about/our-lutheran-commitment/

Gettysburg College
www.gettysburg.edu/about/offices/college_life/religious-spiritual-life/worship-meditation-space/chapel/

Grand View University
www.grandview.edu/aspx/audience/content.aspx?aid=0&pageid=23

Gustavus Adolphus College
www.gustavus.edu/president/vision.php

Lenoir-Rhyne University
www.lr.edu/about

Luther College
www.luther.edu/about/mission/

Midland University
  www.midlandu.edu/basic-page/about-midland

Muhlenberg College
  www.muhlenberg.edu/main/aboutus/

Newberry College
  www.newberry.edu/about-us

Pacific Lutheran University
  www.plu.edu/lutheran-studies/core-elements/

Roanoke College
  www.roanoke.edu/about/purpose_and_principles

St. Olaf College
  wp.stolaf.edu/about/

Susquehanna University
  www.susqu.edu/about-su

Texas Lutheran University
  www.tlu.edu/contact/church-relations/

Thiel College
  www.thiel.edu/about

Wagner College
  www.wagner.edu/ministry/

Wartburg College
  www.wartburg.edu/mission/

Wittenberg University
  www.wittenberg.edu/about/mission.html

Sample Extended Studies of Individual Campuses

Benne, Robert. *The Quest for Soul at Roanoke College: Learnings from its 175-year Venture in Christian Higher Education.* Grand Rapids, Michigan: Wm. B. Eerdmans Publishing, forthcoming.

Bunge, Marcia J., ed. *Rooted in a Distinctive Tradition, Open to the World: Reflections Across Campus on the Heritage, Character, and Ideals of Gustavus Adolphus College.* Minneapolis: Lutheran University Press, 2016.

"Commitment to Interfaith Cooperation." 2014 Annual Report to ELCA Synods and Congregations. Concordia College, Moorhead,

Minnesota: Web http://www.swmnelca.org/PDF/2014%20assembly/2014concordia_college.pdf

"The Five Faith Commitments of Augustana College." Augustana College, Rock Island, Illinois. Web http://www.augustana.edu/general-information/presidents-office/five-faith-commitments-

Kleinhans, Kathryn A. "Wilhelm Loehe's Legacy in Undergraduate Education in the United States: Wartburg College as Exemplum." In *Wilhelm Löhe und Bildung/Wilhelm Loehe and Christian Formation*, edited by Dietrich Blaufuß and Jacob Corzine. Nürnberg, Germany: Vereinfürbayerische Kirchengeschichte and Neuendettelsau, Germany: Freimund-Verlag, 2016. 249-55.

Mattes, Mark C., et al. eds. *The Grand View College Reader: Essays by Members of the Grand View College Community*. Minneapolis: Lutheran University Press, 2006.

Report of the Wittenberg Lutheran Identity Study Commission. Unpublished report. Board of Directors, Wittenberg University, Springfield, Ohio, 2006.

Schwandt, Pamela, ed. *Called to Serve: St. Olaf College and the Vocation of a Church College*. Northfield, Minnesota: St. Olaf College, 1999.

"St. Olaf College 2000: Mission and Identity for the 21st Century." Web https://contentdm.stolaf.edu/cgi-bin/showfile.exe?CISOROOT=/lib&CISOPTR=2388&filename=2389.pdf#search=%22b31177177%22

Torvend, Samuel, ed. *Core Elements in Lutheran Higher Education*. Tacoma, Washington: Pacific Lutheran University. Web http://www.plu.edu/lutheran-studies/core-elements/home.php

VOCATIONS OF THE CONTRIBUTORS

Robert Benne taught Christian Ethics at the Lutheran School of Theology at Chicago for seventeen years (1965-82), and at Roanoke College for thirty years (1982-2012), where he was Jordan-Trexler Professor of Religion, chair of the Department of Religion and Philosophy, and founder of the Benne Center for Religion and Society. He continues at Roanoke as research associate and teaches Christian Ethics at the Institute of Lutheran Theology. He has written a dozen books, including *Quality with Soul: How Six Premier Colleges and Universities Keep Faith with Their Religious Traditions* (Wm. B. Eerdmans Publishing Co., Inc., 2001). But his most important calling is to be husband to Joanna for fifty-seven years, father to four, and grandfather to eight.

Tom Christenson served Capital University faithfully as a professor of Philosophy from 1989 until his death in 2013. Tom first conceived of *Intersections* and was its founding editor, serving in that capacity from 1996 to 2005. He was a leader in Lutheran higher education circles; countless others knew him as a colleague, a teacher, an academic, a philosopher, a poet, a mentor, a storyteller, and a good-humored friend.

Paul J. Dovre served as faculty member, dean, and president of Concordia College from 1963 to 1999. He also served as interim president at Capital University and Concordia College and interim dean of students at Luther Seminary. He edited *The Future of Religious Colleges* (Wm. B. Eerdmans Publishing Co., Inc., 2002) which was the product of a national conference sponsored by the Kennedy School of Government at Harvard. He is the author of *A Holy Restlessness* (Augsburg Fortress, 2009) and *The Cross and the Academy* (Lutheran University Press, 2011). The Dovre Center for Faith and Learning was established at Concordia College in his honor. He currently serves on the boards of Oak Grove Lutheran Schools and Lutheran Social Services of Minnesota and is a volunteer for both Lutheran Social Services and Hospice of the Red River Valley.

Mary J. Henold is the John R. Turbyfill Professor in History at Roanoke College in Salem, Virginia. She teaches American history as well as women's/gender history, and is the author of *Catholic and Feminist: The Surprising History of the American Catholic Feminist Movement* (University of North Carolina Press, 2008). She also founded and coordinates Roanoke College's Mentoring for Mission program.

Darrell Jodock has taught at three ELCA colleges and one seminary. In retirement his vocation continues to be that of a teaching theologian. His other callings include husband, father, grandfather, citizen, friend, and participant in the farm operated by his family since 1874. He is professor emeritus at Gustavus Adolphus College, where he was the first to hold the Bernhardson Chair in Lutheran Studies (1999 to 2012). From 2013 to 2015 he served as the Martin E. Marty Regents Chair in Religion and the Academy at St. Olaf College. Earlier he taught at Muhlenberg College (1978-99) and Luther Seminary (1969-73, 1975-78). He chairs the ELCA Consultative Panel on Lutheran-Jewish Relations, serves on the newly created ELCA Inter-Religious Task Force, and is involved in a number of other Lutheran and ecumenical councils and working groups. His most recent writing projects include *Engaging Others, Knowing Ourselves: A Lutheran Calling in a Multi-Religious World* (Lutheran University Press, 2016), for which he was a consulting editor and co-author, and *Covenantal Conversations: Christians in Dialogue with Jews and Judaism* (Fortress Press, 2008), which he edited and co-authored.

Kathryn A. Kleinhans holds the Mike and Marge McCoy Family Distinguished Chair in Lutheran Heritage and Mission at Wartburg College in Waverly, Iowa. She is the editor of *Together by Grace: Introducing the Lutherans* (Augsburg Fortress, 2016) and author of *Seven Wonders of the Word: Book of Faith Lenten Journey* (Augsburg Fortress, 2010), as well as many scholarly, popular, and devotional articles. A fifth-generation Lutheran pastor, her passion is making Lutheran history and theology come alive for people today. (She sometimes describes herself as living with one foot firmly planted in the sixteenth century and the other planted just as firmly in the twenty-first century.)

L. DeAne Lagerquist is Professor of Religion and Director of American Conversations at St. Olaf College, Northfield, Minnesota. She is the author of *From Our Mothers' Arms: A History of Women in the American Lutheran Church* (Augsburg Publishing House, 1987) and *The Lutherans* (Greenwood Publishing, 1999), and co-editor and contributor to *Claiming Our Callings: Toward a New Understanding of Vocation in the Liberal Arts* (Oxford University Press, 2014). She enjoys recreational cooking, reading fiction, travel, and watching the lake go by.

Jason A. Mahn is Associate Professor and Chair of Religion at Augustana College, Rock Island, Illinois, and editor of *Intersections*. He is the author of *Fortunate Fallibility: Kierkegaard and the Power of Sin* (Oxford University Press, 2011) and *Becoming a Christian in Christendom: Radical Discipleship and the Way of the Cross in America's "Christian" Culture* (Fortress Press, 2016), as well as editor and co-author of *Radical Lutherans/Lutheran Radicals* (Cascade Books, forthcoming). When he isn't teaching or writing, he often feels called to his family garden or to try to keep up with Asa and Gabe, his two children.

Eboo Patel is the founder and president of Interfaith Youth Core (IFYC), a national nonprofit that partners with institutions of higher education to make interfaith cooperation a priority. He is the author of *Acts of Faith*, which won the Louisville Grawemeyer Award in Religion, *Sacred Ground*, and *Interfaith Leadership: A Primer*. Eboo's recent academic work is helping to shape the emerging field of interfaith studies. He is a frequent speaker and guest lecturer at colleges and universities across the United States and holds a doctorate in the sociology of religion from Oxford University, where he studied on a Rhodes scholarship. Eboo lives in Chicago with his wife, Shehnaz, and two sons. When he's not teaching his kids about interfaith cooperation, you'll find him feeding his coffee addiction and rooting for Notre Dame.

Shirley Hershey Showalter, professor of English, served as president of Goshen College (Indiana) from 1996-2004. She then became vice president—programs at the Fetzer Institute, Kalamazoo, Michigan. She wrote a childhood memoir, *Blush: A Mennonite Girl Meets a Glittering World* (2013) and is the Kilian McDonnell Fellow at the Collegeville Institute (Minnesota), fall 2016.

Ernest Simmons is professor of Religion and director of the Dovre Center for Faith and Learning at Concordia College, Moorhead, Minnesota, where he has taught since 1979. An ordained ELCA pastor, he holds a Ph.D. in Religion from Claremont Graduate University and an M.Div. from Luther Seminary, St. Paul, Minnesota. Simmons understands his primary vocation as assisting in bringing the Lutheran tradition into dialogue with contemporary life and thought, particularly as expressed in the academy. His publications include articles on the theology of Martin Luther, issues in science and religion, and the relation of faith and learning in higher education. He is author of the book *Lutheran Higher Education: An Introduction* (Augsburg Fortress, 1998) and a book on science and theology, *The Entangled Trinity: Quantum Physics and Theology* (Fortress Press, 2014).

Martha E. Stortz is the Bernhard M. Christensen Professor of Religion and Vocation at Augsburg College, a position she has held since 2010. Prior to that, she served for almost thirty years on the faculty of Pacific Lutheran Theological Seminary/The Graduate Theological Union. She is author of *A World According to God: Practices for Putting Faith at the Center of Your Life* (Jossey-Bass, 2004), *Blessed to Follow: The Beatitudes as a Compass for Discipleship* (Augsburg Fortress, 2010) and most recently, *Called to Follow: Journeys in John's Gospel* (forthcoming). She writes on ethics, spirituality, and pilgrimage.

Samuel Torvend is professor of the History of Christianity and holds the endowed University Chair in Lutheran Studies at Pacific Lutheran University in Tacoma, Washington. He is the author of *People of Wondrous Ability: The Origin and Gifts of Lutheran Education* (Pacific Lutheran University Press, 2015); *Luther and The Hungry Poor: Gathered Fragments* (Fortress Press, 2008; Wipf & Stock, 2017); *Flowing Water, Uncommon Birth: Christian Baptism in a Post-Christian Culture* (Augsburg, 2011); and *Daily Bread, Holy Meal: Opening the Gifts of Holy Communion* (Augsburg, 2004). Since 2012, he was worked with Radicalizing Reformation, an international network of academicians promoting social justice, peace-making, and reconciliation through scholarship and activism.

Mark Wilhelm is executive director of the Network of ELCA Colleges and Universities, an association of the twenty-six colleges and universities related to the Evangelical Lutheran Church in America. His prior work focused on graduate theological education, serving as churchwide staff for the ELCA, and as associate director of the Auburn Center for the Study of Theological Education at Auburn Theological Seminary in New York. He is an ordained minister in the ELCA.

THE VOCATION OF
INTERSECTIONS

Intersections is a publication by and largely for the academic communities of the twenty-six colleges and universities of the Evangelical Lutheran Church in America. Each issue reflects on the intersection of faith, learning, and teaching within Lutheran higher education. It is published by the Network of ELCA Colleges and Universities, and has its home at Augustana College, Rock Island, Illinois, the institutional sponsor of the publication. *Intersections* extends and enhances discussions fostered by the annual Vocation of the Lutheran College Conference, together lifting up the vocation of Lutheran colleges and universities. It aims to raise the level of awareness among faculty, staff, and administration about the Lutheran heritage and church-relatedness of their institutions, especially as these intersect with contemporary challenges, opportunities, and initiatives.

All issues of *Intersections* are available online at digitalcommons. augustana.edu/intersections.